VD STYLE PUBLISHING, LLC
PO BOX 24586

This is a work of fiction. Any reference or similarities to actual events, real people, living or dead or real locales are intended to give the novel a sense of reality. Any similarity in other names characters, places and incidents is entirely coincidental.

Cover design: Jay Covers
Edited by Tina Nance

DEDICATION

This book is dedicated to my daughter Dalejah. Still doing my best to make you proud of me.

SPECIAL THANKS

I would like to give a special thanks to my homey, Duke, for giving me the talk when I needed to keep pushing. Also, special thanks to Michele Dawn Mellette, Nicole Davis, Allison Essence M Edwards, Al Saadiq Banks, Michel Moore and Lakelia Deloach. Thanks for the support, the knowledge, and just for showing love. I appreciate it.

Connect with me on Facebook: Author King Benjamin
Follow me on Twitter: @KBWordplayz

GANK MASTERZ

A King Benjamin Novel

CHAPTER 1

The stench from the house slapped Lil Stink in his face before he even reached the threshold. Holding his breath, he knocked on the door. The cardboard piece of paper that was wedged between the door and the frame fell to the ground. The door made a slight squeal as it crept open just a few inches. The smell of bad feet and mildewed clothes wafted through the opening and assaulted his nose.

Stink pushed the door open and walked in. He stepped over a bunch of 40-ounce bottles and JT's crack head uncle, who was asleep on a mattress in the living room before he got to JT's room.

JT was stretched across the foot of the bed. He was turned on his backside with his mouth open, snoring lightly.

Stink grabbed his shoulder and began to shake him violently. "Wake up, man! Get up!"

After about ten seconds, JT rose from the dead. "Huh?"

"Get up, nigga. We gon' be late for school."

"Fuck school!" JT rolled over on his stomach.

"Come on, man." Stink shoved him again. This time

even harder. He needed JT to wake up because he couldn't face school without him.

Stink grabbed JT by the ankles and began to drag him out of bed.

Donald Morehouse and James Taylor had been friends since the first grade. They just clicked during their very first conversation, and the rest was history. Six and a half years later, they were more like brothers than best friends.

"Aiight man, let me go! I'm up. I'm up."

JT rose from the bed and went under it to search for his shoes. He slung two beat up pair of Converse out of his way before he found the shoes he'd been looking for. They weren't that much better than the shoes he'd slung to the side, but they were his best pair. He slid his Pro Wings on, and with that, he was completely dressed for school. He grabbed his brush with the broken handle and headed to the bathroom.

Stink laughed at his attempt to brush his hair. "Yo' shit is too nappy." Stink said, standing behind him in the mirror.

"Fuck you, nigga!"

"Maaan, brush yo' teeth before you say anything else."

"Ain't no toothpaste."

"Damn... well at least rinse yo' mouth out or something. Yo' shit banging."

JT tried to clean himself up as much as possible,

under the circumstances. Within a few minutes, he was ready to roll. He still had on the same clothes he'd slept in, and his breath was still tart, but it was a normal day for Stink and JT.

They headed off to school, pushing and shoving, joking and laughing all the way.

JT was dark skinned and a little tall for twelve years old. Stink was brown skinned with dimples. He was average height, but his bowlegs made him a little short. They lived in the area of Detroit, nicknamed The Black Bottom. The neighborhood had truly earned the name over the years, because there was nowhere to go from there, but up.

As they walked up Chene on the way to Knudsen grade school, they ran into Dusty and Romell. Dusty and Romell didn't have it as bad as Stink and JT. They looked decent in school, most days. Dusty got his name when he fell in the school playground, two summers ago, and came up with dirt all over his clothes and face. Stink and JT, being the biggest pranksters and jokers of the school, had fun with it all summer. After that, the name stuck.

As the foursome walked to school, JT always bombed first to keep cats off his ass. "That nigga, Stink, came over my crib talking bout he put on some deodorant. Y'all know damn well, his mama ain't went out and bought no deodorant!"

They all laughed.

"Shut up, bitch! Tell yo' mama to get that raggedy ass door fixed. I knocked on this nigga door this morning and fell in the living room. Raggedy ass house."

Everyone laughed at Stink's comeback, except JT. JT couldn't think fast enough, so he went on to his next victim.

"What the fuck you laughing at, Dusty? I knocked on your door last week, and a roach answered the door, nigga! Roach talking bout, who you looking for?"

Now everyone was clutching their stomachs and laughing, including Dusty. It was obvious that JT was in a zone and ready for anyone who wanted to challenge him. Once they arrived at school, the joke was on Stink and JT. Although they had enough wit to match anybody in the capping game, they gave people a lot of ammo because of the way the dressed and their personal hygiene. Boys and girls alike would sit in the corner of the class and snicker about Stink's clothes and JT's breath, or JT's clothes and Stink's body odor.

The only thing that kept people from trying to make a show of it was the fact that the two were the kings of capping jokes. Everything that was said about them was kept to a whisper, but they could hear the giggling, and they both knew when it was about them. A lot of the jokes about them went unnoticed by the rest the classmates who couldn't hear them from where they sat, but still, it was a hard pill to swallow on a daily basis.

Lately, they had begun to jump at the chance to shower after gym class. JT didn't have hot water at his home, and although Stink had hot water, most of the time, there was no money for soap.

The last class of the day was the typing class they had together. They enjoyed the typing class because it was a sign that the day was almost over. It was a chance to unwind because no one ever paid them any attention in typing class. The teacher was a real softy, so everyone was usually engaged in some form of misconduct—spitballs, thumps, knuckles, capping, flirting, and gossiping.

After school, they went to the penny candy store and stole whatever they wanted. Sometimes they'd get caught and have to run out of the store, but that was the fun part. After getting chased, they'd stay away for about a week, then go back and steal some more. So many of the neighborhood kids stole from the candy store, it was hard for the owners to remember faces.

When Stink got home, his mother was on the couch watching General Hospital with his nine-year-old brother.

"Hey baby," his mom said to her oldest boy with a slight smile.

"Hey, Mama. Why you watching the stories with Mama like a fag?" Stink said to his baby brother. His brother paid him no attention.

"How was school?" his mom asked.

"It was ok."

"I need you to do me a favor.

"What's that?"

"Go upstairs and get me a cigarette."

"Aiight."

Stink walked through the kitchen, out the back door and up the back stairs to the neighbor's house. He banged on the door.

Pam came to the door with a cigarette in her hand. She stood, blocking the door with her two hundred and fifty pound frame. She had a look on her face that read, *what the hell your mama want to borrow now?*

"My mama said can you send her a cigarette?" Pam took a drag from her Newport and released.

"Yo' mama gon' have to get a muthafucking job!" She walked away but left the door open without inviting Stink in. She came back with two Newports. "Tell yo' mama, that's all she getting from me today. Shit, I barely got enough to last me the rest of the day."

"Aiight." Stink snatched the cigarettes and took off before she could complain about his manners. He glanced in the refrigerator before he handed his mom the cigarettes. "She said don't ask her for no more today."

His mom quickly lit one. "Fuck that bitch! She better hope she make it through today without choking on a chicken bone with her fat ass."

Stink noticed his mom had cleaned up the house; something she did only when she was in a good mood. He wondered what had put her in such good spirits. He figured his pops had probably gone to work and would be home in a couple hours with some cash.

"What's up, Rob?" He punched his baby brother in

the arm.

"Nothing."

"Go on now, don't fuck with us while we watching General Hospital." His mother then spread her legs across the couch again, propping her feet on Rob's lap.

She still had on her nightgown in the middle of the afternoon, and Stink had to look away as one of her breasts threatened to pop out. Diamond still had her looks, even though she had been doing hard drugs for the last few years. She was slender and petite, with legs to match Tina Turner in her prime. Her tan skin had very few flaws and her stomach bared no scars from childbirth. Stink had picked up his dimples and his sense of humor from his mother.

Later that evening, Rob Sr. came home with groceries and cigarettes for his lady. He didn't bother speaking to his kids. It wasn't that Rob didn't like his kids or that he didn't ever pay them any attention, but Rob had a jones on him and couldn't wait to get a fix. The only Heroin dealer in the area with something strong enough for Rob Sr. was Chemical, and for a bundle, he knew Chemical would deliver the drugs right to his doorstep.

Stink watched his mother scurry to get dressed and head out the door. He knew she was probably going to the rock house around the corner. Stink honestly liked his parents better when they had their drugs. They got along better, and sometimes it seemed like they were a regular family, with the exception of the nodding and tweaking.

As she walked out the door, Diamond yelled back into the house. "Stink, tell yo' daddy, Chemical out here."

Stink peeked through the dingy blinds to see Chemical sitting in a royal blue 442 Cutlass with blue and white piping on the seats.

"Go watch TV," his dad demanded, speeding out the door.

Stink faked a spin in the direction of his room, but once his father was out of the house, he went back to the window to watch the transaction. Chemical was a big, blue-black dude with a menacing presence and a strong baritone voice to match. All he had to do was raise his voice a little to get people in line. More than anything, Stink was admiring Chemical's ride. It was sparkling clean as if he'd just left the car wash.

Stink was so lost in his thoughts that he missed the whole transaction. Where most kids would have been upset and disliked Chemical for selling their father drugs, Stink only felt jealousy. He wished he had some drugs to sell his father, so he could save up and buy a car, or at least a scooter.

That night, JT came over with a marijuana joint for him and Stink to puff on. He knew Stink would be excited about that, because ever since he took his first hit, Stink had fallen in love with weed.

"Come on, dog. Let's go over on McDougal." JT said.

"For what?" Stink replied.

"Just to see who all out there."

"Fuck it, come on."

McDougal was the street that all of the hustlers fought to get control over at the time. About sixty percent of the drug money in the hood went to the hustlers who had work on this block. From the Blvd, all the way down to Mack. There was a beer and wine store on the corner of Theodore that Stink and JT used to steal from. Stink didn't like going in the store anymore. Even though he had earned every letter in his nickname, he swore the Arabs who owned the store were the worst thing he'd ever smelled.

When they got to the strip, the first person they ran into was Lil Scurvy. Scurvy was only eleven years old, but he was way past eleven in street years. He always had a few rocks for sale, but he had to wait until the police chased the teenage hustlers away before he could sell them.

"What up, Scurvy?" Stink said.

"What up, where y'all coming from?"

"Da crib," JT replied. They slapped fives just the way they'd seen the older cats do when the met up on the premises. It was very dark, with only half of the street light working, and the hustlers were out in flocks.

They roamed up and down the streets in hoodies and sweats with their running shoes laced tight. Scurvy was supposed to be helping his uncles watch out for the big four, which was a group of extremely violent narcotics officers who worked the area. If you didn't run when you saw the big four, you might end up with a black eye, a broken jaw and, your wrist in cuffs.

"Let's step in here for a minute, y'all." Scurvy said as he led them into an abandoned house that still had lights and gas on. Drywall was all over the floor, the results of a crazed drug addict punching holes in the wall. Stink noticed the stove with all four burners lit and figured that this must be where people came when the nighthawk became too much to bear.

"Look what I got," JT said, revealing his joint for the first time.

Stink stared at it for a few seconds then snatched it from JT's hand. "Give me that shit, nigga." Stink said, running to the stove to light it.

"Don't snatch nothing else from me, nigga. You almost broke my shit."

"Shut up, punk. I ain't almost break nothing," Stink barked before bending over to light the joint off the stove.

"I see I'mma have to buss yo' head before I drop you back off to yo' mama." JT calmly stated.

Stink paid him no mind; he was busy trying to get high. He pulled long and hard with a concentrated look on his face.

Scurvy had his back turned, and it seemed he was also rolling a joint. Stink passed JT the weed and walked over to Scurvy, trying to observe his technique. After Scurvy laid the weed across the paper, he went back in his pocket. He pulled out a small plastic bag with four crack rocks in it. He took one out and began to crush it on the countertop with a spoon.

Stink scowled and shot JT a look. Scurvy used the cardboard from his weed papers to scoop up the crushed dope and lace his weed with it. He licked, rolled and lit his joint without paying any attention to the eye screws he was getting the whole time. Stink and JT weren't the brightest bulbs in the chandelier, but they knew what Scurvy was doing was just plain stupid. The smelled of the laced weed made them both leave the kitchen and head back to the living room of the abandoned house.

"Y'all don't wanna hit it?" Scurvy yelled out.

"Naw, we good," JT stated."

"Don't speak for me, nigga. I could have wanted to hit it." Stink joked.

"And soon as you do, I'mma hit yo' ass."

"What's up, then? Hoe ass nigga!" Stink balled up his fist as if he was preparing for a real fight.

JT grabbed him in a bear hug, knocking the joint from his lip. And the tussle began.

"Aww hell naw! Get off my dog!" Scurvy yelled when he heard the commotion.

He ran into the living room, not knowing exactly who he was going to side with, but he definitely wanted in on the fun. He grabbed JT in a headlock since he was the closest.

JT bit Scurvy on his rib cage, freeing himself quickly.

"Aaahhh bitch!" Scurvy yelled.

Stink grabbed JT's legs and yanked them out from under him. He hit the ground hard, and the pain shot straight to his tailbone. Angry now, he grabbed Scurvy by his pants legs and pulled him to the ground. Scurvy came crashing down to the floor and bang! The sound froze the three of them. It was too loud to be a fire-cracker, which meant it could have only been one thing.

Lying stiff like wax figures in a museum, Stink and JT glanced at each other first to see if either was hit. Then they glanced at Scurvy who was lying flat on his back, staring buck eyed at the ceiling.

"Scurvy, you aiight?" JT questioned.

"Oh shit, I'm hit!" Scurvy said before bursting into laughter.

After a few seconds, they all began to giggle away their fears. The twenty-five automatic in Scurvy's pocket was still burning his thigh.

CHAPTER 2

JT was getting downright sick of being at home with his family. The gloomy environment was depressing and there was never anything to eat in the house. Lately, he'd been hanging out at Stink's house more and more. After school, he wouldn't even go home. He'd just go straight to Stink's house. He knew Stink's people liked him a lot, and never cared if he ate at their house, as long as there was enough food.

JT had a secret crush on Stink's mom, along with every kid in the neighborhood that knew her. JT would always sit and listen to her tell stories and crack jokes until Stink would want to go outside and hang with the hustlers.

"I gotta piss," JT said as they sat on the front porch.

"Go piss in the backyard." Stink said.

"I think I gotta shit too, doe. Now I don't mind shitting in yo' back yard, as long as I got yo' permission and some toilet paper to wipe my ass."

"I wish I would catch you squatting in my backyard shitting. I'll beat yo' ass!"

"I'm serious, man, I gotta shit. I'm sure of it now!

"I think my pops still in there, let me go check."

Stink went inside to check for his dad in the bathroom. He called out to him, but there was no answer. He called out a second time; still no answer. He banged on the bathroom door to no avail. He twisted the knob and eased the door open with fear clenching his throat. His father sat slumped over the toilet on his knees, motionless.

"Pop!" he yelled, but there was no response. He began to shake Rob with all his might, harder and harder until he finally came to."

"Hey, hey what's going on?" Rob said in a slurred tone.

"I gotta use the bathroom. Can you go lay down in yo' room?"

Rob was still trying to pull himself together. He had just been brought back to planet earth. He struggled to his feet. "Oh, ok. I'm sorry, son." Rob tightened his belt and stumbled off to find the bedroom.

Stink's mind went back to the idea that had been stuck in his head. He was thinking that with all the money his pops spent on drugs, he could make a killing in his house alone.

He wouldn't ever have to worry about if they were going to buy deodorant or soap because he could buy it for himself. His mother, Diamond, didn't spend much on crack –her drug of choice– but it still took a lot away from the household. He sometimes wished his mother would get off the drug, but in his mind, it was too unrealistic to entertain the thought. As for his pops, who had been a heroin addict for as long as Stink had been alive, the thought of him being anything but a blow head never crossed Stink's mind.

He sometimes wondered if Rob was his biological father. He frequently asked himself why he didn't favor Rob or Rob Jr., and why he would name his second son Jr. and not the first. He knew that he favored his mom a lot, so as he got older, Stink just decided to not question any of it.

Stink loved his dad, mainly because he was always around. But every once in awhile, he'd catch Rob and Rob Jr. standing side by side; Rob Sr. being tall and dark skinned and Stink being short and light brown, and he'd have that thought again.

After JT finished with his business in the bathroom, he came back out to the porch. As if he had read Stink's mind, out of the clear blue, he said, "Man, we should try to get some dope."

"From who?" Stink said.

"I don't know. Maybe we could get some double ups like Scurvy be doing."

"Fuck dat! Scurvy don't be having no money. The only reason he be fresh is cause all his family sell dope."

"Well, we need to get some money in our pocket some kinda way."

Just then, Chemical's Buick bent the corner, banging E.P.M.D'S "Strictly Business". Their eyeballs stayed glued to the Buick as it rode up the block until it was out of their sight.

As Chemical passed, Stink noticed that 40 Grand was in the passenger seat. 40 Grand was a slim, yellow hustler who used to be plain old Eric until he broke up a high stakes dice game at Club 800 on Vandyke. The story was, he walked in with a thousand dollars to his name and left with 40 Grand. That night, the nickname, and a flashy new guy was born.

"We should ask Chemical." JT suggested.

They knew Chemical was probably headed to his baby mother's house since she only stayed around the corner from Stink.

"Come on, we probably can still catch 'em." Stink said as they both jumped off the porch and took off running.

They ran through the field, trying to catch Chemical and cut him off before he reached his destination. JT ran behind Stink, stumbling over empty juice bottles and bricks stuck in the dirt. When they reached the next block, Chemical was headed in their direction.

"Aye, aye aye!" They both screamed and waved their hands wildly trying to get his attention over the loud music booming from the sound system.

Chemical passed them by at first, but then he slowed to a halt, reversed, and came to see what the baby G's could possibly want. He rolled the window down and silenced the music.

"What the hell wrong with y'all lil niggas?"

"Nothing, we was just trying to catch up with you," JT said.

"Catch up with me for what?"

Since this was JT's idea, Stink decided to let him do all the talking.

JT paused because he was expecting Stink to say something first. After all, he was the one who broke his neck getting off the porch to dash through the field.

Chemical was staring at JT now as if he was wasting his time. "What's up, man? You fucking with me?" he asked

"Naw, we needs some work. We tired of being broke," JT finally said.

40 Grand burst into laughter.

They didn't understand what was so funny.

"Y'all tired of being broke? Shit, y'all just learned how to count money. How the fuck y'all tired of not having none?" Chemical questioned.

"We need money for shit, man. We ain't even got no food in the 'frigerator at my house. Shit, look at my shoes." JT pointed down at his beat up Pro Wings as exhibit A.

Chemical understood exactly where JT was coming from. He too had come from a household where he had to fend for himself. He also understood that Stink wasn't much better off, with Rob spending his money on the blow packs that he supplied.

"Man, y'all niggas is kids." 40 Grand said, trying to reason with the youngsters, but Chemical cut him short.

"So, what that mean? I hate to tell you this, but kids grow up to be killas too. Them lil niggas wanna work, they can work. I don't give a fuck. Y'all gon be a lil late for school though, cause my custos need that fix early in the morning, you know?"

"Man, fuck school!" Stink said.

"Aiight, that's up to y'all." Chemical said shaking his head in amazement. "Meet me back at my baby mama house in an hour. I'll have something put together for y'all 'lil niggas. Man, these lil niggas crazy." He pulled off, laughing at the infestation of the hood.

JT and Stink laughed also, even though they didn't know why.

Stink and JT sat around at the meeting spot on the front porch for three hours before Chemical finally showed up. He took them to the stroll on Jos. Compau and introduced them to some young hustlers that they only knew by face. All of these dudes had at least a few years on Stink and JT. Chemical told them it would be best to start fresh early in the morning when the rush came. Things slowed down for the heroin the later it got because most the fiends would be asleep unless they were cross-addicted and took uppers or smoked crack to stay up.

Stink and JT were both high and sleepy themselves, so neither protested about starting first thing the next morning.

JT spent the night at Stink's house for the second

night in a row. No one came to look for him or really cared. JT had been shuffled around for most of his childhood to different relatives who would deal with him as long and they could, then he would go back home with his mom, who was actually his cross-addicted aunt. She only wanted a check for him, but none of the responsibility of raising him. If not for him bouncing around so much, JT knew he would be a ward of the state by now. It all hardened him at a very young age and gave him little compassion or sorrow for other people and their problems.

The next morning, Stink and JT were up and at it with a newfound zest for life. Today was going to be the day that changed everything. They had one bundle each to start with and they were supposed to page Chemical for more when they were done.

Stink and JT would make 20 dollars each, plus their tops off each bundle. The top would be charging 12 dollars for a ten-dollar pack to those who would go for it. When they got to the block, he saw that only one guy had made it there before them. His name was Hammer Head, but everybody just called him Hammer. He was a big guy to be only fifteen, but his head was unjustifiably big. When he laughed, he had extra meat on his forehead that made him look Sharpieish.

Hammer slapped fives with them and began to school them on the things Chemical might have left out or failed to mention about being on the stroll.

"Y'all gotta dip if y'all see the hook, cause we supposed to be on our way to school right now. That's why I always stand between these two houses so they can't see me.

"So where is all these early morning custos Chemical was talking about?" Stink asked.

"Oh, they coming trust me. Just give it a few minutes."

Just as Hammer had guaranteed, five minutes later, they got bombarded with a rush of early morning traffic. It was seven o'clock in the morning and they had cars lined up like they were serving coffee out of a McDonald's drive-through. As the customers sat patiently waiting to be served, the trio hustled to get the cars in and out without a long delay. The most important thing was keeping an eye out for the police while completing the transaction.

It only took a few seconds for the police to hit the corner and hop out, knowing something illegal was going down. Keeping correct change on hand was hard, but they had to, because not having correct change only prolongs the transaction.

JT was immediately annoyed with the correct change part. "Why don't we tell these muthafuckas to have the correct change when they get here?"

"It's not gonna work, dog. They still gonna bring you fifties and hundreds and only spend twenty dollars off it." Hammer said.

"But if we don't serve 'em, then they'll start to remember to have correct change, I bet."

"Naw, they gonna go somewhere up the block where muthafuckas ain't complaining about having the correct change. Plus, I love having small bills, cause it make my knot look fatter."

JT hadn't thought about it from that perspective. Once he did, he decided he wanted a lot of small bills too. Hammer showed him how his roll would have a few hundreds on top, and the rest would be fives and singles. When he flashed it quick enough, it looked more like a thousand dollars than five hundred.

In less than two hours, everyone was out of drugs, but Chemical came through quickly with more. This time, he left Stink and JT two bundles each. They decided to skip school for the day and get all the money they could.

By then, a couple more hustlers had shown up that worked for 40 Grand. These guys had a different agenda because they had a different boss. There was no teamwork with these guys; it was every man for themselves. They went after every sale and every customer, but the trio was too quick and aggressive to let it go down like that.

Stink noticed that Hammer's package was a lot bigger than his. When Stink and JT ran out of packs, Hammer supplied them with more. They hustled for close to 12 hours straight, from 6:30 am to 6:00 pm. When it was over, they had cleared about two hundred dollars each. They left the money that belonged to Chemical with Hammer, as ordered, and abandoned the stroll, feeling better than ever about themselves.

They went straight to the supermarket were they bought soap, deodorants, toothpaste, and lots of food. This was the most money either of them had ever possessed and there was an opportunity to make the same amount, if not more, tomorrow.

Stink and JT were overwhelmed with the joy of possibilities. Things could only get better from there. JT took all his food and hygiene products to Stink's house. He sure as hell wasn't about to take it to his house so somebody could steal and sell them.

"Shit, you might as well move in with us, dog. You always here anyway," Stink said.

Actually, JT had already moved in, but he thought it was good to be invited.

They puffed on a dime bag they had gotten from the Jamaican who lived down the street. "Just think if we can make this much money every day, dog." JT said.

"If we do, I'm going shopping this weekend."

"Shit, me too. I'm getting some Jordans."

"Hell yeah, and some Air Max."

"You seen them new Rockport Gortex boots?"

"Oh yeah, Fat Mark got some. Them bitches sweet. Nigga, I'm getting bout ten pair of kicks." Stink informed JT.

"Nigga, you ain't gonna have that much money. You still gotta buy gear too, stupid ass."

"Watch me."

They hustled hard all week, not attending school at all. Friday night, they outlasted everyone on their stroll, trying to get all they could before they went home. They still had packs to move and money that belonged to Chemical in their pockets.

The next morning, they caught the bus to Eastland Mall and went crazy. They both got the Jordans and the Air Max, but JT said he couldn't afford the two hundred dollar Rockport boots. He spent the rest of his money on clothes.

Stink got the Rockport boots along with a Nautica Jacket and five outfits.

All the young girls were in awe of the little dusty looking cats walking around with too many bags to carry at one time. They had so many bags, they had to catch a taxi home, which Stink paid for.

JT was thinking about all the money Stink had spent as they rode home in the taxi. They had made about the same amount of money all week, but Stink had spent almost double what JT had at the mall. JT could add and subtract pretty well, and something wasn't right. There was only one way he could have been able to spend that much money.

Back home, JT decided to question Stink about his splurging. "You spent Chemical money didn't you?"

"What? Naw, shut up man!"

"Yeah right, how much money you spend at the mall?"

"Don't worry about how much I spent. How much you spend?"

"I spent about six hundred dollars and I only got a hundred left. You spent way more than that, and I know you ain't have that much money."

Stink had an exposed look painted on his face. He didn't think JT was counting his pockets like that. Once he was in the mall, he just couldn't help himself. There were so many things he wanted; so many things he could never afford. Once he started, he just couldn't stop. Stink was beginning to realize that he had gotten himselfinto some shit.

Stink's mom came in and saw all the shopping bags all over the place. She was speechless for a moment.

"I just hope you lil muthafuckas ain't went out and robbed nobody! Just tell me that! Please just tell me y'all ain't went out and robbed nobody!"

"Naw, Mama —"

She interrupted. "Hold up, what the fuck is going on? Y'all muthafuckas been buying food, weed every day, now this shit. Somebody betta tell me something right now."

Stink didn't care. He knew he had brought more money in the house in the past week than his father did. So as far as he was concerned, they should be thanking him.

"We got some dope." he said bluntly.

"Y'all got some what? From who?"

"Chemical," Stink answered.

"Oh my God. Robert!" Diamond called out to her husband who was busy nodding out in the bedroom.

She went to the bedroom and shook him hard to get his attention. "Robert, did you hear this shit? These lil muthafuckas done started selling dope."

A few minutes later, Rob Sr. came into the living room were Stink and JT sat. He flopped down on the couch next to his son. "Talk to me, what's going on?" Rob said.

"We got some dope." Stink reiterated.

Rob wasn't really feeling up to making a big fuss about it at the moment, but he put up a small front for his wife's sake. "Un uh, I don't like this shit. I don't like this shit. Ain't nobody talk to me about nothing." His voice was garbled and low, almost as if he were talking to himself instead of the kids.

"I'm bout to page that muthafucka, Chemical, right now and cuss his ass out," Diamond said.

"Baby, I'll take care of it."

Diamond reached for the phone. "What's the number, Rob?"

"Baby, I said I'll take care of it."

"This some bullshit!" Diamond spat before storming out of the living room.

The whole uproar lasted less than a half-hour. After that, it was pretty much like nothing ever happened. They never paged Chemical to ask why he had twelve-year-olds selling drugs for him and they never asked Stink and JT to stop. It was too beneficial to the household for them to stop.

The next night, Diamond made Stink and JT promise that they would not stop going to school. She told them if they wanted to sell drugs, she knew she wouldn't be able to stop them. Stink had given the rest of his blow packs to his father. He knew he wouldn't be able to pay Chemical the money he owed him, unless JT helped him out.

CHAPTER 3

Monday morning, they went to school, fresh from head to toe. Stink kept stopping and profiling for invisible cameras every five minutes on his way to class. He gave true meaning to the saying, acting like a nigga who ain't never had shit. They sat in the back of each class, with Dusty and Romell, making fun of everybody. It was what they did anyway, but now that they were fresh and had money in their pockets, it was ten times worse.

JT was rocking some black and grey Jordans with grey Nautica jeans and a black and grey top. Stink had on black and grey Jordans with an all-black Jordan Jumpsuit. They had fresh haircuts for the first time in months, and it was obvious to everyone in the know, what had happened in the past week. They even had on some Polo cologne they had picked up from a crackhead on the stroll. Today, they were flawless, and it felt so good.

Everyone noticed the transformation as the bell rang and they headed to their next class. They saw player haters zooming in on their shoes and gear, looking for signs that something was fake and bootleg. They saw girls staring, who usually never look their way.

“So what you gonna do about Chemical?” JT asked, ruining the moment on the way to math class.

Stink stroked his hair with his new Diane wave brush “Man, fuck Chemical!”

“Aiight, you keep saying that and watch what happens. I’m trying to help you out.”

“How the hell you gon’ help me out?”

“Cause, I rolled all day yesterday, so I got like two hundred now. How much you got?”

“Man, I got about fifteen dollars and I owe out six hundred. Like I said, fuck Chemical.”

“Aiight, that’s on you. Just don’t say I didn’t try to help you.”

“I don’t care, man.” Stink said, trying to end the conversation.

He walked the rest of the way with his head down, not saying a word. JT couldn’t understand why he was acting so careless when it came to other people’s money.

The hallways were crowded, and everyone was hustling, trying to take care of whatever business they had between classes. Stink wasn’t watching where he was going and he ran dead smack into a young lady.

“Watch where the fuck you going!” she shouted.

He looked up to see Latoya Bankhead wiggling her neck like a rattlesnake.

Stink thought she looked good, but she was way out of order right now.

"You watch where the fuck you going!" he fired back.

Latoya had beautiful light brown skin, with reddish-brown hair, and big, mesmerizing eyes that captured your attention and held it until she blinked. Now, her whole face was contorted because she was feeling somewhat disrespected. She felt like something may be about to pop off, and she was ready for whatever.

"Un uh, you watch where the fuck you going, nigga! I got 20/20 vision in these big brown eyes, baby. I know where I'm going and I know where I'm at, and where I'm at ain't where I'm trying to be, so move yo' ass out my way."

Stink had stopped listening to her after the 20/20 comment and JT was just standing there smiling.

"Did you just call me baby?" Stink said

"What?" Toya said, caught off guard.

"Don't answer a question with a question. You ain't learned shit in this bitch have you?"

"What? Nigga fuck you!"

"Fuck you bitch!"

When Toya heard the b word, she lunged at Stink. JT had to get between the two of them. She took a wild swing anyway, but JT snatched her arm out of the air before it could land. He wrapped his other arm around her waist to prevent her from moving any closer to Stink.

The more dramatic things got, the more Stink

laughed. It was just too funny to see a chic coming at him like that.

"Fuck dat. Let me go, JT. This nigga got me bent."

"Come on, girl, chill out. Stink, stop laughing, man." JT was trying his best to defuse the situation, but he was also trying his best to get his feel on while he was holding Toya back from Stink. Even mad, she was still fine and she smelled like no other girl he'd ever known.

Stink finally apologized. "Look, I didn't mean to call you no bitch. That just slipped out."

"See, he apologized. Now be cool." JT said.

She snatched away from JT, but kept eye contact with both of them as she walked away. They maintained eye contact with her, but they both had lust in their eyes while she wore fury in hers.

They were waiting for her to turn around so they could get a glimpse of her bottom in its early stage of plumpness.

"Damn, I wanna hit that," JT said once she was gone. He had made a mental note that she called him by name. He didn't know how she knew his name, but he was glad of it.

"Why you ain't holla at her?" Stink asked.

"How I'm gon' holla at her when I was trying to keep her off yo' ass?"

"Man I woulda knocked that bitch out if she woulda hit me."

They continued to laugh about the incident as they

made their way into math class.

After school, they hung around trying to get girls phone numbers, even though Stink was sure the phone would be cut off today unless they somehow paid the bill. He'd seen the shutoff notice and had intended to give his mother the money before he splurged.

They were not shy about approaching women at all. Half of the girls in the school had already shot them down. Today was different. The same girls who had ignored them all school year were now giving out their home phone numbers. Stink and JT knew they were handsome guys; they just needed to clean themselves up. Now the proof was in the swag.

"So, how many numbers you get?" Stink asked.

"About five."

"Nigga stop lying!"

"I ain't lying, sucker."

"Let me see five phone numbers."

JT went in his pocket and pulled out all the different numbers written on notebook paper with females' names on them. There were five in all, and Stink was a little bitter because he only had three numbers. He shook it off.

"So what did Chemical say yesterday? Did he ask about me?"

"Yeah, I told you he asked me where you was at, and I just said I don't know."

"Did he act like he thought you was lying for me?"

"Hell yeah!"

The bus came and they went straight home and changed clothes. JT changed into some old clothes to go hustle on the stroll. Stink changed into another brand new outfit and shoes.

Even though JT slept on the living room couch, most of his clothes were neatly put away in Rob Jr.'s room. While he was changing, Stink walked in brushing his hair intensely.

"Let me borrow twenty dollars."

"For what?"

"In case I get into something. I'm bout to call some of these numbers and see if they real. Whoever gave me a wrong number, I'm cussing they asses out tomorrow."

JT handed Stink the money, and went on his way to the stroll.

Stink was sitting in his room getting his last few strokes to his head and staring at a poster of Eazy E on his wall, when his mother popped up in the doorway.

"Stink, I need ten dollars."

"All I got is twenty, Ma."

"Hmpt, you done let them lil' hoes get they hands on you already, huh?"

"What? Be quiet, Ma. You don't even know what you talking about."

His mother continued to try and slick talk her son out of the money she needed for drugs. "All I know is, blood is thicker than water. So if you can give them lil' thirsty ass girls some money, you can give me ten dollars. Now give me that twenty so I can get some change from the store."

"I'll give it to you when I get back," Stink said.

"How long you gon' be?"

"About twenty minutes."

His mother gave him a skeptical look before leaving.

Stink looked outside and noticed it was beginning to snow. Even though it was the middle of February, the weather had been unseasonably warm. The snow on the ground had almost melted, but now the falling snow was creating new layers of whiteness.

Stink threw on his Nautica coat and prepared to leave. He picked up the house phone just to make sure it was cut off, and it was. He headed off to the corner store to call Sherida from the payphone. He picked her to call first because she was the better looking of the three girls he had to call. Sherida was high yellow with dark hair and high cheekbones. He was still a virgin, but if he had his way, she was going to be his first.

Stink walked into the beer and wine store with a scowl on his face. "It stank in here," he said, looking repulsed as if he were some type of aristocrat.

"That's cause you just walked in, Stinky," the Arab joked.

He mean mugged the Arab standing there with his Hawaiian shirt buttoned halfway, exposing all his chest hairs. "Man, shut the fuck up and give me eight quarters!"

"You gotta buy something."

"I don't want nothing out of this stanking ass store. And why the fuck you got on a Hawaiian shirt in February?"

"If you not buying nothing, get the fuck out!"

"I'll beat yo' ass!"

"Get out!"

"Give me my change and I will."

"Buy something."

Stink saw that he wasn't going to be able to call anybody unless he bought something, so he grabbed two packs of Now & Later and shoved the twenty-dollar bill through the change slot. As soon as he got his change, he decided he couldn't leave without having the last word

"You a bitch!" he barked on his way out. Dogging the Arab that worked the corner store had a certain appeal. It made him feel good to be able to talk to a grown man that way and get away with it.

He walked over to the payphone on the side of the building and checked it for change before he inserted his quarter. He dialed Sherida's number. The phone rang four times before an older woman answered.

"Hello."

"Is Sherida there?" he asked in his most polite and mild mannered voice.

"Who is this?"

"Stink."

"Stink? Why they call you that? You stink?"

"No, it's just a nickname my mama gave me."

"Okay Stink, well Sherida can't have no boys calling here unless I meet them first. That don't mean you can come visit her either. That just means you can come over here and introduce yourself to me, and if I like you, then you can call her on the phone."

"Okay, so when you wanna meet me?"

"Oooh, I see you ain't shy."

"No ma'am."

"Okay, well, I'll tell you what. You can come over this weekend if she agrees to it, and then me and you can talk. But be warned, I don't play."

"Ok, so can I just talk to her now for a minute?"

"Hell naw, you can see her in school tomorrow. Bye."

JT was posted on the stroll with Hammer and one of 40 Grand's workers who wasn't really getting any sales. The police drove by really slow but didn't see anyone because they had all ducked between the houses and hid. This kind of hustling was not for the slow niggas. You had to be on P's and Q's at all times.

"You think we hot?" JT asked Hammer.

"Naw, I think they just making they rounds."

They stepped back out to the sidewalk and spotted the 442 bending the block. JT's heart began to pound because he knew what Chemical was about to say. He hated Stink right now for putting him in the middle.

Chemical pulled up, staring directly at JT as he rolled the window down with 40 Grand riding shotgun.

"Where that lil' fucker, Stink, at with my money?" He sounded more pissed off than he looked. Even 40 Grand seemed to be annoyed.

"He said he'll be over here later," JT lied.

"Later? That muthafucka been gone for two days. I doubt if he got my money, I know he don't. He playing fucking games."

"I don't know, man. I'm just trying to make sure my count right," JT said, trying to distance himself from his underhanded right hand man.

"You a good guy, JT. So far so good with you. Matter of fact, Hammer give JT the rest of them packs and come ride with us."

Hammer looked confused, but he followed orders and gave JT his packs. As 40 Grand stepped out of the car to let Hammer in the back seat, he called his worker over to collect some cash. It wasn't much, but 40 Grand didn't complain.

JT watched them drive away. He was really afraid for Stink. This whole problem was not going to just go away. He cursed Stink under his breath for being so stupid.

Stink violently banged the payphone receiver against the base. He was upset. Every number he had called, either the mother or father had answered and said their daughters couldn't talk to boys on the phone. He was confused as to why the girls had given him their numbers in the first place.

As soon as he pivoted to turn the corner, he spotted the last car in the world he wanted to see. Chemical pulled right up to the phone booth without ever looking in Stink's direction. Chemical was looking straight ahead as if he were waiting for Stink to make the first move. Stink thought if he took off now, he had time to run. He considered it for a moment. He knew he couldn't run forever, so his only option was to lie like a killer in a homicide investigation.

"You fresh as hell. I hope you got my money," Chemical finally yelled out.

40 Grand opened the passenger side door and maneuvered so he could let Hammer out of the back seat. Hammer was fifteen, and much bigger than Stink. He could see it all happening like a prophecy. Hammer had come to do Chemical's dirty work.

"Where my money at, Stink?" Chemical asked again.

Hammer was now approaching, and Stink was frozen like a deer caught in headlights.

"You ain't got the money, man?" Hammer asked with a bit of sympathy in his voice. He was really hoping Stink had the money so he wouldn't have to go through with it.

"I... somebody in my house got me, man. Somebody stole that shit, cause when I woke up in the morning—"

Pow! Hammer socked Stink so hard, he stumbled backwards and fell into the slush that covered the street. Dazed and confused, he couldn't move for a moment.

While Stink was trying to figure out where he was, Hammer was coming to beat the debt out of him. Stink tried to roll over and get to his feet, but Hammer just sat on him and punched him in the face a few more times. Then he wrapped his huge hands around Stink's head and began to bang it on the curb.

Just as Stink was about to pass out, he heard 40 Grand call out, "Aiight man, that's enough."

Hammer calmly walked back over to the car, hopped in, and they quickly sped off.

Stink was stretched out on the curb as if he had been stabbed or shot. He was too light headed to feel all the pain that had just been inflicted on him.

Scurvy walked up and helped him to his feet. "What happened, man?" Scurvy said.

"Hammer knocked me out," Stink answered, walking and dusting himself off slowly.

"Damn, that's fucked up. Hammer knocked me out before too, doe."

"He knocked you out?" Stink asked, not really car-ing.

"Shit, I ran off with some money. I used to roll for Chemical a few months ago. It only lasted about a week though."

Stink's head was pounding and thumping. It felt like he had been dropped on it.

"Damn, man. Yo' face is swoll up like a muthafucka!"

Stink could feel that one of his eyes was swollen almost shut, and he had knots on his head from the smacks on the curb. Deep down inside, he was just glad it was all over and he hoped that was the end of it.

There was no working washer and dryer in Toya's modest home, not too far from the Black Bottom. When there was no money for the laundromat, Toya had to hand wash all of her clothes and hang them to dry on the clotheslines in the basement. It was hard work being poor and still trying to stay fly. But Toya had mastered this art. Luckily, her mother was a con/stick up artist who sometimes came into lump sums of cash.

In her heyday, Letia had been notorious for scoping out drug houses and copping from them long enough to get everyone relaxed and used to her face. Then, she would strike. Truly a wolf in sheep's clothing, coming up, Letia was known hands down as the baddest chic in her hood.

She was an older version of her daughter, Toya, who

had sat up many nights eavesdropping on conversations about hitting licks and smooth getaways. Letia's key to survival was that she never stayed stationary. She moved from one hood to the next, feeling everything out before she laid down a play. When it was time to leave, she didn't hesitate, even if meant leaving the state for a while. In the long run, Letia's Heroin addiction got the best of her, and nowadays she was neither as calculating nor as breathtaking as she used to be.

"Got dammit, I said stop!" Letia screamed at her daughter who was standing over her flicking drips of ice water in her mother's face. Letia had a hot box and had sent her daughter to make a glass of ice water. "If you don't give me my water, I'm bout to smack the shit out of you!"

Toya just giggled and continued to dip her fingers in the water and spray her mother's face. She knew her mother was too high to get up and do anything about it.

"Here, here, here." She giggled and flickered more water.

"So you just gon' keep sticking yo' nasty ass hands in my water? Okay."

Just as Letia was about to make an effort to get up and lay the smack down, Toya stopped provoking her. "Aiight, aiight. Let me stop messing with you, old lady. Here you go.

"I'm gon' kick yo' ass before tonight is over with."

"So what? You too old to still be getting high. That's played out, Mama!" Toya spat.

"So what? I'm still a good mama, bitch!"

Toya burst out laughing at her, as she usually did when the subject of motherhood came up. Toya loved her mom, but she was far from what a mother was supposed to be. "Let me get the rest of my clothes from downstairs so I can iron, cause you is craaaaazy."

"Yeah, just don't forget who bought all them clothes."

Toya propped her hand on her hips and spun around, intending to give her mom a piece of her tenacious mind. "So! That's your job. That's what you supposed to do." It wasn't that Toya was ungrateful for the things her mother did; she just hated when Letia acted as if she deserved a mother of the year award.

As Toya grew older, her and Letia bumped heads more often, due to their similar personalities. Letia was thick skinned and loud and crazy at times. Toya was her body double and character twin. The thing that upset Letia the most, were things like the ice water incident. She constantly complained that her daughter didn't know when to stop playing. Since the age of ten, Toya had been giving her mother mustard mustaches when she was off into a deep nod.

"Mama, I hungry," Toya called out as she exited the basement.

"See, now you want me to cook for your black ass, don't you? Ain't shit up!"

"Ok Mama, I'm sorry. I'm foreal, come on now," she pleaded.

"Hell naw! You play too damn much. Go cook your own got dam food!"

"I can't cook none of that stuff in there."

"Well, I guess you gonna starve til Bryant show up. And he might not feel like taking you to get something to eat, so you might still be shit out of luck."

Toya wished she hadn't aggravated her mother so much. Now she would have to eat bologna and cheese sandwiches. Toya knew the chances of her mom's sugar daddy taking her out for a meal was slim to none. She didn't particularly care for Bryant anyway—didn't like the way he looked at her.

After she finished ironing some clothes for school, Toya ran some bathwater. She still had not eaten anything and was starting to feel lightheaded. McDonald's still sounded better than bologna sandwiches.

She got in the bathtub and held out for Bryant's arrival. She always soaked in the water for fifteen minutes before bathing.

"Calgon, take me away," she said out loud.

She began to think about the boy that had been on her mind lately. The thought put a smile on her face and she closed her eyes, listening to the front door shut. It was probably Bryant coming in. She heard Bryant and her mother talking, but she couldn't make out what was being said. From the bathroom, it sounded like mumbling.

About ten minutes later, she heard a knock at the bathroom door.

Before she could say anything, the doorknob was turning and the door came open. She thought it was her mother until she saw the silhouette of a tall dark man wearing an old school brim come in to view.

"What the hell you doing?" she shouted and tried to cover her bare breasts with her hands and knees.

"Oh shit, baby girl. I didn't know you was in here." Bryant replied as he stood there staring with lust in his eyes.

"Get yo' old ass outta here. You did know I was in here!" she yelled.

"Yo' mama didn't tell me you was in here, baby girl. I swear to you."

"Get out!"

Bryant slammed the door, pretending to be appalled by the accusation. He cursed and ranted until he was out of her audible range.

Toya wished her mother would find a man her age. While Letia was still a youthful twenty-nine, Bryant was pushing fifty. She sunk down low in the bathtub and sighed. It was beginning to look more and more like a bologna and cheese night.

CHAPTER 4

Stink stayed home and recovered from the beating for as long as he could. He hadn't been to school in over two weeks, but no truancy officer ever showed up. The assault left Stink with one black eye and the rest of his face swollen. Once the swelling went down, his skin turned dark on one side, and it made him appear to have a huge birthmark on his face.

Diamond bought him a cocoa butter stick, and she was good about making sure he applied it at least three times a day. Rob Sr. never called Chemical to buy drugs from him anymore, but it didn't make a difference. He could get the same drugs from JT.

As JT continued to hustle, eventually Chemical suggested that Stink come back to work for them as well.

Stink was fiending to get back to the block. Even though he was bitter about the beat down, against his better judgment, Stink agreed to come back to the block. The minute he got a taste of the dope boy lifestyle, he was hooked. He was hooked on everything from ducking the cops and making money, to getting girls' phone numbers and shopping at the mall. He was hooked on all of it.

Stink sat on his bed lacing his Rockport boots up.

"Where you going?" his mother asked from the doorway.

"I'm going to holla at JT."

"Don't take yo' ass around that corner trying to sell no dope."

"I'm not." he lied.

Diamond was trying her best to sound like her impression of a concerned mother. Honestly, she was almost hoping that he did go back to hustling, so she would have her get high money every day and wouldn't have to worry about it.

"When you see JT, tell him to send me some cigarettes," she shouted at Stink on his way out the door.

Stink was about to walk from his house to Jos. Compau, but as he walked up Ferry St., he could hear a voice yelling from the bushes.

"Po Po!"

Stink's vision zoomed in on the bushes, but he couldn't see a face.

"What?"

"Po Po." The familiar voice repeated.

"JT?" Stink asked.

"Yeah."

Just then, a blue and white patrol car bent the corner, followed by an all-black unmarked vehicle. Stink walked away from the bushes and tried not to make eye contact with the police. Once they were right in front of him, he glanced up to look inside the last car. Hammer was in the back seat, looking roughed up and appeared to be still resisting arrest.

When the police cars were out of sight, Stink turned around to go back for JT, but JT was already dashing from the bushes and running towards the alley.

He signaled for Stink to follow him. As he ran, he couldn't help but wonder why JT was running back to the same spot the police had just left?

Out of breath, Stink arrived back at the stroll about twenty seconds behind JT. He leaned against the vacant house while he caught his breath.

"What you come back here for?" Stink asked, exasperated and exhausted.

JT lifted the old gas meter box up and removed bundles of blow packs. He held it up for Stink to get a good look at it.

"This what I came back for. Come on."

They shot back down the alley from which they had come and ran all the way home. The two walked in the house, sweating like boxers in the twelfth round.

"What the hell? What happened?" Diamond spat.

"Police swooped on us," JT explained.

"See, you lil' hard headed muthafuckas gon' be in juvenile somewhere. Keep it up."

They walked past Diamond without responding to her comment. They reached Stink's room and closed the door behind them. JT pulled all the packs from his four pockets and tossed them on the bed. He went through all the packs to make sure each bundle was still a whole one. It turned out to be over two thousand dollars in drugs.

"Chemical gave you all this shit?" Stink asked

"Naw, most of it was Hammer's. Hammer was supposed to take care of you when you got there, so this is all of it right here."

"You gon' tell Chemical you still got all of it?"

"Hell yeah, I got to."

"No you don't. You could say the police found it."

"What about when Hammer get out and say they didn't find shit but a few packs? I ain't tryna get my ass beat like you did."

Stink knew JT was right, but he wasn't thinking clearly, staring at all the bundles of heroin on the bed. Considering the risk factor involved, he might have to just follow JT's lead on this. Getting another beat down was out of the question.

"This is what we gon' do," JT said.

Stink was all ears. Whatever JT came up with, he was all in, whether it was a good or a bad idea.

Stink called Chemical and met up with him a few hours later. He ran down an elaborate story about how he was the one who secured the drugs after the police left the scene. Chemical was very thankful that he didn't have to take another loss along with the bail money and lawyer fee he may have to kick out for Hammer. He was also happy that Stink was learning how to be true to the game instead of the little slickster he had started out to be.

He gave Stink 50 dollars and told him he could start getting paid again the following day.

The next day, JT went to school and left Stink to deal with the hot ass block. JT hung out with Romell and Dusty, relishing in the attention he was getting from all the girls that used to pay him none at all. He saw Sherida at lunch. She asked why Stink had not come over to meet her mom yet. He told her he didn't know, but that he would gladly come over if Stink didn't want to.

Sherida gave him a look of skepticism.

"I'm just playing." JT said, even though he wasn't.

"Whatever."

"You is fine, doe."

"Thanks. My cousin looks a lot like me but she don't go to Knudsen."

"Dang foreal? Hook it up."

"Okay and you hook it up with yo' boy."

"Okay."

JT walked away, amazed that a girl actually liked Stink—a fine one at that. After that conversation, JT decided that he was going to convince Stink that he needed to visit Sherida asap so he could meet the fine cousin. As the school day went on, JT did little work. He knew how to do the work, but now that he was so popular, he thought it was better to have a girl do it for him or at least give him the answers.

After school, he didn't rush home. Instead, he posted up with Romell and Dusty, flirting and whispering mannish things to everyone in a skirt. When the school grounds were almost empty, the trio turned to leave. JT spotted Toya and two of her friends headed their way. She was looking too good to let her pass by.

He stepped to her. "What's up, Toya? Don't be acting like that, girl."

"Acting like what?" Toya asked.

"Like you don't know nobody."

"Boy, I don't even never see you in school. What is you talking about?"

Romell and Dusty distracted Toya's friends, leaving JT alone to talk with Toya.

"So where you been at?" Toya asked.

"I been chillin'."

"Where yo' boy at?"

"Who, Stink? I think he came down with the flu or something. But let me ask you something. How did you know my name?"

Toya waved him off. "Boy, please. Everybody know y'all bad asses cause y'all always in some shit. I always said you was cute, but you used to be dusty as hell!"

JT's eyes widened in shock. He couldn't believe Toya had just blazed him like that. He couldn't think of a comeback, so he slapped her school books out of her hand and onto the ground.

Toya bent down to pick them up, cursing the whole way down. “Why the fuck you just do that? Ignorant ass lil’ boy.”

She was still grinning so he knew that she wasn’t really upset with him. She seemed to always have a slight grin on her face like she was thinking of something funny that happened.

“Shut up, you shouldn’t have called me dusty. That’s Dusty over there.” He pointed to Dusty who was trying to get his mack on.

“Dusty been clean for a while now, too. What y’all been up to?” she questioned.

“Mind yo’ business, kid. What’s up with me and you?”

Just then, two girls came walking up from out of nowhere.

“JT, you fake as hell!” one of the girls spat. She looked upset and JT didn’t understand why. He knew the girl, but he had just met her.

“What I do?” he asked.

“I thought you said you was gon’ call me.” He couldn’t believe that was what this was about. She was clearly trying to throw salt in his game with Toya.

“I did call you yesterday. Yo’ mama said you was gone.”

“Yeah right, fuck you nigga!” the girl said as she walked off.

"Fuck you too," he shot back.

Toya gathered her girls so they could get off the school grounds and head home.

"Where you going?" JT asked.

"Um, you too player for me."

"What? I don't like her. Why you think I ain't called her?"

"It's cool, you still my nigga doe. But I'ma holla at you." Toya gave him a pound and walked off.

JT stood there looking puzzled.

Stink had rented a red Ford Taurus from a crack head who was friends with his mom. He wasn't very experienced with driving, so he picked up lil Scurvy who was already a pro. He was supposed to be hustling instead of joyriding. So, to cover his tracks, every once in a while, he'd park the car long enough to sell a few packs in case Chemical showed up looking for money.

He drove up and down the same eight blocks all day. Scurvy was showing him the ropes. He'd drive past the owner of the car, who would try to flag him down in hopes of getting more money to buy more drugs. Stink just blew the horn and drove right past.

"Let me drive again, dog." Scurvy pleaded.

"Watch out man, I just got back under the wheel."

"Come on, man," Scurvy begged.

"Fuck dat, I'm bout to drive up to the school."

"Hell yeah, they just letting out too."

They headed off in the direction of the school. Once on the main road, Stink began to swerve in the lanes. Scurvy argued that he shouldn't be driving, but Stink refused to relinquish the wheel. It only took them about five minutes to get to Knudsen, and Stink immediately spotted JT, who was standing at the bus stop on Chene.

As Stink zoomed in on the female Stink was talking to, he was excited to see Sherida. He bust a wild and shaky U-turn and pulled up at the bus stop. The *Above the Rim* soundtrack thumped from the car's stereo system.

Stink put the car in park, and instead of speaking to Sherida or JT, he just sat there rocking to the beat. He was profiling his gear *and* the rental.

JT was shocked to see Stink driving, but he didn't let it show. He opened the passenger side door and told Scurvy to get in the back seat. Scurvy didn't argue. He was looking for a reason to get out of the car so the girls at the bus stop could see how fresh he was.

Stink could see that Sherida was eyeballing him, but she was also trying to play it cool and not look as impressed as she was. The other girls at the bus stop didn't try to hide their enthusiasm.

"What's up, Sherida?" Stink finally said.

She moved closer to look inside as if she didn't know who was talking to her.

"Oh, hey Stink. I didn't know that was you. Who car you driving?"

"My pop's," Stink lied.

"Can you give me and my girl a ride home?"

Stink glanced at the girl standing next to her. She was decent looking, but not as fine as Sherida.

"Where your girl live at?"

JT punched Stink in the arm to signify that it didn't make a difference where the girl lived. He just wanted them in the car. What was the point in having a car with no girls in it?

"She lives right down the street from me," Sherida said.

"Come on," Stink said.

The girls climbed in the back seat and snuggled in with Scurvy.

They looked too uncomfortable to JT, all cramped up with Scurvy's punk ass. "Scurvy, you gotta walk, dog." JT said.

"Yeah right," Scurvy said, thinking it was a joke.

"I'm for real, dog."

Stink was thinking the same thing, but he wasn't going to mention it. After all, Scurvy had been with him all day, teaching him how to drive. On the other hand, he didn't want to draw any attention to the car if he was going to be leaving the neighborhood.

"Yeah, he right doe, Scurvy. We might get pulled

over, five deep."

"Man, you better make these hoes walk!" Scurvy said furiously, as he realized that they were not joking. He was heated, and now because of his disrespectful comment, the girls were too.

A screaming match ensued in the back seat while JT opened the door and calmly waited for Scurvy to exit the vehicle.

"Man, fuck y'all!" Scurvy yelled as he maneuvered from the back seat. "Y'all gon' make me walk, so they can ride? That's some bullshit!" He stormed up the block, mumbling profanity.

"Man, it's only ten blocks to yo' house. Quit tripping." JT said, laughing at Scurvy.

They made another U-turn. All four of them giggled at Scurvy as they drove past. Stink and JT didn't care at all that Scurvy was mad. Although they were friends, his choice to mix crack cocaine in with his marijuana made them view him in a different light. Without realizing it, they had lost respect for Scurvy.

They arrived at Sherida's house and she invited them in. They were not expecting to be invited in the house, and now Stink was nervous.

"Where yo' mama at?" he asked.

"She gone to work. She won't be back for a few hours."

They followed her inside and went straight to the kitchen and in the refrigerator.

"What y'all got to eat in this muthafucka?" Stink hollered from the kitchen.

Stink's lack of home training was evident everywhere he went.

"Look in there and see," Sherida hollered out back to him.

JT thought Sherida's friend was okay, but he was holding out to see what the cousin looked like. In the meantime, he showed the girl that was sitting next to him very little attention. She finally got the hint and left.

Sherida called her cousin, and she was there within the hour.

When she walked in, Stink and JT had to take notice. She was short with caramel skin and green eyes.

Sherida made the introductions. "JT, this is Kizzy. Kizzy, this is JT and Stinky butt."

"I'll be Stinky butt, funky ass!" Stink replied.

They all shared a laugh, which was a great icebreaker and gave JT the opportunity to move in and get his mack on. He couldn't stop grinning as he began asking all the normal questions about her age, school, etc. The four of them all naturally clicked, and the boys made sure they kept the girls laughing their hearts out the whole time.

Normally, neither Sherida nor Kizzy went for guys their own age, but they considered these boys to be different. Different in a sense that they were driving at thirteen years old and they wore expensive shoes and clothes like the older boys.

Neither was actually thirteen yet, but their birthdays were right around the corner, so they lied to keep up with the girls who were already officially teenagers. Stink tried to introduce them to weed, but both girls declined. He then asked if they could smoke. Sherida told them to take it outside.

Outside, they made comparisons to see whose girl was on who the hardest. They attempted to roll a blunt, which neither was good at yet. By the time the blunt was rolled, it was completely in shambles.

"It's smokeable," Stink said.

As they puffed on the disfigured blunt, a car came cruising up the block that looked vaguely familiar. As the car got closer, it no longer looked vaguely familiar; it looked just like Chemical's car. The car slowed and pulled over in front of Sherida's house. By now, the marijuana had decreased their response time, but it was definitely Chemical. Not knowing what else to do, Stink tossed the weed and went inside.

JT followed behind him, not knowing what to expect next. Technically, he hadn't done anything wrong, being that he'd just left school. Stink, however, was surely on the clock and would probably have some explaining to do. They obviously had been made on the porch. *But, how did he know?* JT thought.

"I bet Scurvy bitch ass told 'em where we was," he said, moving through the house, still following behind Stink.

"What's wrong with y'all?" Kizzy asked, puzzled.

"Scurvy don't know where she stay," Stink reminded him.

The doorbell rang and Sherida ran to peek out the curtains before answering the door.

"Oh, this my uncle y'all. It's cool." Sherida said.

The guys sat down on the couch and remained stiff as boards while Chemical walked in nonchalantly, ignoring them both.

"Hey niece," he said, hugging Sherida and greeting Kizzy. He then turned to the couch JT and Stink were plastered to. "Small world, huh fellas?" He shot a malicious grin at the dynamic duo who were becoming more shook by the moment.

They didn't know what to think, because they didn't know if Chemical was upset or not. Stink felt like a six-year old about to be sent to his room.

"Whatchu doing over here?" Sherida asked.

"For some reason, your mama told me to come by and check on you. She told me you been becoming more and more sneaky lately, and look at this shit here. Why you ain't call yo' mama when you got home?" Chemical stood in the middle of the room silent, waiting for an answer.

"I forgot."

"Yeah, I see why you forgot."

"You know my peeps or something?" Sherida asked her uncle, referring to Stink and JT.

Chemical's neck went back and one eyebrow lifted.

"Yo' peeps? Them my peeps."

"Yeah right, how they yo' peeps?"

"Oh, you don't believe me, huh? Watch this. Let's go fellas." Chemical snapped his fingers and pointed to the door, while his workers shamefully got off the couch and followed their boss out of the house.

"Aiight y'all," JT said as he reached the door.

JT was embarrassed, but he knew it could have been a lot worse, especially for Stink. Stink, on the other hand, was more upset than embarrassed. He didn't like people telling him what to do and when to do it. JT didn't take it that personal. He felt they had a good deal going, and they should try to keep up their end of the deal and be where they were supposed to be.

From Sherida's house, they followed Chemical back to the block. Stink was told to take the car back and hit the stroll, so he did as he was told. He and JT stayed out on the strip until almost midnight.

CHAPTER 5

Over the next few weeks, the block became an inferno. The police constantly chased them. They barely avoided capture and were always hiding in bushes and vacant houses or behind cars. The money was good, but it was becoming too much to handle.

When Hammer got out of jail, he was bumped up to lieutenant. He mostly just picked up and dropped off. Scurvy took his place on the block, and together, the three of them did less and less hustling every day. None of them wanted to go to jail, but no one wanted to quit either. With his pockets getting noticeably thinner, Chemical finally got fed up and sent Stink and JT to his spot on the Westside that sold heroin and crack cocaine. 40 Grand also had a stake in the house. The crack belonged to 40 Grand, while the Heroin was Chemical's. So now, they had two bosses instead of one.

Once Sherida and Kizzy figured out that the youngsters actually worked for Chemical, they were infatuated. The hard part was trying to see them from the Westside

They had all but dropped out of school, and only talked to the girls on the phone from time to time. After countless conversations from the neighborhood payphone, Stink, Sherida, Kizzy, and JT all lost their virginity one morning at a skip party held at Sherida's house.

Stink fell hard for Sherida and it showed. He went to the phone booth two or three times a day, staying gone for an hour each time.

JT held his composure a little more, even though he did like Kizzy a lot. However, they had sex every chance they got, after the first time. It was an immediate addiction for them both. Chemical would fuss about them missing sales at first, but he wouldn't be too upset. Eventually, the boys' racing hormones began to cost him too much money and something had to be done to keep them sitting still.

Chemical boarded up the front door to the house and put bars on all the windows. The back door had an armor guard gate, which stayed locked at all times. Chemical and 40 Grand were the only ones with keys to the gate.

Stink and JT were locked in the drug house with no way out. They still had the option to quit, but then it was back to the life they were living before hustling.

They hated being trapped in the spot like this but didn't see any other options. They were making money but didn't have any time to spend it on anything. Chemical brought them a change of clothes, and food when they needed it. All they did for weeks, was sit in the spot selling drugs out of the back door through the armored guard gate. They smoked weed all day to pass the time.

"I ain't feeling this shit," JT finally confided.

"What?" Stink asked.

"This, sitting in the spot, all day every day. I mean, I know we need the money, but shit! When he gon' let us leave? I ain't got no pussy in two weeks."

"I'm hip, me neither." There was a knock at the back door. "Your turn," Stink said.

JT shook his head in denial. "I got the last one."

The weed had made them both lazy, and now, instead of fighting over sales, they were fighting to give them away. They were losing the enthusiasm they had started with. It was all work and no play, which made for two dull boys. The knocking on the door continued until JT finally got up to answer it. When he peeked through the peephole, he couldn't believe his eyes. *What was she doing standing on their back porch?* He thought.

"Stink, it's yo' mama," JT said.

He opened the door. He was speechless as Diamond stood at the threshold with her mouth twisted and her eyes looking dead tired, as if she'd been up for days.

"How my babies doing?" Diamond said, peeking through the armor guard to see what and who was in the background.

"We good, Ma, but how you get over here?" JT asked.

"My friend is outside in the car. The one that Stink rented the red car from that time. He wanna know do y'all want to rent it again?"

Stink made his way to the door and eased past JT. "What's up, Mama?"

"Hey baby, open the damn door. Why y'all got me standing outside like I'ma rob y'all or something, shit!"

"We can't open the door," Stink said.

"Why not?"

"We don't got a key to the gate."

"What? You mean to tell me y'all locked in this muthafucka?"

"Yeah," Stink said, feeling a little embarrassed.

"Damn, the man wanted to rent his car tonight. You mean to tell me we drove all the way over here for nothing? Y'all need to get up out of here and come back to the eastside, 'cause this shit ain't right." She was talking and thinking at the same time. Thinking on how she couldn't leave empty handed.

"Let me hold a couple stones, and ten dollars for gas."

"Aiight, I'll give you the ten dollars," JT agreed.

"Aiight."

Stink went off to his stash to grab his crack sack and retrieve two rocks from it. Stink realized his mother's habit was getting worse. She had a look of desperation in her eyes, and her appearance was slowly declining.

Later on that night, Hammer came by to drop off some White Castle and some more drugs. The two voiced their concerns about when they were going to be able to come and go as they pleased again. There wasn't much Hammer could say or do, considering he was a worker just as they were. Since they never knew when Chemical or 40 Grand would stop by the house, he did agree to relay the message about their concerns.

Born three days apart, Stink and JT both had birthdays coming in April. They vowed that they wouldn't be sitting in the spot selling drugs for their thirteenth birthdays.

"If they don't wanna let us go, I'm leaving anyway. Fuck them niggas!" Stink said.

"Yeah, fuck them niggas." JT agreed.

By midnight, they had smoked a few blunts and were high as kites when the crack traffic began to pick up substantially.

They hid the money in a hole in the couch and continued to hustle. The next knock on the door was strange; almost like a code. It was JT's turn again, so he wandered to the door, thinking about the odd knock. He peeked through the hole and saw a shadowy figure.

"Take yo' hood off so I can see you," JT ordered.

The man complied, and JT saw that it was crackhead Leon, a regular customer. He opened the door and Leon stuck a twenty dollar bill through the gate.

When JT reached to grab it, another man appeared, dressed in all black and yanked JT's arm through the bars. JT's head banged against the iron gate and he felt the barrel of a gun on his forehead.

"Give me all that shit, nigga, and what you got in yo' pockets."

Stink heard the scuffle and ran to the back door to see what was going on.

"Back the fuck up, you lil bitch!" the gunman yelled. He pointed the gun at Stink. He had no choice but to cooperate.

JT wasn't strong enough or stupid enough to try and struggle free from the gunman. He gave up the dope sack and the money in his pockets. The man shoved JT to the floor and took off running. The crackhead, Leon, on his tail.

At first, JT laid on the floor, propped up on his elbows in a daze. For a moment, he was just glad to still be alive, but then his anger began to rise as he realized that he had just been bullied out of his sack that quickly.

"You aiight?" Stink asked.

JT rubbed the knot on his forehead. "Yeah." He got up and kicked the kitchen cabinet as hard as he could.

"I tried to tell them niggas we needed a gun," Stink said.

Chemical disagreed wholeheartedly. In his mind, if they killed someone, the spot would be shut down permanently. He'd rather take the risk of getting robbed, than trusting two kids with guns.

"Man, them niggas don't give a fuck about us," JT said.

They sat in silence, feeling sorry for themselves until Stink spoke.

"How much they get?"

"About five hundred altogether, money and dope."

"You know they gon' doc yo' pay for that?"

"Man, that shit wasn't my fault, I ain't paying for that shit!"

Stink had something on his mind already, but this time, he figured it was best if JT came up with a plan. His last move got him an unforgettable beat down.

"What you wanna do then?" he asked.

JT pondered the question before he spoke because he knew what Stink was asking. "We can get out of here if we really wanted to... you wanna?" JT said.

"And take everything?"

"Hell yeah, them niggas don't give a fuck about us. I could've got killed tonight, and you think I'm bout to pay them niggas 'cause I got robbed? Fuck that!"

Stink didn't really need convincing. He was already on the same page.

"Fuck it, come on!"

The two gathered up all the money and drugs they had left. They searched the house until they found enough bedsheets to make a tight rope. Once in the attic, they pushed an old bed over to the window, then tied the homemade rope to the bed frame. They tossed the rope to the ground, and in less than two minutes, they were free.

Now they just had to figure out where they were going to hide out.

Toya had to sleep with one eye open these days. She was growing more and more leery of Bryant's old, ugly, perverted ass. The more her young body developed, the more he began to gawk at her lustfully. He'd brush up against her backside in the kitchen or get drunk, and try to get her to sit on his lap as if she was five. She knew if she mentioned any of this to her mother, Letia would kill him and go to prison forever.

When the door crept open, she thought it was her mom coming to tell her she had made it home from wherever she'd been. To her surprise, Bryant entered the room with his bathrobe wide open, revealing the fact that he wasn't wearing anything under it, with the exception of some tight briefs.

"What the fuck is you doing?" Toya asked with one eye open.

"I need to talk to you."

Bryant staggered in and she could tell he was drunker than usual by the way he swayed from side to side before flopping down on the bed.

"Turn on the light." she said, finally sitting up in her bed and wrapping her blanket around her body.

He didn't make an effort to get off the bed. "I ain't worried about that right now," Bryant said in a drunken slur.

"Why you won't turn the light on?"

"I ain't worried about that. I need to talk to you

about... now me and yo' mama is gon' have to talk too... cause I'm sick of this shit. Do you think you can talk to her for me? Cause, cause I need you to talk to her for me."

"About what?" she said as she finally jumped up from the bed to turn on the light herself.

Bryant threw up his hands in a helpless gesture.

"Talk to her about what?" she repeated.

"Well, for one, she ain't never here. I'm tired of sleeping alone —"

"Aiight. I'll talk to her, bye."

"I'm just saying, I get lonely at night, you know?"

"I said I'll talk to her. Bye, I'm trying to go to sleep.

"Why you do me like that, baby girl?" His breath was, horrendous and the alcohol was spilling from his pores, smothering the air in the room.

"Do you like what? I'm trying to sleep."

"Aiight, I'm gon' get up outta here so you can go to sleep." He tried to stand, but was too dizzy and weak, and had to sit back down.

Toya tried to help him up.

"Give yo' Uncle Bryant a hug, you know I love you."

He leaned in, but she waved him off. "I don't want no hug. Just get out my room, dang!"

Once on his feet, he kneeled over her and wrapped his arms around her anyway. The cheap liquor blasted through her nostrils as she tried to push him off.

"Get the fuck off me!" she yelled. It took all her strength to push his dead weight off her. Bryant collapsed on the bed and exhaled. "Get out my bed right now, Bryant!"

As she gave the order, she slid the kitchen knife from under her pillow.

"Wait a minute girl. Can't you see I'm drunk?" Bryant said, not seeing the weapon.

Toya stood over him and exhaled slowly. "I'm giving you til the count of three to get out of my bed."

"Or else, what?" He taunted as he stretched out on the bed, leaving only his feet on the floor.

Toya was enraged and didn't have any patience left.

"One... two... three!"

She jabbed the knife wildly into Bryant's thigh. He let out a shriek that could be heard in the neighbor's basement. She removed the knife from his thigh and jabbed it into his stomach. Toya went to jab again, but somehow, he managed to grab her wrist. He held her wrist with one hand and his stomach with the other.

"Please stop," he begged.

Toya snatched her arm free and ran from the house.

JT and Stink had twenty-five hundred dollars' worth of crack cocaine and heroin, as well as two thousand dollars in cash. Most of the money was actually their own, being that they never left the spot to spend any of the pay.

They went back to the Eastside, but knowing they couldn't go home, they ended up hiding out at a crack-head named Yvette's house. She lived far enough for them to feel a little safe, but close enough to the block that they could still get there and hustle without too much trouble.

They were basically on the run from Chemical and 40 Grand, so they had no choice but to give the dope to the people they believed would be trustworthy to sell the dope and pay them the money owed. They called in Romell, Dusty, and yes... Lil Scurvy.

"You seen Lil' Scurvy?" Stink asked.

"Naw, not since yesterday." They hopped in the car they had rented from another dope fiend and went to the block that Romell and Dusty hustled on.

"We shouldn't keep this car too long. People are going to start saying they seen us in it, and next thang you know, them niggas a be rolling up on us." JT said.

"We straight. We just gonna use it to get to the block and back, that's it."

"We need some guns."

"I know. We should see if Romell know somebody."

They knew that no one would be able to sell them guns without the word getting back to Chemical. Romell was probably their only hope.

When they got to Romell's block, they spotted him and Dusty in the middle of the street. It was April, and there was a light drizzle outside. Dusty and Romell wore hoodies over their heads, but you could always spot the two when they were together, because of the difference in size. Romell was tall, and looked older than he was, while Dusty was short with more of a baby face. They were supposed to be hustling for Romell's older brother, but had agreed to push Stink and JT's drugs on the side, for a cut of the profit.

"Happy birthday, nigga!" Romell said to Stink who was turning thirteen.

"I'm telling you now. Don't try that birthday lick shit with me, nigga!"

"Aww man, ain't nobody bout to—"

Bam! Romell punched him in the shoulder as hard and he could.

"That's one, I got twelve to go."

"Might as well get it out the way now," JT said, throwing the car in park.

Stink tried to climb in the back seat, but Dusty had the door open, already waiting for him while JT grabbed his legs and held him down. They beat his ass like he'd stolen something, and then made jokes about the way Stink was screaming like a girl. The four of them had a good laugh, and although Stink was in a lot of pain, he knew it came from love.

Romell and Dusty paid some of the money they owed and informed the two that they hadn't seen Scurvy. In all the excitement, they forgot about the guns. They didn't realize it until they found themselves outside at a phone bank, trying to get in touch with Sherida and Kizzy. They watched every car as they drove by. To them, every blue car looked like Buick 442 Cutlass. They were glad they had decided to leave the spot, but now they were realizing the hardest part of it all was going to be watching their backs.

They didn't know what kind of car to look for as far 40 Grand was concerned, because they only saw him with Chemical.

Still, it was all well worth it. They had fresh fades, and Stink had just copped some white on white Air Force Ones with a pair of black Girbaud jeans. A lot of cats around the hood their age were hustling, but none of them were walking around with thousands of dollars in their pocket.

"Them bitches still ain't answering the phone, dog." JT complained.

"You think we should just go over there?"

"Naw, we called 'em both and they ain't answering, so they must don't wanna be bothered no more."

Either out of respect for Chemical or for the safety of JT and Stink, the girls stopped taking the calls after they ran off from the spot. The still managed to party the whole weekend and celebrate each other's birthdays. They met some older girls at the mall and lied about their ages to get them. They got drunk and high and had sex with fifteen-year-old chicks every night until the middle of the week, which was three days past JT's birthday.

They finally caught up with Scurvy, and he only had

half of the money he was supposed to pay them. Scurvy looked nervous as if he was expecting a beat down. Stink and JT had already agreed not to hurt Scurvy because he was their friend. They never factored in that Scurvy had a slight drug problem of his own when they gave him the drugs. They had to cut Scuvry off.

A week after they had run off, almost all the drugs were gone. Stink had already spent almost all of his profits, except five hundred dollars. He spent most of the money on clothes. It was obvious that he loved to look good. JT had done a little better with his money and he still held on to almost a grand. They still had money to get from Dusty, and he was nowhere to be found. It was starting to look like Romell was covering for him. Romell had promised he could get them matching 32 automatics, but now it seemed he was reneging on the deal for no real reason.

Dusty owed them five hundred. JT wasn't tripping about it, but Stink was in dire need of his two-fifty. He wanted to be able to cop at least an ounce. That night, he went out looking for Dusty and decided he would stop by Dusty's house one last time.

To JT's surprise, Diamond popped up at Yvette's house. She never really liked Yvette, but this day, she played it as if they were best friends.

"Heyyy girl!" She slid in the door and hugged Yvette.

She came with a fifth of Thunderbird, knowing

it was Yvette's favorite. JT came out of the backroom when he heard the familiar voice. He was counting money, but once he spotted Diamond, he quickly tucked it in before she could leech. Diamond had on a low cut top and a mini skirt, with her hair in a wrap. She wore lipstick, which was a rare sight in itself, but JT was most surprised to notice her nipples poking through her halter-top.

She moved briskly past Yvette to give JT a hug, like she hadn't seen him in months. When he hugged her, he noticed she was also wearing perfume. If he didn't know better, he would have thought she was about to go on a date.

"Where you coming from, Ma?"

"Ain't this a bitch! Last time I checked, I was grown. You said the right word, ma, so mind your bizness, son." She finished with a forced laugh, while glancing at Yvette.

JT was just hoping that she hadn't started tricking for crack. It didn't take him long to figure out she didn't have any money, so he ruled out tricking for the moment.

Diamond and Yvette sat in the kitchen making small talk and JT provided them with the entertainment—one rock to split between the two of them. *That is just like Diamond to find a way to get in where she fit in,* he thought. She knew the chances were high that Yvette would be getting high for free since JT and Stink were posted up at her house.

JT chilled in the bedroom smoking on a blunt

watching re-runs of *Married with Children*. Just as he was dozing off, he felt someone shaking his leg. He opened his eyes to see Diamond standing over him, tipsy off thunderbird.

"Baby, I need some dope."

"Ain't got nothing."

"Come on, JT, cut the bullshit.

"I'm serious," JT said.

Diamond straightened and placed her hands on her hips. She looked flustered, embarrassed, and disappointed. She didn't like to beg. "You got something, I know you do."

"I'ma be honest with you, I got two rocks left and those are Yvette's. She told me to keep them until you left so she could smoke by herself."

"Man, fuck that bitch, JT! Let me get 'em. At least one." she insisted.

"I can't do that to her and we sleeping in that lady's house."

Diamond's eyes rolled around in her head as if she were brainstorming. Then she started to sway her body back and forth, as she questioned JT about Stink's whereabouts.

"I ain't seen him in a few hours. He was out looking for Dusty."

Diamond began to brainstorm again. It was obvious she wasn't about to give up easily. "Why he looking for Dusty, he owe some money or something?"

"Yeah, something like that."

She casually strolled over and closed the bedroom door. She came back and stood over JT, who was still lying down. He was high as a kite and wishing Diamond would just leave.

"How about this..."

She eased one hand under his shirt and another on his zipper. She slid his shirt up just enough to kiss his navel and unzipped his jeans at the same time.

JT was bewildered, but his little head quickly took control of the big head. Nobody had ever sucked his dick before, and he had heard enough about it to know it was supposed to be a wonderful experience. At that moment, he just wanted to know what it felt like, so he didn't resist as Diamond's mouth engulfed his penis. JT's conscience gave way to ultimate bliss.

At that moment, Diamond wasn't his best friend's mother. She was just a woman he'd secretly lusted for and now he was having his way with her.

Five minutes into it, he heard Stink's voice somewhere in the house. "Where JT at?" he heard Stink ask Yvette.

JT and Diamond shuffled around the room trying to organize themselves as the footsteps came closer. JT decided to fake sleep, while Diamond opted to act as if she was watching TV.

Stink entered the room. "Hey, Mama. JT wake up!"

"Hey, baby, where you been?" Diamond replied with a guilty look plastered on her face.

Luckily, Stink's mind was on other things. "Looking for this nigga, Dusty, that owe me some money. JT get up."

JT rolled over, wiping his eyes. His penis was still hard.

"What's up?"

"We gon' have to fuck Dusty up!"

"Okay!"

"I'm for real!"

"Okay, I'm with you." JT didn't feel one way or the other about hurting Dusty. He was more of an associate than a friend.

"Son, I need ten dollars." Diamond said.

Stink reached in his pocket and gave her ten dollars. JT was now wondering why didn't he just do that instead of what had taken place. He knew he had committed an unforgiveable act.

The next day, Stink and JT looked for Dusty all morning. They went to the school, they searched the blocks he hustled on, and they went to his house several times and knocked on the door. JT was feeling extremely guilty, and he thought whooping Dusty's ass would make him feel more like a friend than he did right now. He told himself it wasn't his fault. She came on to him.

They ran into Scurvy, who swore he had seen Dusty ten minutes ago. Stink stomped on the gas, determined to catch up with Dusty once and for all. When they pulled up in front of the arcade, there was a big crowd outside as usual; mostly the girls and boys from the neighborhood that never went home after school.

JT hopped out first, and ran down the side of the building. He knew there was a pile of two by fours over there. Stink followed him, not knowing what he was doing until he saw the pile of wood.

JT grabbed one and Stink grabbed another. Someone must have tipped Dusty off, because by the time they made it back to the front of the building, he was making his escape.

JT ran out on to the main street, dodging traffic as he snuck up behind Dusty.

Bam! Clocked him once in the back of the head.

Bam! Stink followed with another one.

Dusty fell into the street between the yellow lines. Cars swerved around the group of kids pouring out into the streets to witness the assault. They continuously took turns pummeling Dusty over the head, back, and legs.

Dusty tried to block some of the blows, but was unsuccessful. The crowd of onlookers, who were laughing at first, were now stunned and terrified as the two continued to beat Dusty's limp body.

Some kind of killer instinct had taken control of them and everyone in sight knew it. Nobody could stop them and no one tried.

They beat Dusty until he passed out and eventually died from the repeated blows to his head.

CHAPTER 6

Within four hours of the beating, Stink and JT were in police custody. Then came four hours of incessant bullying that doubled as an interrogation. There was no pacifist to intervene, just bad cop and evil cop. Stink threatened to sue, every time the big burly one collared him up.

JT laughed in his face until he found himself on the floor. It was all pointless, because no matter what they did, neither Stink nor JT planned to talk to them.

The next day, they appeared in juvenile court and were charged with Dusty's murder. They were issued a court appointed lawyer. The magistrate presiding over the hearing was a beautiful black woman who couldn't have been over thirty-five.

"Donald Morehouse, can you rise please?" The magistrate signaled him to stand.

"Do you understand the crime you're being charged with?"

"Yes."

"You may be seated. James Taylor, please rise."

JT stood, nonchalantly staring around the courtroom, counting heads.

"Do you understand the crime you're being charged with?"

JT nodded.

"Is that a yes? I need you to speak to me because I don't do body language."

"Yes." JT finally stated.

The court appointed attorney was hesitant to discuss any kind of strategy on how to fight the case until he talked to their parents. The police had unsuccessfully attempted to contact JT's family members. They did get in touch with Diamond and explained that her son was in jail for murder. She never made it to the station, and by the time she made it to juvenile court, Stink and JT were being escorted out of the room after entering a not guilty plea.

The case was in the bag before it even got started. There were over thirty witnesses, and five were willing to testify. Stink and JT had no real defense or explanation for their actions. They had beaten a kid to death in the streets. They were convicted of manslaughter, and sentenced to juvenile until the age of eighteen.

Both would start serving out their time at Wayne County Juvenile Detention Facility. They were given black jumpsuits and placed in the Malcom X pod with the most violent offenders.

Stink and JT adjusted to juvenile like the hoodlums they were. They hooked up with the most notorious and violent cats the jail had to offer.

"Big Pooh, you playing cards or what, man?" Stink said.

Big Pooh was only sixteen and was already 6'1" and 240 pounds. He was light skinned with wavy hair and a thick goatee.

"Yeah, I'm playing." Big Pooh said as he continued to reenact another armed robbery story for all who would listen. "We beat this nigga's ass sooo bad dog!" He pounded on his fist for emphasis.

"Man, them niggas ain't trying to hear that shit, come on!" JT commanded.

"Naw, this ain't no bullshit. This real shit. We be coming for the loot." He was serving time for armed robbery, and all of his fantastic tales impressed everyone except Stink and JT. The way they saw it, he hadn't done anything they weren't capable of doing.

Big Pooh finally strolled over to the card table and joined them. "I'm hungry as hell." Big Pooh said.

JT grabbed his penis with his right hand. "I got something you can eat, you hoe ass nigga!"

Everyone who was in listening range burst out laughing, with the exception of Big Pooh.

"Keep talking. I'ma knock your punk ass out." he shot back.

"Nigga, don't nobody care 'cause you used to box." Stink put his two cents in.

"I'll hit you so hard, yo' mama's mama will feel it."

Big Pooh taunted.

"Play cards, lame, and shut up." Stink said.

"If you see a lame, smack a lame."

"Don't do it, Stink. He ain't worth it." JT joked.

It was all jokes and never taken seriously amongst the youngsters who had mutual respect for each other. That was what it was like every day, all day, in juvie. Young boys with growing balls and testosterone, testing their homies' wit and sometimes patience. They played cards and Dominoes and had gym hours that they spent lifting weights or playing basketball.

JT woke up pissed. He had new school hours, which meant he had to wake up earlier than usual. He looked at the clock and realized he was late. He tried his best to stay out of trouble, because the more trouble you got into in juvie, the earlier you had to retire to your cell. He was trying to work his way up to a level four, so he'd be able to get as much free time as possible.

He threw on his jumpsuit, brushed his teeth, washed his face, and stroked his waves with the wave brush before heading to class. The afternoon teacher was cool, but the morning teacher was a real lame. Middle aged white dude who loved cracking corny jokes that no one laughed at. JT would do his class work most days. There was nothing else to do in class, but work. No girls to flirt with, and nobody to crack jokes with.

After being in class less than twenty minutes, he asked to be excused to use the bathroom. The teacher gave him permission. On the way down the hall, he peeked in the girl's classroom, as he always did. The girls were separated from the boys at all times, and the only way they knew the girls were there was because of the school.

The girl at the teacher's desk looked familiar. Her hair was in her face, but then she swept it behind her ear. He slowed his pace and continued to eyeball her from a distance. She must have felt him watching her when she glanced up in his direction. Toya and JT eyes locked and they were both in disbelief at seeing each other.

Toya gave him her signature grin and JT gave her one back. After that, he kept it moving, knowing he wasn't allowed to talk to the girls. He wondered what she had done to get herself locked away in a juvenile. How long had she been there? When class was over, he couldn't wait to get back to his pod and tell Stink what had happened.

"Guess who I just saw?"

"Yo' mama!" Stink spat.

"Quit bullshitting, I'm serious."

"Who?"

"Toya."

"Fuck is Toya?" Stink questioned.

"Toya Bankhead. I just saw her in school."

"Damn, for real?" Now Stink was excited too. "How she look?"

"She still look good as hell."

"I wonder what the bitch did?"

"I don't know. I was thinking the same thing."

Toya sat in her cell that night with JT heavy on her mind. She hadn't had much time to think about boys since she had been on lockdown. It was the farthest thing from her mind until today. She hadn't seen the streets since the night of the stabbing.

Bryant pressed charges and she was sentenced to three years for assault with intent to do great bodily harm. So far, she had only done six months of the three years. The time was passing by extremely slow, and seeing JT brought an excitement to her life she hadn't felt since she'd been there. She thought about how good he was looking. He had put on some pounds and was taller.

As she went deeper into thought, she began to feel herself getting horny at the thought of him. Technically, Toya was still a virgin. She had let a dude finger her one time, but that was as far as it went.

It was mandatory that inmates set their jumpsuits outside their cells at night, so Toya laid in her cell in her bra and panties, rubbing her index and middle fingers across her clitoris. Her nipples expanded as she pictured JT in bed with her. She slid her panties off and eased the two fingers inside her. She used her free hand to continue to stimulate her clitoris. The pleasure that ran through her body put an arch in her back and made her moan much louder than she had intended.

She didn't care; she was caught up in the moment. One hand now caressed her breast as she envisioned JT's firm chocolate body thrusting in and out of her. She came with shivers that traveled through her body and out of her mouth. She laid in the bed, feeling her heart rate decrease, trying to ignore her own wetness, breathing heavily. Every time Toya had masturbated, she had envisioned a different guy. But after that one, she knew she was going to go steady with JT for a while.

The next day, Toya looked for JT but didn't see him. It was hard, because the girl's bathrooms were inside the classroom, so she could only move around in the classroom. She made several trips to the teacher's desk and to the restroom in hopes of seeing JT in the hallway again. The whole time she was in class, she kept her eyes on the classroom across the hall, which contained all boys.

After school, she vented her frustration over a game of scrabble to a girl named Trouble, who lived up to her name.

"Why don't you just write him?" Trouble asked.

"That's a good idea, I think I will."

"Yeah, tell him you wanna be the first to hit that when he come home."

"Shut up, bitch. I ain't about to say that."

Trouble was a sixteen-year-old girl who was model tall and yellow like the sun. She had big breasts and no ass, but her face was gorgeous. Trouble and Toya had both witnessed each other scrap with broads in the rec room, and had developed a mutual respect because they both had a knuckle game.

"That's not a word, bitch!" Toya spat from the across the table.

"That is a word. Look it up."

Toya scanned the dictionary until she found the word, voila. It didn't sound like it was spelled, and she was still confused about the word, but didn't let it be known.

"You know when a magician saw somebody in half and then they yank the sheet off him? They always say, 'voila!' "

Toya understood what she was saying, but she was still confused as to how Trouble knew how to spell the word.

"I don't even wanna play no more, cause you getting stupid with it." Toya said, knowing that she was defeated.

"Here come your auntie." Trouble said, pointing to sergeant Landrum who was her mother's sister, but did not bear the Bankhead name because of a rocky marriage that left her separated.

Toya had lived with her aunt for a few months in the eighties when her mom had tried rehab unsuccessfully. Keisha stopped by the card table to say hello to her niece as she always did.

"What's up, Keisha?" Trouble said.

"What I tell you about calling me that?"

"Sorry, Sergeant Laaandrum." She dragged out her last name like she didn't want to say it. Trouble was the only one who knew that Toya and the Sergeant were family. They kept it quiet, just so they would be able to get away with certain things.

"You want some KFC?" Sergeant Landrum asked Toya.

"You already know I want some."

"Ok, I'll be back. I gotta warm it up. Don't let nobody see you with it either."

"I'm not, I promise."

"What about me?" Trouble asked.

"That's up to Toya if she wanna share."

"Hold on," Toya said, getting up from her chair. "I need to talk to you."

"What's wrong?"

"Nothing, I just need a favor," Toya said walking beside her. "It's this boy I went to school with. I think his name is James Taylor."

"I know wanna be bad ass, JT!" Keisha said louder than intended.

"You do?" Toya said excitedly. "I want to write him this letter and I want you to give it to him. Please, please, please? You know you my favorite lady in the world, besides my mama."

"You like that old thug, shit huh? You gon' learn... but I'll give it to him. You better write it now and give it to me when come back with your food."

"Okay," Toya replied feeling excited.

Stink sat in the front of the pod watching Pamela Anderson on *Baywatch* running up and down the beach in a red bathing suit, making him hornier by the minute. She was all tits and hair, but it kept his mind off the reality of his world. He may have laughed and joked most of the days away, but inside, Stink was miserable.

He was literally laughing to keep from crying. Stink felt like there was a world of opportunity out there that he was missing out on. Now that he knew how to hustle, it was all he could think about. But more than that, it was the money he thought about and all the things he could do with it. New gear, weed every day, and most of all... girls.

"Man, y'all need to turn this shit off!" Stink complained frustrated now.

"Ain't shit else on," another dude responded.

He knew the dude was right, but Baywatch just made him think about girls. He couldn't take it. "Turn to the music channel," he said.

Someone thought it was a good idea, so the TV ended up on a Wu Tang video called "C.R.E.A.M" Everyone began to nod their heads. It was Stink's first time hearing the song, but he immediately fell in love with it.

When he heard the chorus, Stink jumped to his feet, bowlegs slightly bent at the knees, hands waving in the air. "Hell yeah!" he shouted excitedly. It represented exactly how he felt, and what was important in life to him.

At that moment, he felt like the Wu had wrote that song strictly for his enjoyment. It became his theme, and every day he'd try to keep the TV on the music channel until the song came on. When it came on, he'd sit there nodding his head, while picturing himself in all kinds of fly whips with JT riding shot gun.

Today he got mail from Sherida who he hadn't heard from in a few months. She had been keeping in contact, but it was like for every five letters he wrote, he might get one back. He was excited as he ripped the envelope open and read the first page.

"What the fuck?" he shouted to no one.

The letter started with the usual about her and Kizzy's school life, but then went into a detailed account of her uncle, Chemical, being murdered. Sherida informed Stink that her uncle had been shot fifteen times and found dead in his brand new Mercedes Benz. Stink was in shock for a moment, so he sat back in a daze.

After the shock wore off, he began to admire the way Chemical had died. He had lived and died like a gangster. If you had to go, that was the way to go.

"Taylor, you got mail." he heard the staff call out.

He saw that JT had just come in from school and was about to pick up his mail. If his gut was right, it was probably a letter from Kizzy giving him the same information he had just received.

JT sat down in the day room to read the letter. Stink sat quietly close by as JT read to himself. About a minute into the letter, JT glanced over at Stink, and the look confirmed what he had been thinking the whole time.

"I already know, nigga!" Stink said.

"You know?"

"Yeah... I got a letter from Sherida today."

That's fucked up!"

Stink nodded in agreement. "Real fucked up."

CHAPTER 7

Toya and JT had been corresponding through Sergeant Landrum for weeks. On her off days, if Toya wanted to get a message to JT, she would leave a letter in a certain math book and he'd get it when he went to math class. Today, he was feeling down because Stink had been sent to the Calumet facility to do the remainder of his time there. JT was hoping he was next on the ride out list.

He checked the math book to see if he had a letter, and he did. As he read the letter, he quickly noticed that it had a different tone than the rest of the letters she had written him. It was the first time she was sexually explicit in a letter, and it turned him on. She told JT she wanted him to be her first. She went on to give details of how she wanted him to do it and what she wanted to do to him. He couldn't believe how openly she spoke about fucking, and doubted that she was a virgin, even though she was.

After school, he ran straight back to his pod to show off the letter. Only the niggas in his immediate circle knew about him and Toya. He knew that if the word got back that Sergeant Landrum was the go between, somebody would hate and snitch.

"Look at this shit!" JT said, handing Big Pooh the letter.

Big Pooh examined the letter as if it needed his stamp of approval to be authentic. He was skeptical of the whole story from the beginning. Didn't believe JT had enough game to pull it off. "Damn this bitch a freak!" he said with bucked eyes.

"She claims she a virgin."

"If you believe that, my nigga, you a clown."

"Bitch only fourteen. What is you talking about?"

"Dog... she a freak-a leak."

"I know she is." JT snatched the letter from Big Pooh. "Why you think I let you read it? I'm bout to go write my response to this shit right now."

Later that evening, JT sat in his cell reading the novel, *Whore Son* by Donald Goines. Every time he read one of those Donald Goines or Iceberg Slim books he would get some bright ideas. He'd even stolen some of the dialogue from the books and tried to pass it off as his own. He was believable except to Big Pooh, whom the books actually belonged to. Every time he read something he thought was slick, he'd put it in a letter to Toya.

When he considered the logic that made a pimp rich, it made sense to him. He began to believe he might have pimping in his blood. The more he read those books; it seemed to iron out the details in his mind of what and who he wanted to be in life. His conversation became slicker and his vocabulary extended. He knew that a pimp had to be a charming individual, so he was determined to be the charmer of his circle. He wasn't sure if he wanted to be an all-out pimp, but he really loved the idea of using manipulation to get what he wanted.

The changes benefited JT in a lot of ways. He began to get along with all the staff and break the rules with a little savvier. He considered himself smarter that a lot of the guys he was doing time with and he wanted it to show.

He rose to a level 4, which meant he was a model inmate. He was rewarded with more free time and recreation and he took full advantage of access to the weight room.

One day, after doing a few sets of flies and presses, he sat up for a minute to admire his new biceps. His shit was starting to look good and he knew it. Just under fourteen now, he imagined himself looking like a boxer or a professional wrestler when he came out of jail. He wished Toya could see him with his shirt off right now.

As he sat on the bench, thinking of her, he imagined she was sitting in her cell thinking of him. He had plans to pimp her when he got out. He would make his own moves and get his own bread, but any girl in his life would have to break bread with him. He'd be eighteen at the time of his release, and JT felt he'd have a lot of catching up to do. There wouldn't be time for anyone who wasn't assisting his overall plan. He was almost fourteen, with the mind of a thirty-year-old gangster.

Toya had passed her classmates and was learning quicker and easier than expected. She changed her schedule and started attending a more advanced class. She hadn't seen JT in weeks, and it was killing her. Just to get a glimpse of him walking past in the hallway every blue moon would make her weak. Her aunt would no longer pass along her messages, and she was now begging for one last favor.

It was a huge favor to ask, and Sergeant Landrum couldn't even believe she had fixed her mouth to make such a request. Something like this could cost her job, so at first she refused.

Toya continued to beg, and when her aunt saw how good she was doing in school, Sergeant Landrum decided she was going to do something she might regret.

"Come on, Bankhead," Sergeant Landrum said, keying Toya's cell door.

As they walked down the long corridor, Toya was so jubilant, she began skipping and singing praises to her favorite aunt.

"Shhh! Shut the fuck up before I turn around and take yo' ass back."

"Alright alright. Sorry," Toya said.

"You just as crazy as yo' damn mama."

"I'm glad you noticed," Toya mumbled.

They arrived at the outside door of the weight

room and looked each other in the eyes.

"This is a one-time deal, so don't ever ask me again." Sergeant Landrum said.

"I know. I won't... I promise."

She had agreed to let Toya go in and talk with JT for fifteen minutes. Toya peeked in and saw JT with his back turned. She immediately felt the big grin that spread across her face as she grew nervous and excited. Her heart was pounding in her chest. She couldn't control it; didn't want to.

"You got fifteen minutes. Don't make me have to come get your ass, either."

"I won't, I won't."

Toya slid inside the weight room and glanced around anxiously.

JT spotted her and his eyes grew big with shock. "What the fuck?" he said, as Toya scurried over to the weight bench he was seated on. He turned around to face her and she sat next to him.

"How you get down here?"

"I'm connected," she said, scooting closer until their shoulders collided. "Miss me?"

"For real, how the fuck you get down here?"

"My auntie, dummy."

"Where she at now?"

"Right outside."

JT felt himself getting nervous. He didn't know if it

was Toya, or the fear of getting caught with her. But, who was going to tell with Sergeant Landrum right outside? They stared in each other's faces for a while, just enjoying the reunion. Right then, they knew they had a connection beyond words. JT was still crazy about her caramel skin and sexy lips. The slight grin she always wore instead of a full-scale smile.

"So you didn't miss me?" Toya asked.

"My man, Big Pooh, say you can't miss what you never had."

"Shut up, punk." She jabbed him in the shoulder.

"I'm just playing," he said, wrapping his arm around her small waist.

"So you been thinking about me?" she rephrased.

"Yeah, I been thinking about you a lot."

She batted those pretty brown eyes at him. "You getting big." Toya said, squeezing his bicep.

"Why I ain't seen you in school?"

"Oh, cause I'm in the advanced class now, so I got a new schedule."

JT cut his eyes at her then raised one eyebrow. "Smart girl, huh?"

"Brains and beauty... you could have it all," she said, laughing at her own arrogance.

JT had to laugh himself. There was moment of silence that became uncomfortable after a while. During that time, they both chose to stare at the floor.

"So how much time we got to be alone?"

"She said fifteen minutes."

"You think she'll get mad if I kiss you?"

Toya looked back at the door to see if her aunt was watching her. She was nowhere in sight. She grabbed JT by the hand and led him into the corner where they couldn't be seen. He slid his arms around her and then palmed her ass.

They began to kiss. Toya's lips were soft and moist, just as he had imagined them. As they massaged each other's tongues, JT freed one of his hands and slid it inside her jumpsuit to caress her breasts. Her breasts were warm and smooth.

She felt his erection and began to rub on his dick gently.

JT was rock hard before he knew it. It occurred to him that this was probably a one shot deal. After this, there was no telling when he'd see her again. He began to pull the buttons open on her jumpsuit and she did nothing to stop him. JT kissed Toya's neck as she continued to wiggle out of her jumpsuit until her one piece was down around her waist. He sucked on her breasts, opting from one to the other excitedly.

"Help me," Toya said, fumbling with her bra.

They were both scared to death, but they couldn't stop. There was no time to waste thinking about the consequences. After removing her C cup bra, he was dying to be inside her.

JT laid her on the floor and removed her jumpsuit

completely. He gazed at her nipples, shocked at how big they were.

She pulled his gym shorts and boxers off with one swift yank.

Hearts pounding, lying naked on the floor, JT eased on top of her. He kissed her hard while sliding off her panties. Realizing they didn't have much time, JT grabbed his penis and attempted to insert it in her. Only the head would fit.

As she grabbed his dick to guide him, she was amazed at its heaviness. His dick felt enormous, and while Toya was a virgin, she had grabbed a couple of dicks in her day. They tried together to maneuver him inside her, but neither had any luck. It just wasn't working.

"Damn!" JT said frustrated.

"Hold on," Toya said as she grabbed the head of his tool and rubbed it against her clitoris. She may have been a virgin, but she was a master at masturbating.

She began to moisten a bit more, and slowly he penetrated her pussy. She cried out in pain at first, almost telling him to stop. She held her hand on his stomach, forcing him to be gentler. The pleasure she had been anticipating began to consume her. Every time he went too deep, she would shriek out in pain. JT covered her mouth so he could concentrate on coming and not getting caught. It was slow and steady grind.

They heard a knock on the door as JT stiffened and began to pound her aggressively. It took all Toya had not to yell at the top of her lungs, as JT quickly exploded inside of her.

After knowing what sex was like and having it taken away from him, this was by far the best sex JT had ever had. Having nothing to compare with her experience that afternoon, it was the best sex and the only sex Toya had ever had.

CHAPTER 8

4 years later

Toya had been home almost a year and a half, and she still hadn't found a dude that could compare to JT. Since her mom was doing a bid for armed robbery, she moved in with her aunt Keisha, who still worked as a sergeant for the juvenile facility. As smart as Toya was, she had no interest in school once she was released. She could have easily finished, but it just wasn't high on her priority list.

At age seventeen, Keisha began to put pressure on her to work and be independent. She worked a few fast food jobs, but always managed to get fired because of her attitude. Toya was now eighteen, and she got most of her money from the young hustlers she dated.

She sat at home, trying her best to piece together the events that took place the night before. She had drank too much to remember, so she called Trouble to clarify a few things.

"What up, bitch?" Trouble answered.

"Bitch, where did you go last night?"

"I left with Tank fat ass. I told you I was leaving."

"So how did I get home?"

"You was that drunk, bitch? You really don't remember?"

"Hell yeah I was. I don't remember shit!"

"You said you was leaving with 40 Grand. He called Tank and said you fell asleep in the car, so I guess he took you straight home."

"Damn... I gotta call that nigga and thank him." Toya knew 40 Grand was a true baller. She had never snagged a dude of his caliber.

"Girl it was so many money getting muthafuckas up in that spot last night, that shit was ridiculous," Trouble said.

"Yeah, now that I know we can get in, we gotta hit Floods up more often. Fuck club 2000 and all that other wack shit."

"Yeah, you right. So what's up for today?"

"Ain't nothing up, bout to lay my ass back down. My stomach is killing me. Do you know how to get in touch with 40 Grand?"

"His number should be in your phone."

"Hold on, let me check." Toya sat the house phone down and went to grab her Nextel. She roamed through her phone book, and sure enough, there was 40 Grand's number. She didn't remember taking his number, but was glad she had it. She went back to the house phone. "Girl, I got it."

"You gon' call 'em?"

"Later."

"Aiight den, call me tonight."

"Aiight." Toya hung up and laid back down in her bedroom. She began to think about her mother, and promised herself she would sit down later to write her and send her some money. Toya held no bad feelings towards her mother. They way she saw it, you can't choose your family, and she had no doubts about her mother's love for her.

Stink had only been home for 3 days, and already, he was mad at the world. For starters, his father, Rob, had abandoned his mother and Lil Rob. He hadn't been seen in years. His mother's drug habit was way out of control and he was shocked that she still had legal guardianship of his brother. Stink was short and stocky now. He had become the push up king his last year of doing time. His chest and back was wide and his biceps and calf muscles were huge. He wore his head clean-shaven, believing it gave him a more intimidating look.

As he roamed through his mother's house, he was glad to have some alone time. He couldn't stand to see his mother living the way she was, and his brother was shaping up to be a follower who ran with a group of car thieves. They mostly stole small, inexpensive cars just for the air bags.

The only thing that made him have a good vibe today was the fact that JT was getting out. Both were released on their eighteenth birthdays and both knew exactly what they wanted to do when released. They had two years of probation, but only had to report every other month.

Stink opened the refrigerator door, expecting to see a change. He didn't. Same old KFC bucket that was there before he came home, and a pitcher of ice water next to a box of baking soda. He slammed the door back and checked his shoddy plastic watch for the time.

Every time he looked at the cheap watch, he thought about how he was going to be rocking a Rolex before the year was out. He went on the porch to see if there was any signs of JT. JT hadn't had much contact with his family while away, so Stink was sure JT would come straight to his house.

As soon as he stepped out on the porch, he spotted a tall, dark skinned dude strutting up the street. It had been almost four years since they'd seen each other, but Stink knew JT's black ass when he saw him. It was a little nippy outside, being late April, but still JT wore a black wife beater, showing off his biceps. He had put on some weight, but he was more cut than mass. He still wore the tan khakis and state shoes.

When they made eye contact, they both began to smile. They were coming home to nothing but each other, but somehow, they knew that was enough. JT walked up to the porch and they embraced in a tight hug.

"Damn baby, we gotta hurry up and get you out of them hoe ass state shoes." Stink said.

"I know. Who bought your gear?" JT said, noticing

that Stink was fresh.

"My lil brother and his crew chipped in and got this shit for me."

"Straight up? What bro out here up to?"

"Stealing cars and shit. Wait til you see this nigga doe, he 'bout tall as you."

"Foreal? Fuck dat, you got some pussy yet, nigga?"

"Hell naw, I can't catch up with nobody."

"You ain't even had no dome yet?"

"Oh hell yeah, I had some of that toothless dome last night from this fiend name Tracy. You ain't had that toothless dome yet, that shit is outcold, boy."

"How you know what I had, nigga?"

"Don't start lying already, JT."

"Nigga fuck you!" JT instantly remembered the time he had gotten a blowjob from Stink's mom, right before they went away. He began to feel guilty all over again and changed the subject. "You got any money?"

"I got twenty dollars, and no, you can't have it."

"Let's go get some weed."

"Come on." They started off the porch. "Hold on," Stink said.

"What's up?" JT asked.

Stink pointed at JT's feet. "Them states, baby. We can't go nowhere til you get up out of them."

After JT changed into some of Rob's shoes and gear,

they headed toward the weed house. Stink had already been there a couple times, but always with his brother. As they walked, the conversation was all about money. How to get some, where to start looking, and who had the most, according to the word on the street. Rumor had it that Romell was getting a lot of money in the hood. He was selling weight and had a couple of crack spots.

Stink told JT that Big Tank had money now, according to Rob and his crew. JT remembered Big Tank, who popped up in the hood about a year before he went away.

"Yeah, they said Big Tank got everything. Weed, 'cocaine, blow, whatever."

"We need to holla at him then."

"I don't know that nigga like that."

"What's up with Scurvy?"

"Man, they say Scurvy owe everybody money and he somewhere hiding out."

"Mmmph."

After copping the weed, they went to the liquor store to get a blunt. Diamond was standing outside of the store, along with several other addicts. *She probably trying to turn a trick,* Stink thought.

When she spotted Stink with JT, she took off running in their direction. She ran up and gave JT a big hug that lasted a while.

"Hey Moms," JT said.

"I'm so glad I finally got my babies back, I don't know what to do!" She turned to the other addicts on the corner and smiled. "Y'all see I got my babies back?"

JT was happy to see her, but it was a downer to see what the drugs had done to her. There were still hints of how beautiful she used to be, but she was so unkempt, it would have taken a serious extreme makeover to bring it out.

A Lexus GS400 pulled up and parked in front of the fire hydrant like he was above the law. JT was the first to get a look at the driver. He tapped Stink. "That's Romell."

Romell eyeballed the onlookers outside. Stink and JT caught his eye immediately. If the two weren't standing right next to each other, he probably wouldn't have made them so easily.

He stepped out slowly, rocking a Sean John velour sweat suit and Louis Vuitton gym shoes. A platinum chain hung from his neck with a diamond piece sitting proper on his chest.

Stink instantly felt a hint of jealousy flow through him.

"What up doe?" Romell said in voice much deeper than the one they remembered.

"Whassup, whassup?" JT replied.

Stink's reply was late and dry.

They slapped fives.

"How long y'all been out?"

"I just got out today, Stink got out a few days ago."

"I see you got the 360 waves beating, all cut up and shit. What's good?" Romell said.

"Yeah, yo' shit beating harder than mine. You got that mixed nigga hair," JT replied.

Stink was ice-grilling Romell without even realizing it. He didn't mean to, but as he counted the diamonds in his damn chain, he couldn't help but want to cut to the chase.

"What up, Stink?" Romell said turning to face him.

"Shiiit, I'm trying to eat out here, my nigga. What's up with that work?"

"Oh yeah, I know you boys came home to get that paper."

As they moved the conversation inside of the store, the subject quickly changed to the girls that were better looking now, and who was beefing with who. Stink couldn't help but notice Romell hadn't said anything about the work he referred to outside.

Romell bought some blunts, then they sat in the Lexus and smoked his weed instead of theirs. They learned a lot about what was going on in the streets.

On the outside, things were cool, and everybody was still homies—just like old times. On the inside, everyone knew that Romell had feelings he was harboring. The fact was, the dude they had killed five years ago was Romell's closest road dog.

Stink and JT were hoping there weren't any hard

feelings, but realistically, they knew it would be. *If the shoe was on the other foot, Romell would be dead already,* Stink thought to himself.

"So where y'all niggas staying at? I'll drop y'all off if you want."

"We at my old bird's spot for the moment. You remember the house," Stink said.

As they rode in the Lexus, Stink sat in the passenger seat, thinking it was best not to mention the Dusty incident if Romell didn't bring it up.

JT, who sat in the back, held a different opinion. JT felt like they should get it all out on the floor instead of waiting down the line to find out they had a real enemy to deal with in Romell.

"Aye dog, you know that shit with Dusty was an accident, man." JT said. "The whole thing just got out of control, but that was our man, too."

Stink cringed, and Romell's face hardened. He tried not to reveal his hand, but they all knew it was a bad idea to bring it up this early into their reunion.

"That's water under the bridge dog, water under the bridge." Romell said.

"This the crib right here," Stink said, pointing to the shack he dwelled in.

"I'll be through in the morning so we can talk business." Romell stated.

When they got out of the car, JT was optimistic, but Stink smelled a spin move in the making. After he

broke it down to JT, he agreed. Romell wasn't coming back in the morning. Stink and JT had to think of another avenue to get on.

They decided to split up for a while. Stink went to look for Scurvy and JT went back to the liquor store. It was possible to run into almost anybody if you stood there long enough. Their plan was very simple; get dope and turn Diamond's house into a spot.

Stink had half suspected that someone else would have already taken over his mother's house by now, but he was thanking God that wasn't the case. They knew all of the addicts in the neighborhood, and the newcomers they didn't know; Diamond did. JT ran into a few dudes he knew from school, but no one seemed to be doing any better than he was. As time went on, he grew tired of watching police roll by and giving him the mean mug, so he followed his gut feeling and got ghost. The last thing JT wanted to do was go to jail on his first day home.

As he walked down Chene, a light drizzle began to fall. He pulled the hoodie over his head. He wasn't ready to call it quits just yet. His internal compass told him to go up Fredrick St. As he obeyed, he thought about Toya for the first time all day. She hadn't written him in years, but he still had her home address in his property that he brought home. He wanted to go see her, but not broke; he had to get some paper first.

When he got closer to the corner of Fredrick, he zeroed in on a Cadillac Escalade on big chrome rims. He immediately began to rack his brain, trying to remember who lived in that corner house. Before he could recall, a big boned, brown-skinned girl came out of the house followed by a six-five, fat, dark skinned guy. A closer look at fatboy revealed a platinum chain with a diamond pendant shaped into a capital T.

As fatboy wobbled down the steps and headed towards the Escalade, JT tried to think quickly. He knew he was looking at Tank, who was supposed to be a major player now, but he didn't think Tank would remember him. Shit, he barely remembered Tank. He still couldn't think of reason to not go over and talk to the guy.

Tank watched the dude approaching him with a hoodie on with a cautious eye. JT caught the look on Tank's face and removed his hoodie before approaching.

"What's up, Tank?" JT said as if they were old friends.

"Who is you?" Tank asked with one hand on his door handle.

"Oh shiiiid, I'm JT. You might not recognize me 'cause I been gone away for some years. I went to jail for the incident at the arcade back in the day." Tank's eyes rolled toward the sky as if he were trying to recall the incident.

"You mean when the lil nigga got beat to death?"

JT was a little uncomfortable with the topic, but he was the one that brought it up. "Yeah, yeah, some shit got out of hand, you feel me? But that's old news."

"Yeah, so what's new?"

"I just got out and um... I'm trying to get on with some work, you feel me?

"Aww shit. I can't help you with that, dog. I ain't doing nothing."

Tank quicky piled into the Escalade and started the engine. As he began to pull away from the curb, he rolled down his driver side window.

"Good luck with that doe, homey."

He pulled off and left JT standing in the middle of the street with a pocket full of bruised pride. If he had a gun, he would have taken the truck and that bitch ass chain. He walked home feeling devalued, deflated and deprived.

Later on, JT searched through his property, looking for Toya's address. He found an old letter she had wrote him and read it out of boredom. He was always impressed by her penmanship. It was so unique. When he was finished, he slung the letter on the floor. He couldn't believe it was nightfall and he still didn't have a dime to his name. JT could only hope Stink had better luck than he did.

JT heard footsteps outside. More than two. He ran to the shades to peek out and see what he could see. By the time he made it, Stink and Rob were headed through the front door.

"What up, Lil Rob?" JT said, happy to see Rob for the first time.

"It's big Rob now, nigga." Rob said.

JT was amazed at how much Rob had grown. He was

becoming a mirror image of his father. He really was big Rob now.

"You have any luck?" Stink asked

"Hell naw, I was about to ask you that. I ran into Tank bitch ass and he was acting like he wasn't doing nothing.

"What?" Rob cut in "That nigga is the man around here now."

"Fuck that nigga! I gotta a better idea anyway," Stink said.

"And what is that?" JT asked.

Stink pulled out a seventeen shot chrome Smith and Wesson nine, and Rob followed with chrome 357 Magnum.

"Where the fuck y'all get those?"

"Climbed in a nigga window while he was out of town," Rob said bluntly.

"Yeah, Rob showed me these muthafuckas as soon as I got out. We got a whip outside too, that bitch hot, but fuck it! We gotta do what we gotta do," Stink said.

JT peeked out the shades for a second time and spotted the Chrysler Concord parked out front. What was understood didn't need to be explained to JT. He was down. The plan was simple. They needed money and they needed it fast. Rob made some calls to a few dudes who lived outside of the area. They found some dudes who were willing to buy the guns at the asking price.

Rob drove, while Stink and JT held the burners. When they arrived at their destination, instead of selling the guns, they robbed the buyers for everything they had.

They were pissed that all they got was fifteen hundred dollars to split three ways, but fuck it! Something had to be done.

CHAPTER 9

Five hundred dollars each wasn't gonna get Stink and JT very far, and they knew it. The very next night, they decided to rob the weed house they had been buying weed from. They had noticed the two guys who ran the weed house never had pistols on them. The house was a two-family flat with the downstairs unoccupied. You had to ring the doorbell and then the weed man would come down and let them in. No masks or hoodies on, they would just ring they doorbell and pretend they wanted to buy some weed.

They rang it twice, then they heard someone coming down to let them in. After gazing through the peephole, the weed man cracked the door and let them in to the stairway where the business was conducted. Stink and JT assumed the house had at least a few pounds inside, considering the amount of traffic. They made eye contact with each other, which was the signal to up the burners.

Click Clack! Just as they were about to draw down, they heard the 12 gauge racking and peeped the dude standing at the top of the stairs, daring them to be stupid. Apparently, these dudes took more precaution at night than they did in the daytime.

"What y'all need?" the weed man asked.

Luckily, they had money.

"Couple of dime bags, cuz."

They copped the weed, and was leaving when a Cadillac DTS pulled up. The driver hopped out, moving a mile a minute. They made eye contact with him as he headed towards the front door. They paused. The driver of the Caddy paused.

"Scurvy?"

"The fuck? I know that ain't Stink and JT!"

"Whassup, nigga!" JT said as they all began to slap fives and hug.

The reunion was quickly filled with jokes and laughter, just like old times. Stink had felt Scurvy's pistol poke him when they embraced. Scurvy looked good, like life was favoring him at the moment.

"We been looking for you, nigga. Where the hell you been?" Stink asked.

"Shiiid, I don't come out in the daytime at all. I got niggas on my heels." Scurvy said with a grin.

Stink's eyebrow rose.

"Oh yeah? Well where you headed to now?"

"I got something on the floor, matter of fact..." He paused for a second. "Let me go grab this weed right quick, and y'all can wait for me in the car."

"Bet," JT said.

Scurvy hit the auto locks on his Caddy and headed

into the weed house. When Scurvy came back out, he hopped in and sped off quickly, heading straight to the freeway.

"So what's been up, dog?" JT asked.

"Nothing much, just trying to survive out here." He passed JT some blunts in the backseat and JT noticed his diamond bezel Rolex.

"It looks like you doing a pretty good job of it, nigga!"

"Don't let this watch fool y'all. I pawn this bitch damn near every month."

"This your whip?"

"Naw, this my bitch car."

As the conversation continued, they realized Scurvy wasn't doing that good at all. He was actually doing bad, but he kept his fronts up so people would think otherwise, therefore trusting him with a large amount of dope. He gave them more information about what was going on in the streets. He told them about their old flames. The word on street was that Sherida was a gold digging hoe who stayed hob knobbing with all the major hustlers, friend and enemies. Kizzy had moved to Atlanta.

The car fell silent for a moment, and it appeared Scurvy had something on his mind. His cell phone rang.

"Hello...Where you at? Okay, I'm gon' call you soon as I get to the city." He hung up.

"What you got up, dog?" Stink asked for the second

time.

Silence.

"Is y'all niggas strapped?" Scurvy asked.

"Yeah, what's up? What's popping?" they said.

I got these niggas coming in from Battle Creek and they wanna buy a brick. I ain't got access to no bricks, but I used to sell weight in Battle Creek and they think I still got it like that."

"So what, you wanna rob 'em?" JT said.

"Naw, hopefully we won't even need the guns.

Once Stink and JT heard the word, "we" they knew they were about to be on to something good. They were ready for whatever, as long as they had some money by the end of the night.

CHAPTER 10

Scurvy made them promise on their lives they wouldn't tell anybody where he lived. He was ducked off in a low key apartment building in Southfield. They watched him move methodically through the house, looking for a variety of things. A car funnel, a bag of flour, some duct tape, and a razor blade. By now, they had figured out that Scurvy was about to manufacture a fake kilo. The paraphernalia that laid on the kitchen counter must have come from a real kilo. It had been split open with precision to make sure no damage was done to the packaging.

"So, how many of these niggas is supposed to show up?" JT asked.

"I don't know. I didn't want to scare 'em off, so I didn't even ask. But that's why I need y'all niggas with me. I was gonna hit this lick by myself if I had to, but I sure didn't want to. And don't worry, y'all gonna get y'all cut."

"Oh, we wasn't worried about that," JT said with a cold look in his eyes.

Scurvy was his man, but he'd give him the business if he tried to play them. He had a rough idea of how much a kilo of cocaine cost, and he'd be damn if he put his life on the line and didn't get what he had coming. When scurvy finished with the fake brick, it looked so good, everyone in the room had to admit they would buy it, no questions asked. Stink and JT had never seen a brick in real life, but they'd seen enough on television to know how they were supposed to look.

Scurvy's cell phone rang and he looked at the caller ID. "That's them," he said.

They met on the eastside in a neighborhood that only had fifty percent of its streetlights working. If these dudes were any dumber, Stink would have backed out of it, thinking they had to be cops. But Scurvy said he knew them well, and Stink took his word for it. It took all of sixty seconds for the deal to go down. The out-of-towners pulled up alongside Scurvy in a dark Sedan. Scurvy tossed the fake kilo to the driver. He looked it over for a second and tossed Scurvy a shopping bag full of money. Just like that, they had been Ganked.

"I'm telling you, I'm not going to no Club 2000. That shit was wack as hell," Toya spat. The new millennium club had bust the doors open before the millennium had even kicked in, but it was getting mixed reviews.

"Fuck it den, we can hit Floods." Trouble said as they got close to the downtown area.

Trouble took one hand off the wheel to reach in her jacket pocket and pull out a sandwich bag of pills.

Toya's eyes bucked in confusion. "Bitch what you doing with all them E pills?"

"I been slanging these muthafuckas. I'm on one tonight, doe."

She tossed the bag in Toya's lap. Toya quickly untied the bag and took one out. "We on ex tonight, huh? Fuck it bitch, let's get crunk! I'm bout to be on some other shit tonight, I'm telling you."

It was Saturday night and Floods was flooded with ballers and beautiful women. Trouble and Toya blended right in, because they each had wardrobes to match some the best gold digging hoes Detroit had to offer.

Toya spotted a petty hustler she had shot the wrong number the last time she was here. She maneuvered past him, nice and easy, trying not to be seen. She didn't really go for the run-of-the-mill hustlers. Mistakenly or not, she considered herself to be top notch and worthy of a rich nigga.

She and Trouble arrived at the bar with money in hand. They weren't the type to wait on a nigga to buy them a drink. They could get themselves drunk; they wanted money.

"Double shot of Bombay with cranberry," Trouble shouted over loud music.

"Damn girl, you ain't playing!" Toya said.

"Sure not."

"And let me get a bottle of Moet." Toya told the bartender.

The ecstasy had them feeling a little dehydrated. As soon as Toya got her bottle, she turned it up like a forty ounce. Once she wet her whistle, she poured a drink and tried to act like a lady. They sat at the bar, sipping and studying the crowd, and feeling the music. As Toya studied herself on the stool, her skirt rose up her thigh a little more. Juvenile's "Ha" got mixed in with BG's "Bling Bling" and the dancefloor went nuts. All the ballers threw their ice in the air. Toya wore a small necklace with a heart shaped diamond pendant, which she flashed every time Lil Wayne said, "Bling Bling."

Toya knew as the night went on, she would have to monitor Trouble's alcohol intake as well as her own. She wasn't trying to have another episode like last weekend when she woke up and couldn't remember a thing. After killing almost the whole bottle of Moet, Toya found herself on the dance floor backing that ass up on some dude whose name she had forgotten. She had a slim frame, but her ass was fat enough to make it clap when she wanted to. The pill she had taken earlier was in full effect and she was getting loose on the dance floor. When the song ended, she looked around to see if Trouble was still on the dance floor with her.

"I'll be back," she said to her nameless companion.

"Come here girl where you going?" he said grabbing her arm.

"I'll be back!" she said, yanking away.

Toya left the floor in search of Trouble in the front, but came upon some familiar faces at the far end table. She moved slowly, enclosing all the familiar faces inside her periphery. She calculated the timeline in her head and it confirmed her suspicions. Stink, Scurvy and JT sat at a table in the corner covered with champagne bottles. She couldn't believe she had let JT's release sneak up on her like that.

She spun around and headed back towards the bar, wearing her infamous grin. She took the last hundred dollars she had to her name and bought a bottle of Moet. She scurried back towards the table, getting more excited by the second. There was no doubt in her mind that JT was going to be ecstatic to see her.

When she arrived at the table, she slyly moved in, trying to get the element of surprise. "Welcome back, niggas!" She screamed so loud that it startled everyone at the table as well as some onlookers. She shook the bottle until it began to spray all over the place like somebody had just won a championship.

"Yeah, yeah, yeah. Whassup mutherfuckas!"

They finally realized who the crazy girl party crasher was. JT's eyes lit up as he hopped out of his seat and pulled Toya into a bear hug that lasted forever. She hugged Stink and Scurvy as well, because she hadn't seen either of them in a long time. Once her champagne settled, she filled their glasses and took a step back to get a good look at JT.

He was bigger, taller, and sexier. He wore a Roca Wear button up with blue jeans and some Louis Vuitton sneakers, just like the ones he and Stink had seen Romell rocking. Stink was rocking a button up and jeans, but he had on ostrich skin Cole Haans. Scurvy had kept eleven thousand of the twenty one they made off the lick, leaving them with ten thousand to split between the two of them. They had already spent half of the money on clothes.

"What's up, my nigga? Why you ain't been to see me?" Toya asked.

"Why you think I'm here now? I was looking for you." JT shot back.

"Fuck outta here. Like you really knew I was gon' be at Floods."

"I did. Damn you wearing the fuck outta that skirt though!"

"You like?" She did a spin around to make sure he saw how plump her ass was now.

"Yeah, I do. I like you in them heels too, you looking real lady like."

"Scoot over," she told Stink as she squeezed between him and JT.

Scurvy was drunk and he kept touching and grabbing on all the girls walking by. JT just laughed, thinking about how his approach was all wrong. The E pill had Toya downing glasses of champagne every five minutes, but the alcohol wasn't having any effect on her. It just made her want more.

"I can't believe my niggas is out. We bout to be clowning!"

She got up and started dancing seductively in the aisle and on JT. He got and instant hard on. Stink and Scurvy tried to not to stare but her gyrating was turning them on too. She noticed the eyes on her, but she kept it going until she was finished. Toya couldn't sit down to save her life. She was jumping around rapping every word to every song as loud as possible.

JT was just glad to see that she still had the same zest for life he loved about her. He had no idea she was geeked up. "Who you here with?" he asked.

"Oh shit, I forgot all about..." Toya shot off, giving JT the one-minute finger. She was moving so fast, she didn't see the big, light skinned dude coming her way. They ran right into each other.

"Excuse me!" Toya said as curtly as possible. He was about to flirt with her, but then light skinned made eye contact with the dudes sitting at the table she had just left.

"Whassup, you big fat muthafucka?" Stink shouted out.

"Hell naw they done let my niggas out the box," Big pooh said as the reunion ensued.

Big Pooh was with gang of cutthroat looking niggas from the Mack and Grey area, his stomping grounds. Introductions were made, more drinks were ordered, and phone numbers were exchanged.

Once Stink saw Big Pooh, he felt like everything was falling into place. This was the beginning of what he and JT had talked about in many letters and face to face conversations over the years.

Toya came back a half hour later with a tall red bone who nobody was familiar with.

"This my girl, Trouble, y'all."

"Trouble? I thought that was my middle name," Stink said.

"Well, we got something in common, don't we?" Trouble said.

Big pooh gave out daps and pounds and made his way towards the exit.

"Why don't you come over here and see how much we got in common," Stink flirted.

Trouble obliged and sat down. She snuggled up next to Stink. She liked his baldhead and dimples, although she thought he was kinda short. At 5'9, she was three inches taller than he was and tonight she was wearing heels. But Stink's presence was much bigger than his physical form. He was a dude who wouldn't be overlooked by anyone. At age 18, he had the swagger of a man ten years his senior.

"So why they call you Trouble?" he asked.

"Why they call you Stink?" she shot back.

"It ain't cause I stink, you can believe that."

"That ain't answer my question, doe."

"I asked you first." Stink reminded her.

"You sure you wanna know?"

"Ha! I don't scare easy, baby."

It was obvious they were feeling each other by the suggestive looks they were shooting back and forth. Then the suggestive looks became suggestive comments, so Stink suggested they get a room.

At the hotel, Stink was mesmerized by Trouble's long flowing legs and big perky tits. Her shoulder length hair smelled inviting, mixed with her Chanel perfume. His cell phone rang and he rose from the bed in his wife beater and boxer shorts. He checked the number and saw that it was a chick he had banged the night before. He turned his phone off.

Trouble eyed him as he moved about the room. She had to admit, he had a nice body that made her eager to see what was inside those boxers.

"I didn't know you were bow legged," she said.

"It's a lot you don't know about me, baby."

"Aiight big timer, just get over here and strip." she said, peeling off her panties.

She didn't have to twist Stink's arm. As soon as he saw the panties drop, his manhood jumped stupid hard and he stripped naked. The two locked horns and went at it like wild beasts. Stink kissed her neck and chest eagerly while rubbing his fingers around her clit.

She rubbed his bald head and ran her calf up and down his butt cheeks. Her body was soft, but firm in all the right places.

He kissed her stomach and sniffed his finger on the sly checking for odor. The smell was pleasant and that was all he needed to confirm before he dove in head-first. He took the plunge, by teasing her a little bit with his tongue, then sucking on her inner thighs. She moaned in pleasure, running her heel down his spine. Everything she did was turning him on. He began to taste her, hoping she could keep a secret. He didn't want JT to find out he was a lick 'em low lover.

Toya mounted JT's massive pole slowly, and it filled her completely. She steadied herself by placing both hands on his chest as she began to ride him. His dick was still overwhelming, but she could handle it much better now.

He thumbed her big pretty nipples and stared in her eyes, waiting for her to blink, but she wouldn't. She matched his gaze with intensity, putting her back in to it. She let out a shriek.

He grabbed her by the waist and flipped her on her stomach. This was the kind of fuck he had been waiting on. Finally, someone who could compete with his fire. He manhandled her, grabbing her waist and pulling her up to her knees. He began stabbing at her backside like this was the last piece of pussy he was ever going to get. He could hear her screaming his name, but his mind was in a zone, and the only thing he could focus on was the tattoo on her back that read, princess. He slowed his pace as it got so good to him, he didn't ever want it to end.

"That's right. Fuck me like you miss me, nigga." Toya commanded.

"Shut up! Take that!" he slapped her ass and pulled her hair, pumping harder and harder.

Thirty minutes and five positions later, JT and Toya exploded in climax at the same time. JT collapsed on top of her, panting.

"Get yo' black ass up off me," she said shoving him off. "How you just gon' fuck me like that? Like you the only nigga that can fuck me right."

"I am," he said, pulling her close.

Her cell phone rang and she grabbed it off the nightstand, flipped it open and closed it back. "I wonder what he want this time of night," she said, hoping JT took the bait.

"Who?" he heard himself say.

"This nigga 40 Grand." She just had to get that out. She needed it to be known that she had a major player hot on her trail.

"40 Grand!" JT jumped out of bed. "Call him back."

"For what?" Toya asked confused.

"I been looking for that nigga." Toya thought about it for a second. This wasn't the reaction she was expecting at all. She gave JT a stare down and then made the call. "Hey, what's up?" she said, using her sexy voice.

"What's up, girl? Where you been at?" 40 Grand asked.

"Hanging, you know me. But hold on a minute, I got somebody wanna holla." She handed the phone over to JT.

"What's up 40?"

"Who dis?"

"This JT from the hood. I used to work with you and Chemical back in the day."

"Lil JT that use to be with Stink?"

"Yeah nigga, what's up? And before you say anything, I know me and Stink owe out a few dollars, but don't worry about that. It's nothing."

"When you get out?"

"I got out last month man, we both did."

"Oh, Stink out here too, huh?"

"Yeah we been trying to get at you."

"Ok, well, you got my number now, so call me in the morning and we'll hook up. Matter of fact, I'ma call Hammer and we can all get together in the morning."

"Oh, you still fuck with Hammer?"

"Why wouldn't I? Real niggaz stay down fo life."

"Right, right."

"What's up with you and Toya? That's yo' piece?"

"Well you know, we shared a moment here and there. You know how mafuckas do."

He heard Toya snatch the bathroom door open, but didn't bother turning to face her.

"We just finished fucking, JT! That's how you gon' do me?"

He ignored her. "I'ma let you go, 40, but I'll be at you first thing in the morning," JT said.

"Aiight, one."

JT hung up the phone, feeling better than ever. He knew 40 Grand wouldn't be tripping about the chump change they ran off with five years ago. Besides, they were kids that didn't know anything about staying down or being a team player. He wondered how Hammer was doing now. If he'd been on the streets with 40 Grand this whole time, he should be doing pretty damn good by now. He knew Hammer was no dummy, so he probably had made the most of his opportunities in the street.

Toya came out of the bathroom rolling her eyes.

"What you have to say all that for?" JT asked.

"All what?"

"We just fucked. He don't need to know our business."

"We did just fuck!" she snapped.

"So what that mean?"

"You talking about we shared a moment here and there. What you trying to say, we fuck partners? Cause if that's the case, I sure would have liked to know it ahead of time. Yeah, that's what you should've said. We fuck partners!"

JT had no idea what she was upset about, but he found her rambling humorous. Toya on the other hand was already feeling JT, and hadn't even realized it yet. She wasn't a girl that was easily thrown off her square by a nigga, yet here she was, as far away from her square as could be.

"You crazy." JT said, smiling at her.

"I ain't crazy, mafucka, I'm real."

JT would find out soon enough just how real she was.

"Come here," he told her and she obliged even though she was still pissed.

KING BENJAMIN'S PERSPECTIVE

Hmmmm. I'm just wondering if I'm the only one feeling a certain way about these cats by now. I honestly and truly believe that they are cut out for the shit they trying to do. If for no other reason than to get up out of that shack they live in, Stink and JT have the right mindset going into this. I only hope they learned a lesson from the past about loyalty and anger management, because they're about to enter the world of soul selling sin.

CHAPTER 11

"I'm serious about this pimping shit!" JT told Stink as they sat on their front porch the next morning." His eye were wide and he looked dead serious.

"Whatever, hoe ass nigga. You gon' handcuff that bitch Toya first chance you get."

"Your name is boo boo the fool if you think I'm bout to handcuff any bitch. Me and Toya is fuck partners and that came from her mouth, not mine."

"She said that for real?"

"Yeah man, Toya wild, I'm telling you. She ain't on that other shit. Even if she was, she know I ain't on that, so it would be a waste of her time. I think should could be like my bottom bitch, doe."

Stink waved him off.

"Light that blunt, nigga, don't talk me to death."

"Don't talk about it be about it huh? That's what you trying to say? Aiight, I'ma show you, nigga, 'cause you don't believe shit stink until it's on your mustache. I ain't showing these hoes no love out here."

JT lit the blunt as a black luxury sedan pulled up in front of the house. The passenger side window rolled down, and Hammer stuck his huge head out ofthe window.

“Put that backyard boogie out and come smoke like a player.” Hammer said.

Hammer looked like he had formed into a grizzly bear since they’d been away. His neck shoulders and biceps were monstrous. 40 Grand sat behind the wheel looking pretty much the same, but older. He wore a simple Dickie suit with a Detroit fitted cap. Hammer wore Dickie pants and a wife beater, showing off his physique. JT and Stink hopped in the back seat and 40 Grand turned the music down.

“Y’all niggas looking good, man. Look like y’all already getting to the money,” he said.

“Naw man, we trying to come up for real. We ain’t come out here to be on that petty shit.” Stink said.

“Oh yeah? Y’all ready to fuck with them birds?”

“Hell yeah!” They both said simultaneously.

“Good, ’cause I need somebody to hold the fort down in Columbus. Hammer and his man was doing it, but they on something else now. Y’all came right on time.”

“That’s what the fuck I’m talking bout! When we leaving?” Stink said.

“Tonight.” 40 Grand said as he threw the car in drive and mashed the gas.

As they rode around, Stink and JT noticed how the atmosphere began to feel unfriendly. They floated blunts around while 40 Grand and Hammer conversed amongst themselves. They wound up at The Steak House, where 40 Grand paid for everything. Whenever he did address Stink or JT, he stared coldly through his Cartier lenses.

Stink wasn't feeling this nigga acting all brand new. They offered him some money to make up for the stuff they had took off with back in the day, but he wouldn't accept it. He told them loyalty was more important than money, and they could repay him with that.

As time went on, they began to realize that 40 Grand was just feeling them out to see if they were worthy of this type of project. He was about to put a lot of trust in them and he had a right to be cautious.

Still, Stink being a cut to the chase type of nigga, spoke up. "Listen man, we understand that we been gone for a minute and we understand that our records got some blemishes on 'em; but we ain't out here to play no games. If you with us, we with you all the way. But if you against us, it's the same thing... and if you ain't feeling that, you can drop us back off where you picked us up from.

40 Grand liked what he heard. It took a lot of balls for Stink to speak his mind like that. He was the same way at Stink's age, so he was sure now that he had some real Gs on his team. Hammer had already put in his vote and he welcomed Stink and JT back into the circle.

40 Grand took a chance.

Toya and her aunt, Keisha, were really growing tired of each other. Keisha was starting to realize that no matter what she said, Toya had no plans to pursue a job, an education, or a career. Meanwhile, Toya was just sick of Keisha's constant nagging. All she ever talked about was who was hiring or what classes were open for enrollment. If she hadn't enrolled in one in all this time, what made her think she was about to start now? Eventually, it all came to a head.

"I'm tired of strange niggas coming by my house all types of night, blowing the horn, ringing my doorbell —"

"Don't no niggas be coming by yo' house blowing no horn," Toya argued.

"You a muthafucking lie! I know what I hear at night. These niggas could be killas or anything, ringing my doorbell. Is Toya here?"

"You act like I be fucking a gang of niggas or something. Them niggas that be popping up over here is niggas I been stop talking to. I told them to stop coming by my house."

"They shouldn't have never been coming by in the first place. I told you to keep that shit out in the streets, 'cause I know what type a niggas you be dealing with. Calling my house at three in the morning, is Toya home? What the fuck you want at three in the morning?" Keisha shouted.

"Auntie, like I said, that be them stalking ass niggas I cut off a long time ago. Everybody know not to call me on your house phone. When is the last time I been without a cell phone? Any nigga calling your house is just stalking and I can't do nothing about that."

"It don't even matter, Toya, because I shouldn't have to deal with it. You get all this money from these niggas and you spend it all on clothes and clubbing. You don't even have a car, so I know you not about to look for no job. I need some help around here and you don't offer me shit!" Toya's eyes widened because she couldn't believe she had just went there.

"This was your idea in the first place, and now you wanna flip the script? This was your idea, not mine, remember? And I told you I have been saving money for a car, that's why I haven't offered you any money and you know that."

Keisha was already waving her hand ready to counter whatever Toya had to say.

"You been talking about you saving for a car for almost a year. That never stopped you from sending your mama money, so it shouldn't stop you from helping me out."

Toya fell silent. She didn't have a response to the truth. There was nothing else to be said, and the only thing she could do now was try and save face. Her pride took over.

"I'll move out, how 'bout that? Will that make you happy?"

"I'm not asking you to move out, but if that's what you wanna do, bye!"

Toya stormed out of the living room and headed

to her room to start packing. Her feelings of anger and betrayal overwhelmed her to the point of tears as she reached for her cell phone. The truth was that she really had been saving for a car because she was tired of depending on people to get around. It was also true that her expensive clothes and partying kept her stagnated. She wanted a nice car, but had only been able to save fifteen hundred dollars.

She was about to call the one guy she'd been relying on for the past nine months. The guy she'd been getting the majority of her money from and basically living off. She had a revelation as she began to dial the number. Toya realized she was spending thousands of dollars a month on nothing, and she didn't even have a car. Her life really wasn't making sense. Her spending habits kept her dependent on dudes, and therefore, leaving them with control. Now she was considering shacking up with a dude and losing all of her freedom.

As the phone began to ring, she shuddered at the thought. She hung up before the second ring.

Toya sat on her bed, contemplating her next move. She thought about Trouble, who lived alone now, since her man was doing county time. She called her instead.

CHAPTER 12

COLUMBUS, OHIO

Hammer set Stink and JT up in an apartment off High Rd., right near Ohio State University. The building was crawling with college students and they fit right in. The apartment was essentially a plush weight house. The living room was filled with convertible glass tables, black leather furniture, plush carpet and a huge flat screen television that stayed on the video channel. The corners held exotic floor lamps and the walls were even decorated with African paintings. In the two bedrooms, were motionless waterbeds and 47" flat screens with PlayStations attached. Redwood dressers with gold latches offset crème colored lamps with gold trim.

For a place of business, someone had paid great attention to detail when decorating the apartment. Even the satin sheets were the exact same crème as the lamps, and there were two extra sets of sheets in each closet. Stink and JT stood out on the terrace smoking weed, feeling blessed to have the opportunity they had.

"This is whassup, my nigga." Stink said.

"Dog, it's so many bitches in this building."

"Yeah, that's the bad part about it."

Hammer had given them three specific rules that could not be broken under any circumstances. The first rule, no fraternizing with the other tenants, male or female. The second rule was only customers purchasing a half a kilo or better were allowed at the apartment. Everyone else would get their work delivered to them. The third rule was that the house was to be shut down by 8 o'clock, meaning no one was able to come by and cop, no matter how much money they had. The two of them had burnout cell phones, two personal cell phones and two pagers. They also had a Lincoln rental car, all provided by 40 Grand. All they had to do was make the money.

They got paid a thousand dollars off each kilo and they were supplied ten at a time. They made extra money by raising the price even more on slow niggas who couldn't see a squeeze play coming. They knew Hammer used to grind out of this same house, and now his pockets were swollen. They intended to do the same.

For a solid month, the two stayed totally focused on the goal. They came and went quietly, and they only left the house to make drop offs. The stayed away from the other tenants and they saved all their money under the mattress in their bedrooms.

At night, they would come into each other's rooms. Every time JT went into Stink's room, Stink would show off his stash under the mattress. JT would show his off too, but not as much as Stink. Stink would even count all of it and make JT watch so he wouldn't be able to dispute how much it was if it came up the next day. Stink had twenty-five Gs and he couldn't stop talking about it, while JT only had twenty-one. JT hadn't made as many side deals as Stink.

After a month passed, they began to feel like they were in jail all over again. To make matters worse, they were working for a guy who had actually imprisoned them before.

Stink found himself driving around the eastside of Columbus, just girl watching and looking for fun. He spotted a girl coming out of a hair and nail salon on her way to her car. She was tall with beautiful brown skin and long wavy, bouncy hair. She wore a dress with one shoulder exposed and stilettos. He pulled alongside her as she keyed her alarm.

"I like the hair, but I can't see the nails," he said.

She quickly flashed her freshly manicured nails at him. They were a simple almond tone that matched her complexion perfectly.

"You like?" she asked.

"Actually, I do. I like the whole package." He slid the Lincoln gearshift into park without pulling over. "What's yo' name?" he asked.

"Naomi," she said, opening her door.

"Hold on, where you going? We in the middle of a conversation."

"I'm going home, and you should get out of the street.

"Take my number and call me later!" he tried.

"No thank you. But it was nice talking to you." She started her car and pulled away from the curb, waving goodbye at Stink.

He waved back, but called her a dumb bitch under his breath. As he drove away and pulled near a stop light, he realized he was lost.

JT felt that if he was going to be a pimp, he needed to start getting his hoes lined up. He didn't want to be a full blooded pimp. He just really wanted to use women to get where he needed to be, and he definitely planned to break a few bitches. He nabbed his first target at the Eastland Mall. She was a chubby chick named Tasha who was ten years his senior. Tasha was really cute, but insecure about her weight. JT looked older than he was, so he told her he was twenty-two. He had read "Pimpology" and he knew this made her a likely prospect.

He planned to present himself as her savior from the heavens above. He hadn't had much experience with women up to this point, but it was a gift, being so inexperienced, because he had no reason to believe his plans wouldn't work. On their first date, he took her to Benihana. He sat across the table, penetrating her with his gaze.

"Why you staring at me like that?" Tasha blushed.

"Because I like what I see," JT responded.

He was fresh to death in Polo from head to soxs, including his cologne. He didn't want to tarnish his image by drinking or smoking until he found out what type of man she was looking for. He already knew enough about her to know she was worth the time and effort he was about to put in. He knew she drove a five series beamer and worked as a Hamilton County Coroner, which paid pretty well. When he found out what she did for a living, he thought it was very possible he could be barking up the wrong tree. She could be as cold as JT thought himself to be, but that remained to be seen.

"So how long did you have to go to school to be able to fuck with dead bodies?"

She giggled at the way he worded the question.

"Well, I studied forensics and anthropology at Ohio State and got a four year degree there. Then I attended Mortuary Science School for a few years while I worked as a coroner's assistant."

"So this is something you always wanted to do?" he asked, honestly intrigued.

"I guess so. At first, I thought I wanted to be a mortician, but then when I really thought about the type of person I am, I knew I didn't wanna be alone with dead people all day. My job allows me to work with police and lawyers; I get to testify in court sometimes. It's fun."

"But it can't be all good, all the time. I mean, I know you gotta see some shit that upset your stomach a little, unless you just a cold ass woman?"

"A little at first, but I do have a pretty strong stomach, that's why I knew I could do it. Yeah, I gotta a big strong stomach," she repeated, rubbing her round belly.

"First of all, your stomach is not that big. You thick and sexy as hell. Niggas love women like you." Most of what JT said was true, but Tasha didn't believe it. It was more important to her that JT actually believed it, than how she felt. He paused for a minute. "Keep it real with me doe, how many dudes you got on deck right now?"

She smiled and leaned back in her chair while wiping the sweat from her palms on to her jeans. "I mean, I got a couple of friends but they don't mean shit. I just keep them around to keep from being lonely."

"Yeah, but you know that's a quick fix and I know you would rather solve the problem completely."

"I didn't say I had sex with these guys."

"I didn't say that either."

"So what did you mean by quick fix?"

This was where he was gonna go hard. He had rehearsed what he wanted to say, hours before the date. It was time to reel her in.

"I mean you want to put your feet on solid ground. I know I'm younger than you, but I understand a woman like yourself wants something real. Something that is not gon' get uprooted every few months and changed like shoes and socks. I dig yo' style and everything about you, so I'm trying to offer you something you can sink your teeth into. Something real."

Tasha felt herself more and more attracted to JT from the first day they met. Her guard was up because she hadn't laid her feelings on the line in a long time.

"I like you, JT... a lot. But I know you got a flipside. You got a mean streak or something. I don't know about you, but most hustlers have an ugly side to their character that allows them to do what they do."

"Don't try to over think things, though. Just get to know me. To know me is to love me," he said with a devilish grin.

Tasha was beginning to think JT was lying about his age. He told her he was twenty-two, but he acted a lot older. It was his conversation that had convinced her to give his young ass a chance in the first place, and so far, she didn't regret taking a chance on him.

The meal came, and they actually ate while discussing some of the gory details of some of her most horrific crime scenes. It didn't bother either of them at all. JT was truly fascinated by death, and Tasha had no problem discussing it while she ate.

JT's cell phone rang.

"What up doe!" he answered.

"What up, man? Y'all still in Ohio?" Scurvy said.

"Yeah, but whass up?"

"I'm trying to put something together, dog. I'm fucked up right now! When y'all niggas coming back?"

"I don't know, Scurvy. We was thinking you should try and get where we at."

"Man, I can't come to Ohio! I owe Hammer about ten thousand dollars."

"Damn! You stay on some bullshit, don't you? But I'm with my lady friend right now so I'm gon' get with you a little later and we can talk then."

"Aiight man, do that." As JT hung up, he thought

about the desperation he heard in Scurvy's voice. He and Stink had figured out that Scurvy wanted to keep them around him for protection. He'd buss his gun in a heartbeat, but he was only one man. One underhanded scandalous man, with lots of enemies. His phone rang again.

"Damn, my bad," he apologized before answering. " Hello."

"You in Ohio giving them bitches my dick?" Toya said.

"Don't call me with that bullshit." JT and Toy usually called each other two to three times a week, but lately she noticed he hadn't been calling her at all.

"Where you been at, my nigga?"

"I'ma pop back at you tonight. I'm in the middle of something," JT said.

"Hmmpt, do that." Click.

JT put his phone away and got back to his date. Tasha was finishing her meal and waiting patiently for JT finish with his conversations. His phone rang a third time, but this time he didn't answer. It was another chick. All the girls he had met since coming home knew he was out of town getting money, so they were relentlessly pursuing him and waiting for his return.

"You got a hot line, don't you?" Tasha said.

"I know, and the thing is, don't nobody even want shit." His phone rang again.

"Goddam!" JT said in frustration. He saw it was

Stink's number, this time so he knew he had to take the call.

"What up, Stink?"

"Where the hell you at?"

"I'm with my lady friend, what up?"

"I'm lost somewhere on the eastside. I don't know how to get back to the crib."

"Why the hell you call me? I can't tell you."

"Who the fuck else was I gon' call?"

"Why you ain't call Hammer?" Stink realized that JT had a point. He had called the one person that knew as little as he did about Columbus.

"Shit, ask yo' friend to give me directions," Stink said.

"Hold on." He gave Tasha the phone and explained the situation.

Stink told her that he was near the Green Bryer Projects and he was trying to get back to High Rd. She gave him clear directions and handed the phone back to JT.

As JT reached for the phone, he leaned in and thanked Tasha with a kiss.

She was really feeling JT.

Later that night, JT and Stink sat around the apartment jokingly arguing over JT's money. "I made the sale while you was out wining and dining that fat bitch, so you don't get nothing."

"Man, you better give me my money and stop playing!" JT patted Stink's pockets, searching for his bankroll.

"Dog! Touch my pockets again, I'mma lump yo' ass up." Stink threatened.

JT pointed his finger in Stink's face as if he was addressing a child.

"Boy, you would neva put yo' hands on a real nigga like me. Fuck you talking bout?"

Before Stink could rebut, they heard a key turning the lock on the front door. The door swung open and Hammer walked in scowling. They weren't expecting him. They didn't they even know he was in town, but he looked pissed.

"Where y'all niggas been at all day? And where the fuck is y'all beepers?

"Mine right here," Stink said, picking it up off the end table.

"Why the fuck you ain't been answering it? Niggas been calling me all day, talking about they can't reach nam one of y'all."

"First off, watch yo' tone, dog. You ain't got no muthafucking kids in here," JT snapped.

Hammer's face bore a look of confusion. He wasn't used to the workers talking back. He looked at Stink and JT, thinking about who they were. He knew they probably held animosity from him beating up Stink back in the day, but business was business. He liked and respected Stink and JT, so he calmed his nerves and addressed them with respect.

"Listen man, I don't know what y'all been out doing, but y'all ain't come here to bullshit. Y'all came here to work."

"We gon' work." Stink interrupted. "We been working. But at the same time, we don't need no babysitter. And we ain't about to sit around this bitch twenty-four seven like it's a crack house. Come on Hammer baby, y'all gotta ease up on a nigga."

"I'm just saying, dog, I had to drive all the way from Toledo just to check on y'all niggas cause ain't nobody answering the phone."

Stink had stop answering his phone when he got lost and JT had turned his off to finish his date. It was a small period, but to Hammer, it appeared they were ignoring him and he had too much at stake right now.

"I got other shit to do, so I can't be running out here to check on y'all. I got spots in Lima, Dayton and Toledo that need my attention. I can't be running out here on some bullshit."

"Don't then, nigga!" Stink said.

JT interrupted.

"Hammer, you can't be serious. I know you don't think we bout to keep posting up in this bitch and not fucking with no bitches or nothing. We ain't in jail no more, nigga."

"I ain't saying that, but what's wrong with the Detroit bitches y'all been fucking with? I know y'all still got some bitches in the city on deck. Send a bitch a bus ticket, cause these girls in Columbus ain't to be trusted.

All they gon' do is get yo' name hot. Every nigga in the street gon' know who you is cause they run they mouth. Fuck these out of town hoes."

What Hammer said made a lot of sense. They were so concerned about the women they were surrounded by, it never registered to them until now.

This wasn't a set up for a stranger. This wasn't the type a thing you just brought somebody new around without knowing their background, because that was a good way to get dead quick. They talked it over and came to an agreement that they would lay off the women of Columbus and call some girls from Detroit to come and chill with them. They needed some chicks that knew how to roll with the day to day operations of the game. Two perfect girls came to mind.

CHAPTER 13

Two days later, Toya and Trouble arrived at the train station were Stink and JT were waiting in the Lincoln. Since the apartment was close to the downtown area, they hung out there for most of the day. They smoked blunt after blunt, getting stupid high, except Toya, who felt weed slowed down the momentum of her alcohol so she didn't smoke. They hit Red Velvet and checked out college night at another spot. Toya immediately fell in love with the vibe of the city. She could tell it was crawling with similar hustlers, ballers and gangstas that Detroit was famous for.

"I fucking love this city!" Toya said as she downed a Hennessy sour and ordered another one.

Two white guys staggered by her. One stopped and threw it in reverse. "Heeey! I seen you around on campus. Candice, right?"

"Nope."

"Your name's not Candice?"

"Mmpt um."

"Aww, come on."

"My name is not Candice," she said with a slight giggle.

She thought he was cute for a white guy, from his short blond hair and blue eyes to his tight jeans and Prada loafers.

“Let me get that drink for you, Candice.” he slurred.

He went into his pocket and paid for her drink. Toya noticed he was carrying a lot of money and it looked like all hundred dollar bills. It was her nature to peep a guy’s stash. She let him pay for the drink before telling him for the last time that she wasn’t Candice.

She looked out on the dance floor and saw JT surrounded by a bunch of girls. He couldn’t dance a lick, and she thought he looked ridiculous standing in one spot throwing his arms in the air.

“I’m fucking smashed.” she heard the white guy say.

She turned her attention back to him. “I know you is cause you keep thinking I’m somebody I’m not.”

“I’m sorry. Maybe you not her, but you look just like her. I need some ex. You do ex?” The conversation had gone in a totally different direction.

“Hell yeah.” she said, knowing she was on one now.

“You know where I can get some?” he asked.

She went into hustle mode. “How much you gon’ pay me?”

“I’ll give you thirty dollars right now. Matter of fact, because I know my friend Brian is gonna want one too. I’ll give you sixty for two.”

“Stay right here.” Toya said.

She went searching for Trouble. It wasn’t so much

the money that excited her, Toya got a thrill out of being involved in anything underhanded. She found Trouble with Stink on the opposite side of the dance floor. They appeared to be arguing. She walked up and grabbed Trouble by the arm.

"Come here, bitch." Toya said, pulling her away from Stink. She went into the rest room.

"I need two pills."

"For what?"

"I'm bout to sell 'em."

"To who?"

"Bitch give me the pills," she snapped. Trouble went into her pocket and pulled out her stash. "What's up with you and Stink?"

"I don't know what's wrong with that nigga, but he getting on my fucking nerves."

Toya didn't have time to play mediator.

"Fuck that nigga, go mingle like I'm doing. But whatever you do, don't start no bullshit up in here." With that, she walked off in search of the white guy.

She found him huddled in a group of four. Two guys, two girls. She snuck up, slid the pills in his back pocket, and slapped him on the butt.

"Oh, hey beautiful." he said, turning around.

"Give me my money."

"Alright, alright." He went in his pocket and fumbled through his bankroll. "Hey listen, can you score some coke?"

The question jerked Toya's head back at first. "How much?"

"Like an ounce."

"Ummm, yeah, I can get it for you.

"Ok cool. Give me your number cause I'm telling ya, my connect just got busted about a week ago, and I need somebody I can score at least a couple ounces a week from."

She was glad he rambled on, because it drove some of her suspicions down. He sounded like a guy that really needed to support a habit. Even if he was undercover, it was too late to turn back now; she had already sold him ecstasy.

JT found a table and ordered a bottle of champagne. At the moment, he was conversing with two gorgeous college girls who attended Ohio State.

"Y'all in a sorority?" he asked

"Hell no. That's for them fake hoes." one girl answered.

JT glanced on the floor and saw Toya dancing with a group of white folks. He loved having her around already. Her energy was contagious, and she was somebody he felt he could really relate to. He didn't know if he could pimp Toya, but he still was gonna try.

A commotion broke out on the other side of the dance floor. Security came barreling through. JT fell in behind them to make sure all his people were safe.

After pushing his way through all the bystanders, he arrived at the scene of the chaos only to find it was Stink and Trouble going at it. Stink had smacked the shit out Trouble and she responded with a Moet bottle across Stink's head. Trouble found herself in a choke-hold shortly after, and now security was trying to pry Stink's hands from around her throat.

JT tried to intervene, but security stopped him short, not knowing his intentions. Stink and Trouble were kicked out of the club, which meant JT and Toya had to leave as well.

Back at the apartment, JT and Toya engaged in wild sweaty sex all night, as did Stink and Trouble.

The next morning, Stink sent Trouble back to Detroit, but Toya stayed. She knew Trouble would live up to her name sooner or later, so she thought it was best. That same week, she began to serve the white guy from the club, ounces of coke at astronomical prices. She drove the rental car to his house and gave JT a cut of every sale.

Soon, she had her own rental car and a steady clientele that expanded from her first customer. JT began to quickly view her differently, but he didn't know what to think of it.

One day, after a night at the bar, Toya found herself floating in her rented Buick LeSabre down High Rd., almost all alone. She pulled up slowly to the red light as a blue and white Dodge Viper pulled alongside her. She peeked at the driver out the corner of her eye. At first glance, he was an Ice-T look-a-like. She could feel him trying to make eye contact with her, but she mashed the gas as soon as the light turned green. She wasn't in a flirtatious mood. Just zoning out, enjoying her buzz, and banging Lil Kim.

She caught another red light, and so did the Viper. This time, he blew the horn to get her attention. She lowered her window and turned down the volume on the stereo.

"What's up?"

"You think us being out here all alone on the road like this is a sign?"

She was confused.

"What kind of sign?"

"I don't know, like maybe the planets are aligned just right and it makes for something special, like two people finding what they been looking for."

Ice-T was tripping.

"I ain't been looking for nothing." Toya said sternly. A month ago, Toya would have been all over this dude, just on the strength of the Viper. But right now, between JT and her new hustle, she didn't give two fucks about him or his Viper.

"Sometimes, you find the best things when you not looking." Ice-T said.

The light turned green, but neither car pulled off. She gave him a once over. He was attractive, so she figured, why not?

"I guess it's only one way to find out, huh?" she said.

"Now we talking. What's yo' name?"

"Toya, and yours?"

"They call me Pretty Mike. Sometimes, just Pretty."

Toya silently laughed at the name.

"Aiight Pretty, give me your number. I'll call you tomorrow."

Toya was walking down the corridor as JT was calling her phone to check on her. He wasn't used to her staying out this late. She answered the phone.

"Open the door, I'm outside."

JT came to the door in his boxers and some Nike slippers. As soon as he opened the door, he looked in her eyes. "Oh you ain't on one tonight, huh?" he said.

"A pill?" she said, strolling in.

"Right, I see yo pupils ain't all dilated and shit."

"I been backing off that shit since I gotta pay for it now. It was cool to pop them bitches for free, but I ain't bout to be paying for 'em."

She followed JT into the bedroom and sat on the edge of the bed. She roamed through her phone to make sure Pretty's number was locked in.

"Did you fuck 40 Grand?" JT said out of nowhere.

The question surprised her. "What?"

"You heard me."

"How you gon' ask me that, after all this time passed?"

JT was beginning to realize that he wasn't cut out to

be a real pimp. The minute he began to question Toya about her relations with 40 Grand, it was a clear sign that he was digging her more than he should be if his plans were to pimp her.

"You know what, you right. I'm tripping, and that's my bad." He sat down next to her and she wrapped her arms around his neck and kissed his face.

"You know you like me, boy," she said.

"Shut the fuck up."

"You shut the fuck up. Now since you brought it up, I'll tell you that I didn't fuck him, but I planned on it. He just always called me late as hell on some two in the morning type shit and I'd be like, call me tomorrow. He would wait another week, call me again at two in the morning. I told him like, nigga I ain't that type a bitch. You ain't bout to get me to jump out the bed at two in the morning for yo' ass. I don't care how much money you got."

"So what type are you?" JT asked.

Toya wasn't ready for that question. They were both eighteen years old, in a fast world, trying their best to figure out how they fit into it. Toya thought for a second. "What type a bitch am I?" she asked.

"Yeah."

"I'm the type a bitch that's gonna do shit the way she feel it should be done. If I fuck with a nigga, he gonna treat me with some respect, and I'm gonna do the same. Yeah, I might fuck a nigga after he spend a couple dollars or whatever, but that's cause it's something I wanna do. My decision."

JT listened and he internally asked himself the same question as he took in her answer. What type of nigga was he? He was still learning, but he knew for sure he was a get money nigga.

"I hear you, and I feel what you saying. Only thing is, we gotta think big, now. I think If you gonna fuck with a nigga that's getting money, you should take something away from it besides a couple dollars. If a nigga can give you some game, then you really winning. And maybe when them dollars run out or he don't wanna give you no more, you got something of value that can get you even more money."

Toya soaked up JT's words like the smart girl she was. She knew a gem when it slapped her in the face, and she knew JT had just dropped one on her. She also knew he was the guy that could teach her something if she stuck around.

The two sat on the bed with all types of thoughts roaming through their heads. The past, the present and the future.

Romell was single handedly increasing the murder rate in Detroit. Word on the street was he and Tank were vying for control of the eastside. Tank wasn't known for his murder game, but Romell, in direct correlation to his success, had grown into a known sociopath.

Currently, he was walking through an empty house

he had labeled the House of Death, with all black on from head to toe. Black hoodie, black Dickies, black Air Force Ones and matching leather gloves.

He had found a way to remedy the problem of all the bodies being found all over the eastside, causing homicide to rear its ugly face. He grabbed a chainsaw from the cabinet under the sink and headed to the Blood Room where his victim lay. His right hand, Fo Tre, who was a crazy California Crip on the run for murder in LA stood over the dead man.

Fo Tre and Romell were cousins, and when Fo Tre fled to Detroit, he quickly became a welcome addition to Romell's crew. After seeing some of Fo Tre's work, first hand, Romell quickly appointed him as one of the top enforcers in his crew. Since coming to Detroit, Fo Tre had become smarter, and paid much more attention to detail when doing his job. He was light brown with braids, and tatted up everywhere but his face.

"Hand me that bitch, cuz," Fo Tre said, referring to the chainsaw.

"Oh, you got this one?" Romell said, handing it over.

"Hell yeah. Back up, cuz!" Fo Tre revved the chainsaw.

"I know you got it, nigga. I'm just here for moral support." Romell yelled over the noise.

Fo Tre noticed the man's foot was sticking outside of the Blood Room.

"Pull 'em inside a lil more," he said.

Romell grabbed the limp body by the ankle and

dragged him to the center of the floor. The blood room was covered with plastic from floor to ceiling. After the work was finished, the plastic would have to be redone, but it only took his man a couple hours to do the job.

The house was located on a small dead end street, where Romell happened to own all of the remaining property that wasn't destroyed or vacant.

As Fo Tre began to dismember the dead man's body, he paused. "Aye cuz, it's eighty-five degrees outside. Why you got on a mafucking hoodie?"

"Cause I ain't taking no chances." Romell answered.

"I'm burning all this shit I got on, even these mafucking Chucks," Four Tre replied.

As Fo Tre continued to saw his victim into pieces, Romell's mind drifted off to Stink and JT. The day after they left for Columbus, Romell had swung by their house to pay them a visit.

His plan was to convince them that he would help them get on their feet, all the while, with intentions to lure them into his little house of horror where sudden death awaited them. Romell had cried himself to sleep some nights after losing his best friend, Dusty, at such an early age. He never forgave or forgot, and he was determined to avenge his right hand man. He had a twenty-five thousand dollar contract on each of their heads and plenty of blood thirsty goons in his squad, ready to collect. Stink and JT had no idea how lucky they were to have left town when they did.

Blood began to spray all over the walls, and Romell backed out of the room to avoid the mess. When he heard the chainsaw stop, he leaned inside.

"Speed this shit up, man. We got other shit to do.

CHAPTER 14

Hammer was in town, and he and Stink had the hottest tickets in Columbus that Saturday night. The Annual City Wide Hair Show was the place to be, if you loved being surrounded by beautiful, sexy, and stylish women. Hammer stepped in the place with over a hundred thousand dollars of ice dangling from his neck and wrists.

Stink was icy, but he felt a hint of jealousy because Hammer was outshining him by far. But he was feeling himself that night, rocking pink and white linen with pink gators. JT called him a fag when he purchased a pair of pink shoes, but Stink didn't care. He liked to wear loud and flashy colors that made him stand out the minute he walked into the room. They had good seats right near the stage, and Hammer had to talk louder than he wanted to just to be heard.

"It's been drama going down in the city," Hammer said.

"What?" Stink said, straining to hear.

"I said it's been big drama on the floor in the D. Tank and Romell is beefing over control of the eastside. Niggas coming up dead left and right."

"Oh yeah?"

"Yeah, and you know Tank is 40 Grand's partna?"

"Whatchu mean like business partna or just homies?"

"40 said if Tank don't handle his business soon, he might need y'all niggas to go down to the D and help out. I was telling him y'all had a relationship with the nigga Romell from back in the day. Whatchu think about it?"

Stink glanced around the room to make sure nobody was eavesdropping. "Tell 40 just give us the word and a good idea what's in it for us, and we can roll." He was still salty about how Romell had treated them when they came home.

Just before the lights dimmed and the show began, a group of females took their seats right in front of Hammer and Stink. The girl in front of Stink glanced back at him for a second... then glanced again. She was trying to figure out where she had seen him before.

"That's kinda rude to not speak to a guy," Stink said smiling.

"I'm trying to remember where I seen you before," the girl declared.

Stink remembered her as soon as he laid eyes on her. It was the girl he had met in front of the beauty salon. "We met a few months back. You was coming out of the shop and had just got your nails done. I was flirting and you shot me down."

The girl laughed. "Yeah, I remember now. What's your name again?"

"I'm Stink, and you Naomi, right?"

"Dang, you got a good memory."

"Especially for things worth remembering, you feel me?"

"I most certainly do." Naomi introduced her friends, but Hammer had already made a connection with the one that held the title of the biggest ass in the crew. *Hammer loved him some big asses,* Stink thought as the host took the stage.

"Well Naomi, I don't wanna rap your ear off, so you ladies enjoy the show. Hopefully, we'll get a chance to talk more, later."

Naomi shot one last glance over her shoulder as Stink relaxed in his seat. He had her and he knew it.

*****

While Stink was at the hair show, JT was breaking down the walls surrounding Tasha's heart. Even though he had decided he wasn't going to be a pimp, he still knew he could get over on a girl like Tasha. In the past two months, he'd been methodical about how he spent time with her. Sometimes, when he was out of dope, he'd spend the whole day with her, giving her back massages and fucking her brains out. Then he'd disappear for a week. He treated her like a queen when they were together, but then he wouldn't answer her calls the next day. This put Tasha on an emotional roller coaster. He made her feel more beautiful than she'd ever felt, and for that, she would reward him greatly.

First, she put a Cadillac in his name and paid the first

note. Then, he ran a story down about how he took a loss and she loaned him eight thousand dollars. Sometimes he'd pop up with an expensive tennis bracelet or a nice purse with some perfume inside. He managed to maintain the image that he was generous and thoughtful, but always needed help at the same time. JT's phone never stopped ringing and his chirp never stopped chirping. Sometimes he'd turn it off just to make Tasha feel special.

At least that's what he wanted her to think. The real reason he turned it off was to downplay all the money that was coming in daily. He needed her to believe in him, but at the same time, be left in the dark.

The two of them laid in Tasha's bed after a draining sex-capade, in which JT was sure Tasha came at least three times. She laid on her stomach, rubbing her fingers across his wide muscular chest.

"You know, you the only nigga that never asked me to lose weight? It seems like every guy I meet starts off telling me how beautiful I am, and end up telling me how much better I'd look if I lost—"

"That shit don't mean nothing to me," he interrupted. "I like you for you."

"But be honest, you don't think I'd look better if I lost like 40 pounds?"

"I mean, if that's how you feel, then that's just how you feel. But if I wanted somebody 40 pounds lighter, I would've went after that."

He grabbed her by her rolls and pulled her closer as she burst into laughter. "Look at me," he said. Tasha gazed into his eyes. "I love you."

The words made her grin from ear to ear, then she pecked him on the lips. "I love you too," she said, meaning every word of it.

JT, on the other hand, couldn't care less about Tasha. He had to admit, he enjoyed the sex, but that was nowhere near enough to keep him around this long. It was all about getting over, so he learned how to make his words count. That was the first night he had ever laid the L word on her. She snuggled up next to him, letting the feeling of being loved sink in. JT thought about Toya and wondered what she was doing.

JT could bring the best or the worst out of a female, depending on who the female was. Since the talk they had in the room that night, Toya had chosen to stop sleeping with JT for the time being and focus on herself. She knew about his little scheme he had going with Tasha and she was taking a page from his book. Neither JT nor Toya complained about the pause in their sexual relationship.

She closed her legs and opened her mind. She learned to tone down her arrogance and strengthen her appeal. Once she realized where she was in life and where she wanted to be, the true Toya emerged. She was in a position to get all she wanted out of life and nothing was stopping her, but her. She acquired a flock of new male associates and kept them all at bay. She presented herself in different lights to each individual. From eavesdropping on JT's conversations with Tasha, she became persuasive in all her conversations, knowing when to flirt and when to play hard to get. She knew how far to go with a nigga to not look easy, but much more than a tease.

Columbus niggas didn't know her background, so she was able to manipulate her past and present. She moved into an apartment in the same building as Stink and JT, so she could focus on her own money and her own goals. JT didn't mind. He was glad to see she was stepping her game up to the next level. She was still helping them flip bricks, so her being in Columbus was beneficial from day one.

Her primary target was Pretty Mike. She had remained mysterious with him until tonight. Mike had been throwing money at Toya for over a month now, with hopes of impressing her enough to have his way with her. But Toya was focused, and she had learned through the grapevine that Pretty was a hustler who flipped weight in the small town of Steubenville, not far from Columbus.

Her plan was simple; she would present herself as a heavyweight drug dealer and find out how much he was paying for his kilos. Whatever he was paying, she was sure JT could beat it and leave her with a nice piece of change. She was dressed to impress this day, in a one piece black Donna Karan jean fit with black stilettos and black Chanel frames perched on top of her long, genuine ponytail. Her one piece hugged her body tantalizingly.

She applied her lip gloss in the rearview mirror, then started up her new rental Caravan Voyager. She chirped Pretty. "Where you at?"

"I'm on the block, whassup,"

"You still gon' let me take you out tonight?" she asked.

"Yeah, I ain't gon' back out on you. It's not often a broad ask to take me out."

She chirped, "A broad?"

"You know what I mean, boo."

"Not really, but we gonna discuss it when I get there."

"I'm looking forward to it. Where are you?"

"I'll be there in ten minutes."

"Aiight."

As she drove to pick up Pretty Mike, she mentally congratulated herself for a job well done. She had a string of Columbus niggas wrapped around her finger, caught in lust and infatuation. She'd never felt more powerful. Stink two-wayed in.

"My nigga."

"Whassup?"

"You should've hit that hair show last night. That bitch was off the chain."

"Fuck that shit," she responded.

"You ain't been out nowhere in minute. Whassup wit you?"

"I'm focused man, that all."

"Fuck you den, holla back!" Stink shouted into the phone.

Toya dismissed his immaturity and got into character as she pulled on the block that Pretty Mike clung to when he wasn't in Steubenville. This was his domain. She put a gangsta lean on her seat, took the P-89 from under it, and shoved it between the console and the seat, so it was in plain view. Pretty was outside waiting in front of a string of luxury cars, conversing with friends.

She paused in the middle of the street, with one stiletto on the brake as Pretty walked around to the passenger side. He hopped in and she sped off quickly.

"You smelling good what's that fragrance you wearing," Pretty asked.

"Thank you, it's Chanel," she said bending a corner.

At nine o' clock sharp, her Nextel rang just as planned. It was JT calling to implement the first part of her strategy. "Hello," Toya answered. "Naw man, I told you, you gotta catch me before eight. After that, it's a wrap." She hung up and stared straight ahead.

She could feel his eyes on her and she noticed when he finally got a glimpse of the P-89 she was packing. They pulled into the parking lot of The Steakhouse.

"Can you hand me that bag out of the glove compartment?"

Pretty opened the glove compartment and spotted the brown paper bag staring him in the face.

"This one?"

"Yeah." She grabbed it, opened it, and pulled out a huge wad of hundreds and took the rubber band from around it.

"Damn, boss lady. I ain't know it was like that!"

She peeled a few hundred off the top. "Yeah, it's a lot you don't know about me, Pretty. Can you put that back for me?" She handed him the bag full of cash.

Inside the restaurant, the curiosity was killing Pretty Mike. It wasn't long before he broke.

"So what's the deal with you?"

Toya took a sip of her red wine. "Can you be a lil more specific?"

"You know, like what's yo' grind? I see you got doe."

"Same as yours."

"Oh ok. So what you flipping? A lil half or something, I can give you a good price."

She took another sip before responding. "Come on now... a lady never tells. Let's just say I can probably give you a better price."

Pretty was taken aback by the statement. He stroked his goatee. "Oh yeah, like what?"

She dunked her jumbo shrimp in the spicy sauce. "Like lower than what you paying now."

"You don't know what I'm paying."

"Don't matter. My daddy is that fucking deal. I ain't heard a nigga with a lower number yet. Stop playing."

"Who is yo' daddy?" he asked.

Toya threw her hands up. "I just told you. That fucking deal." She was expecting Pretty to lie about what he was paying, which was exactly what she wanted. That way she was sure to solidify a deal by the end of the night.

"I'm paying twenty-one."

"I'm lower."

"How much lower?"

She didn't want to seem too eager. She was supposed to be the bird lady, so it wasn't like she needed the money.

"Eat your food before it gets cold," she warned.

After dinner, Toya cut the evening short, claiming she had to be up early in the morning. She could feel her sexual attraction to Pretty becoming too much to contain. She hadn't had sex in a while, and she was starting to feel overdue. She didn't want to give up her edge just yet, so she called it a night.

On the way home, she got a call from JT, telling her to come to his place ASAP. He wouldn't go into detail, which made Toya's mind ramble all the way home. When she stepped in, she was surprised to see Hammer, Stink and JT all in the living room, wearing matching looks of concern on their faces.

She sat her purse down on the end table. "What the fuck wrong with y'all?"

"Shiiid, you about to see in minute." JT said.

Toya didn't know what the hell was going on, but she was getting more nervous with each second that passed. Stink and Hammer sat on the couch, so Toya took a seat next to JT on the love seat.

Hammer flicked through the news stations and stopped at CNN News. Toya was wondering what could be on CNN that would be a concern to her life, or theirs for that matter. She didn't have to wait long for the answer. The first scene was a warehouse with what appeared to be cocaine piled to the ceiling. The scene then switched to a Florida loading dock where dozens of customs agents and coast guards scrambled around after one of the biggest seizures to date. The reporter went on to relay in dramatic fashion, that with help from the DEA and Customs the Cost Guards were able to seize a shipment of over 25 tons of cocaine.

The assistant director of the FBI issued a statement on how this was a defining moment in the war on drugs. He went on to say that the scales were finally starting to tip in favor of the good guys, and that he knew the war was just beginning, but he and his team were in it for the long haul.

Hammer clicked off the television and the room fell silent. Everyone in the room knew enough about the game to know a drug bust of such a substantial amount would have a trickle-down effect nationwide.

"That's some fucked up shit!" Stink said, breaking the silence.

"I think y'all should hold on to that shit y'all got for a minute and see what happens." Hammer suggested. It made sense. If they were going to be out of drugs, then they needed to make as much as they could off the coke they had now.

"Hell yeah. If 40 ask for his money, we can pay him out of pocket. We only owe him like fifty- four." Stink said, and JT nodded in agreement.

"Fuck holding shit! I'm supposed to hook up with this nigga Pretty Mike tomorrow. I don't wanna look like no fronting ass bitch after I told this nigga I got work."

"Who the fuck is Pretty Mike?" Stink asked.

"The Ice T looking nigga with a ponytail." JT answered.

"See if you can stall, 'cause it might get funky, sooner than later," Hammer suggested.

Toya was pissed. Everyone else stood to make a bonus by raising the price on the coke they had left if the drought hit, while she would have to sit around empty handed. If the deal didn't go down with Pretty tomorrow, she'd seem like a fraud. Something had to shake.

CHAPTER 15

The next morning, JT woke up to Toya knocking at the door. Still half asleep, he let her in and she went straight to his bedroom, not even asking if he was alone. She still had clothes in his closet she'd never thought to get until today. For the first time since she had been in Columbus, she was thinking about returning to Detroit.

As JT watched her, he could tell she still had an attitude. He knew she was salty about her deal with Pretty falling through, but it was out of his hands. He really wanted to hold her down, since she was a productive member of the crew. She wasn't just a bitch lingering around, waiting for some crumbs to fall her way. Toya was getting to the money all on her own. He thought about letting her work one of the three kilos they had left, but he would have to get Stink to agree with him, which he knew was highly unlikely.

Toya gathered her things from his closet and made her exit without saying a word.

"Fuck naw, nigga," Stink argued.

"I'm just saying, dog. Toya been holding her own and she been helping us flip that shit faster, so... it's not like I'm asking you to look out for a bitch that got her feet kicked up."

"Well, you give her yours if you feel like that."

"Her being here ain't just benefiting me, it's benefiting both of us. We got one that we got to split the profit on anyway. Lets just give it to her for the eighteen and let her do what she do."

"Why would we do that and we can sit on the bitch and stand a chance to get twenty six or twenty seven? That shit you talking don't make no sense."

JT knew he wasn't making sense, but he felt better, now that he had at least tried to rally for her cause. When he really thought about it, he didn't want to miss out on the chance of an extra seven or eight thousand dollars to split, so he shut up and left it alone.

Toya sat on the terrace, staring blankly into the sky. A bird landed on the guardrail followed by another, and another. They seemed to be oblivious to her presence.

"Get the hell on!" she kicked the guardrail, taking her frustration out on the birds. Her phone rang, and without even looking at the phone, she knew it was Pretty Mike.

It was eating her alive to know that she was so close to her first brick sale and couldn't make it happen. Pretty wanted three bricks, twenty thousand each.

There was three bricks right downstairs at JT's apartment. *How is this possible that she can't make this deal happen?* She had a revelation.

If the news had spread overnight like she believed it did, that meant Pretty knew there was a drought coming. If he was smart, he would get his hand on whatever he could get. He continued to call her, but she didn't answer. Toya was strategizing. If he could get some dope from his regular connect, then she would just have to miss out on the money, but if he couldn't, he'd have no choice but to pay whatever price she insisted upon.

She waited a full twenty-four hours to return his call, and she could only hope she had played her cards right.

"Them chicken dinners went up, my nigga." she calmly said.

"Oh yeah... they went up, huh?"

"Yeah, you know what it is, doe." She paused and waited for his response. It was way too soon for the streets to be dry, but she knew people like Pretty would be thinking ahead. Even if he had some dope, there was still a chance he'd want all he could get his hands on.

"They went up like overnight, huh?"

"Yeah, you already know. I need like four more dollars now. I got one left and it's yours if you want it."

She waited.

"I'm hungry as hell. Fuck yeah, I want it!"

Toya hung up the phone and shot to JT's as fast as

she could. When they let her in, she literally fell to her knees and begged Stink and JT to let her get one brick for twenty- two, so she could make the two thousand dollars. It wasn't the two thousand dollars that made her beg, it was all the thousands she stood to make in the future by establishing herself as a true business-woman.Stink and JT agreed on the twenty-two and let her make the deal. She sealed it a few hours later, and everyone was happy.

The following days, the streets dried up, just as everyone expected. Stink and JT sat on the two kilos for weeks, and then sold them for thirty thousand each. After that, they contacted 40 Grand on a daily basis, but he continued to tell them he had no clue when they would have work again. The first couple of weeks went by without much thought of a crisis. JT kept his phone off most of the time, so he wouldn't have to think about all the money he was missing out on. Stink was able to spend some time with Naomi, and they hit it off really fast. JT met a thirty-five year old real estate broker and he began to juggle his time between her and Tasha. Toya began to hustle ecstasy pills in the club to keep some money coming in.

By the third week, everyone was extremely frustrated with the situation, except Stink. He continued to wine and dine Naomi as if he didn't have a care in the world. He had bought her a five-thousand-dollar necklace without knowing her a month. JT was furious. He couldn't believe Stink had the audacity to parade around town like they were rich, when in reality, they didn't know when they were going to have the opportunity to make money again.

In week four, JT went into panic mode. Stink didn't come home that night, but JT was up early the next morning waiting to have a talk with him.

"Don't you think you spending too much money?" JT said.

"Don't worry about my stacks, guy. Count yo' own pockets." Stink countered.

"I'm trying to look out for your stupid ass. You spending all that money on a bitch you just met. You clubbing again, all of sudden. This the worst time in the world for that shit."

"Fool, I'm out here networking, trying to see what I can come up on, while you sitting around waiting for 40 Grand. What you hurting or something? You need a loan?"

"Fuck naw, I ain't hurting. I ain't trying to be working for 40 Grand forever, either. We supposed to be trying to be our own bosses, remember? We gonna need to stack our bread for that."

Stink looked at him with a lips pursed.

"Is you finished, fuck boy? Don't you ever think for a second that the kid don't got a trick up his sleeve. I just been chillin' and waiting to see how this shit gon' play out."

"So what you saying?"

"I'm saying, first of all... Fuck 40 Grand. I'm tired of working for him already. And I'm saying it's time for us to boss up and get this money. You ready to get this money or what?"

JT's face was twisted. "Don't ask me no stupid shit like that!"

"Check it out!" Stink said as he took off towards his bedroom.

In the closet was a bag. As he grabbed the shopping bag, JT stood in the doorway wondering what he was up to. He dumped the contents of the bag on to the floor. JT was shocked to see that Stink had been saving empty kilo wrappings. There were ten in all.

"Remember that move we shot with Scurvy?" Stink said.

"Yeah, how long you had these?"

"I been putting 'em to the side here and there from the keys we broke down."

JT just stood there for a while with his arms folded, letting it all sink in. This was not what he was expecting from Stink, but it was a good plan, with a lot of money to be made.

"If we do this, you know we gon' be beefing with 40 Grand?" JT said.

"Fuck 'em!" Stink shouted as he tossed the duct tape and the scissors on the bed.

"What about Hammer?"

"I don't wanna pop Hammer, but if he get stupid, fuck him too!"

JT didn't want to fall out with Hammer. He was the guy that vouched for them to make this out of town shit come to life. But the truth was, he only had one real friend, and he was looking at him.

"So... we hit these Columbus niggas up and head back to the D?" JT said.

"Hell yeah, until we can think of something else. So you wit it?"

JT felt a small butterfly in the pit of his stomach. He wondered if Stink was nervous at all about the implications of what would happen if they went through with it. But JT feared no man, and he had a crazy muthafucka that had his back to the fullest.

"It's whatever. Let's do this."

For the next hour, they worked on putting the plan in effect. They slowly funneled flour into the kilo wrappers until they were at the right weight. Next, they sprinkled the top layer with sugar and a vitamin supplement mix, to give the keys a sparkling fish scale glow. They had to make it as believable as possible. Their lives could depend on it.

After they finished rewrapping all ten bricks, they called Toya and told her to stop whatever she was doing and come to the apartment.

When Toya came in, Stink and JT were in the living room searching through their pagers and calling numbers back.

"Yeah, we on now, baby! What's happening?" Stink said into his cell phone.

She looked at JT. "We back on?" Toya said.

"I guess you could say that," he answered and put

one finger to his lip, signaling her to hush up until Stink got off the phone.

Once he was off the phone, they let Toya in on the whole plan. She was one of them now, and this would determine if she was really in this thing for the long haul. This would decide if she was playing for keeps, the same as them.

As they gave her the run down, Toya's eyes went back and forth from Stink to JT. She could see that they were dead serious. What she didn't understand was why they were letting her in on something that they could obviously do without her help. JT provided her with the answer.

"So what about yo' boy, Pretty Mike?" he asked. There was no hesitation in her response.

"Fuck that nigga. I'm wit it!"

An hour later, the three of them hopped in Toya's caravan with her behind the wheel. They tossed the duffle bag full of fake keys on the floor. The first stop was Tico on the south side because he was the easiest and most gullible target. Tico never asked any questions and he never complained about the prices. Some of the dudes that bought coke were used to only coming to the apartment, but to keep anyone from having second thoughts, they just made it seem as if they had too many orders to fill for the high traffic it would bring the apartment. It was a drought and in the end, nobody really cared as long as they got work.

When they hit Tico's stomping grounds, JT called and told him to be outside. They pulled up to the address Tico had given them, and he emerged from the side of the house wearing a fleece hoodie, carrying a brown paper bag.

JT sat in the front passenger seat, while Stink was in the second row of seats with his feet kicked up. He was cool, calm, and collected. He slid the door open and told Tico to hop in the back.

"Y'all aiight?" Tico said to everyone as he got in.

"Hell yeah, we beautiful now that shit is back on and popping."

"I'm telling y'all, man. Y'all the only niggas with work in the whole city."

"That's right, get 'em while they hot," JT added.

Tico tossed Stink the brown paper bag. "That's sixty," he said.

Stink observed the rubber banded stacks closely, not wanting to seem anxious. He unzipped the duffle bag and pulled out the two keys. JT and Toya watched their surroundings while Stink conducted the hand to hand.

"Here you go, my dude. Nice doing business with you as always."

"This shit some butter?"

"Naw, you got fish scale right there, baby."

Tico opened the door to exit. "Be careful out here, my nigga," he said as he departed.

"You too, homey." Stink replied.

They pulled off slowly, with excitement building inside each of them, realizing they had just pulled off an easy lick. In a few minutes, Tico would take his package into the kitchen and bust it open, only to realize he'd been Ganked! This was the beginning of something special.

The next two licks were risky. They had to hit Rakim and Dada, who both hustled on the eastside. They couldn't stick around in one area for two long, because the consequences could be deadly. They decided to hit Dada first, since Rakim's block was closer to the freeway. When they hit the block, Dada was outside as they had instructed him to be, but he was with four more cats.

JT sat his pistol on his lap in case Dada had any bright ideas of his own.

When Stink opened the sliding door and Dada climbed in, his jacket rose above his waist. Stink could see the pistol on his hip.

"What up?" Stink said sternly.

"You got it, player. I got your call right on time, man. I was about to start pulling my hair out."

"Glad we could help, my dude. Glad we could help."

Dada started pulling money from every pocket, including his jacket. JT and Stink watched closely. They didn't know Dada that well, but he seemed to run with some grimy cats. Dada paused and peered through the front window, nervously.

"What the fuck?" Dada said.

Everyone's attention turned to the Taurus with the four deep convoy behind it. All four doors flew open on the Taurus and the occupants dressed in all black piled out, one by one.

"That's the police, pull off! Throw that shit out, throw that shit out!" Dada screamed.

Toya slammed in reverse and stomped the gas. Stink grabbed the duffle bag, ready to start slanging shit, but he noticed the van was slowing down.

"Bitch, what the fuck is you doing?" Dada yelled.

Toya had spotted the old lady as the fourth passenger and the other cars were now pulling around the Taurus. "That's not the gotdam police that's an old ass lady. You see them getting her groceries out of the car?" Toya shouted back.

Dada was in shock to see that it was the old lady that lived next door to him and the men in black were her sons and a friend who all worked for the same security company. They continued to help the old lady with her groceries as Toya pulled over to the curb.

"Man, you just scared the shit outta me!" Stink said.

"Them muthafuckas did look like the police," Dada said, defending his right to panic. "But my bad for calling you all out your name and shit, baby. I thought it was about to go down in this bitch."

"You might need to slow down on the weed or something," Toya replied.

"Just give me my shit so I can bounce. That shit got my nerves all fucked up now. I really need a blunt. I'm on parole and shit, fuck this."

Stink tossed the thirty thousand dollars in his duffle bag full of money, and gave Dada his fake kilo in the other bag. Dada was so shook, he didn't ask any questions. He just tucked away his package and got out the van without saying another word.

"That nigga high as hell!" Toya assured them as they pulled away from the curb.

They hit up Rakim in the projects for another two bricks before they called in the big money deal. By now, their cell phones and pagers were ringing nonstop with people ready and willing to murder them by any means necessary. They began drinking to calm their nerves.

They passed the bottle of Hennessy around, drinking straight from the bottle. The fact that they were still in Ohio had everyone on edge, and praying they made it out alive. It was too late to turn back now, so they continued with the plan. All or nothing. They knew people would be out looking for them everywhere, so they set up the next deal just in time for the daylight to disappear.

Toya agreed to meet Pretty Mike at the usual location–his block. Everyone was strapped up and extremely cautious at this point. One wrong move could make all they'd schemed and Ganked their way up onto come crashing down around them.

When she hit the block, all the same luxury cars lined the street, but Toya wasn't expecting a crowd. There was too much money on the line to do business that way, whether it was a Gank move or not. For a brief moment, she had second thoughts. She called Mike on his cell phone.

"Why so many people, Mike?" Toya said.

"You outside already?"

"Yeah, and I wasn't trying to meet nobody, either."

"You ain't about to meet nobody. This gon' be me and you, but to keep it real wit you, I got some partnas that's spending money on this too. So you know they want that package as soon as I get it in my hands."

"So where they at?"

"Come on boo, this me and you. You ain't got shit to worry about. Now is we doing business or what?"

Toya swallowed the lump in her throat. "I'm on my way in," she said.

After she hung up the phone, she went over all the pros and cons in her head.

Stink and JT watched, knowing what was going through her mind. "What's up?" JT finally said.

She continued to think. This was her deal and they didn't know for sure if she was capable of handling something this big. She was going into this all alone, and there was no way around that. Stink and JT coming along would be an immediate red flag for Pretty.

"Okay listen," Toya finally said. "I don't know how many niggas is in there watching his back, but I know some of them is gon' be in the house hid where I can't see 'em. Stink, let me get your gun with the extended clip, and you take mine."

They made the exchange and Stink looked around at how the cars were positioned in front of each house. One house had three Cadillacs in the driveway.

"How many of these houses have you ever seen him go in or come out of?" he asked.

"All three of these and that one on the other side." she said, pointing to the opposite side of the street.

"Okay, go ahead before he get nervous, we got yo back." JT said, gripping his Desert Eagle.

Toya grabbed the duffle bag with the five remaining keys and walked briskly to the front door. Her Chanel shades masked the growing fear that was apparent in her eyes.

Pretty held the door open for her as she stepped inside and scanned the room and everything in her eyesight.

"You look gorgeous, as usual," Pretty complimented her.

"Thank you," Toya said, resting her duffle bag on the leather sofa.

"Can I get you something?"

"Naw, let's just do this. I got a lot of running around to do."

She began pulling out the keys one by one, stacking them on top of each other in the middle of the floor. Pretty walked over to his entertainment center, turned a speaker face down, and detached the back of it. He pulled out six wads of cash wrapped in rubber bands and placed them on the glass table in front of Toya.

"Each stack is thirty each. Count if you want, while I check these boys out." He picked up the last kilo that Toya placed on top of the stack as Toya's mind began to race.

She didn't know what he meant by 'check these boys out,' but she knew it wasn't good. He placed the kilo on the dining room table and produced some type of kit from the china cabinet. Toya had remained standing because she didn't want the Glock with the extended clip to move around in the small of her back. She wanted it right where it was, for easy access. She began loading the cash into her duffle bag.

"I trust you," she said.

Pretty obviously didn't share her same confidence. He split the duct tape with a razor down the middle. Toya's eyes roamed back and forth from him to the door. She was wishing Stink and JT would come blasting through the door and save her, but she knew this was her deal, and she had to save herself.

Somehow, she knew it would come down to this before she even stepped foot in the house. She drew her gun while he had his back turned.

"Let me save you some trouble," she said aiming at Pretty's head.

"Bitch what the fuck!" he leaned a step in her direction.

"Fuck wit me if you wanna," she warned making Pretty freeze in his tracks.

"Listen, whoever put you up to this—"

"You ever seen New Jack City? Rock-a-bye baby!"

He didn't believe she'd do it, so he lunged forward again while reaching for the gun in his waistline and she rock-a-byed his ass with two shots to the forehead. As soon as his body dropped, Toya could hear the rumbling of footsteps coming from upstairs. She quickly grabbed the duffle bag and aimed her gun at the top of the stairs. As she saw legs and feet in her view, she began firing shots at the staircase and didn't stop until all twenty-eight shots were fired.

She turned and pulled on the double locked doors, praying she didn't get shot in the back. When she finally got the door open, she heard shots coming from every direction.

The caravan door slid open. Stink and JT were crouched down in front of the van, aiming their guns at the house directly across the street from them. Toya ran for dear life towards the van, not knowing if the guys in the house with Pretty were dead or alive. From the grass, she dived in the open door.

"Come oooon!" she yelled at the top of her lungs.

JT stood to his feet and bucked the last few shots from his Desert Eagle as he and Stink made their way inside the van. Toya was so rattled, she stomped on the gas while the car was still in park. As the engine revved, bullets began blasting through the windows. She slapped the gear shift in drive and peeled out, ducking bullets and flying glass.

"Turn at this first street." JT called out.

She bent a hard left and went on to run the next three stop signs and two red lights before slowing down and heading towards the freeway. They hit I-23 to I-75 headed back to Detroit in a bullet riddled rental and the extra three hundred thousand in cash. They knew they had to say goodbye to Columbus forever.

CHAPTER 16

SOUTH BEND, INDIANA

They stayed in Detroit, just long enough to visit the probation office and then hit the road again. The word on the street was that 40 Grand had a contract on their heads. Toya was the only one in the clear, since her business didn't interfere with Hammer or 40 Grand. But she didn't feel safe in the city without Stink and JT, so when they gave her the word that they were headed to Indiana, she put a safe at her Aunt Keisha's house and hit the road.

Big Pooh had extended his hand and invited them to join him in a new spot that Detroit hustlers had found and flocked to in recent years. South Bend was crawling with gang bangers—CVL's, G's, Latin Counts and smaller organizations. Big Pooh wasn't offering any piece of his pie, just access to the city and extra muscle if needed. He already has his camp, The Mack Boys, eating off his plate.

After feeling out South Bend for a few weeks, Stink rented a house in the slums and brought in his little brother, Rob, and his crew to run things. From day one, Stink and Rob didn't get along in a business relationship. Rob was just a fuck up in Stink's eyes, but if you asked Rob, Stink was an arrogant muthafucka who didn't realize that he wasn't a kid anymore.

Stink parked his Benz 430 on 20s at the Steak 'n Shake next to Big Pooh's Suburban. The Steak 'n Shake was a spot where a lot of the up and coming hustlers hung out. Big Pooh and Stink were there for two reasons. One was to get to know some names and faces. The other was to get familiar with enough South Bend niggas to see who was holding some real cash. By now, Stink had come to the realization that a Gank was always better than a grind.

Stink spotted the table with two dudes wearing Detroit Tigers fitted caps and strolled over. "What up, doe?" Stink said to Big Pooh and his partner.

"What up doe?" they returned.

Stink was about to sit across from Big Pooh, but he stopped Stink before he could have a seat. "Aye homey, why don't you sit over there so Stink can sit on this side?"

They swapped seats, and Stink sat next to Big Pooh, scanning the room. He saw some familiar faces, but no one he knew by name. Big Pooh began whispering names and backgrounds of everyone in his ear. The Indiana cats had taken a liking to Big Pooh, so he knew most of the who's who around town. Those that didn't like him had learned to accept his presence.

"What up, Big Pooh?" A young native said as he walked by.

"You got the best hand, nigga." Big Pooh returned. They slapped fives and the youngster kept it moving.

Big Pooh knew what Stink was thinking already.

"That's Nate, he ain't working with shit," he said before Stink could ask.

A chubby, caramel skinned chick came in, and all heads turned in her direction. She wore a beige cashmere sweater with slacks and a beige leather blazer. Stink noticed her looped diamond earrings and her Dooney and Burke handbag. It was just like the one he bought Naomi, so he knew it wasn't cheap.

Big Pooh leaned over. "That's Carmen."

"What's up with her?"

"Her pops got long money, this nigga name Face."

"How old is she?" Stink asked

"Bout twenty, twenty-one."

Carmen spoke to a few people, then went to the counter to pick up her order that had been called in earlier.

"I'm 'bout to creep outside and follow that bitch," Stink said as he began to slide out.

"I know where the bitch stay already," Big Pooh said, grabbing Stink by the arm.

Stink settled back into his seat.

"I just don't know if it's something at her crib or not."

"Who she live with?"

"I think she live alone, but she keep a few free loading bitches hanging around. I ain't really had time to lay on the bitch like I wanted to."

"Well, I got time."

While JT and Toya were chilling at a hotel, Stink cruised around Lakeside aka Little Mexico after visiting a senorita he'd been seeing in the area. He thought about Naomi. He had to stop seeing her, cold turkey. It turned out that Pretty Mike was Naomi's brother that he'd never met. JT's girl, Tasha, had worked on the crime scene and related to JT that three people were killed that night.

The information came by coincidence, but once Stink and JT put it all together, it was clear that no one really knew it was them that did the murders. If anyone found the timing of their departure from Columbus odd, no one spoke on it. It had been over a month since Stink had seen or spoken to Naomi, and he was longing to hear her soft breathy voice. She was the only girl he'd met since the day he came home, that could take his mind off of money and constant hustling for a moment. Stink knew the right thing to do was to cut all ties, but it seemed that he was in the clear for at least the murders in Columbus. Against his better judgment, this day he decided to call her.

She picked up almost immediately, as if she knew it was Stink, even though he was calling from a new number.

"Hello."

"Whassup?" Stink said.

"Hey you," Naomi answered, recognizing Stink's voice immediately.

"I'm just calling to check on you and make sure you straight."

"Yeah, I'm glad you called. I thought you said we were gonna keep in contact, but then you don't call me for over a month?"

"Well, you know shit gets kinda crazy with me sometimes."

"Mmm hmm, well I don't know how you gonna take this, but I got some news for you. Whether it's good or bad news, I'll let you decide."

Stink's mind started to race. "What kinda news?"

"I'm pregnant."

"What?"

"You heard me, I'm pregnant."

There was silence…

"Get the fuck outta here with that bullshit," he snapped.

"Whatchu mean? What bullshit?"

"Maaan…"

Click!

Stink hung up the phone, furious at her and himself.

Toya pulled her indigo Jaguar X Type into the liquor store parking lot next to JT's Cadillac DTS. She tucked her Glock in her skinny jeans and locked the door. JT looked her outfit over. Pink and grey puffy vest, grey jeans and pink and grey Timberlands. He loved how she seemed to have a different look for every day of the week. Toya and JT had a spot they ran together on the southside.

"You looking cute," he said as he got out of his vehicle.

"Don't I always?"

"A nigga can't just take a compliment." He shook his head.

"Hell naw!"

They made their rounds like this every day. They left the cars at the liquor store and took off on foot. They walked down the street and JT put his arm around her shoulder, making sure they looked like a couple in love. They stopped at each corner to talk and embrace before continuing their stroll. To the untrained eye, it appeared they were nothing more than two youngsters lost in a world all their own. But the southside hustlers were feeling the decline in their crack sales, and starting to investigate. JT spotted a crack head knocking on the front door to his spot, which was a big no no.

"You see this shit?"

"Yeah, I see it," Toya said.

JT pulled out his cell phone to call Lil Rob who had quit working for Stink and only worked for JT now.

"Go to the back door." Toya yelled at the crackhead.

"Who is you?" asked the man looking for a fix.

"Bitch don't worry about it. Just do what I said."

JT shot her a look and she calmed down. She had forgotten that quick that they were supposed to be in character. She was just the young girl in love, knowing nothing about the dirt that was going on around her.

"Hello Rob? Why the hell you got muthafuckas knocking on the front door?"

Toya could hear Rob trying to explain why it wasn't his fault. Cars began to pull up back to back with crackheads hopping out in a rush to get what they needed.

"Come on, let's bounce," Toya said.

A squad car bent the corner and cruised by. JT put his arm around Toya and ended his call with Rob. They noticed how the police had slowed down, taking notice of all the cars in front their spot and in the surrounding area. JT thought they might double back.

"You got anything on you besides the strap?"

"Never dat," Toya said.

They both knew the likelihood of JT being searched if they were ever stopped, so he never carried a gun when they walked the hood, nor did he ever stop by the spot. Together, the two had a strong, consistent efficacy. They headed to check on another spot that Toya was thinking about pursuing.

The alligators in Romell's basement were full grown now, and their jaws held two thousand pounds of pressure when chomping down on dinner. There was no need to dismember bodies with a chainsaw anymore. Just toss them into the pit and watch the show. Romell had the basement steps knocked out in the house of horror, so once someone was in the pit, there was no getting out.

Fo Tre dragged in the disloyal subject who had violated. He was still kicking and screaming. He had no pride left and openly begged for mercy.

"Shut the fuck up!" Fo Tre smacked him with the pistol, while still dragging him by the neckline of his hoodie.

Romell wandered in from the kitchen as Fo Tre shoved the man inside the blood room.

"Sit yo' ass down," Romell ordered.

"Listen man—"

"Shhh! Don't talk, just listen. Matter of fact, make sure he don't talk, Tre."

Fo Tre quickly produced some duct tape and wrapped it around the man's mouth. Romell waited patiently until he was finished.

"Now... nobody makes it here to the house of horror by chance. If you find yourself here, that means you fucked up, big time." He strolled across the floor as if he were a college professor, lecturing his students.

"How do that saying go?" He glanced at Fo Tre. "Oh yeah, excuses is like assholes; everybody got one. But in this muthafucka, ain't no excuses, just consequences. So let me start by being real with you. I never really liked you that much to begin with. It was my manz idea to put you down in the first place. Now you owe him ten thousand, you owe me thirty thousand, and that ain't even the worst part."

The subject placed his hands together in an attempt to pray, seeing his final hour approaching.

"Put yo' muthafucking hand down! The worst part of it is, you been running yo' mouth. Telling muthafuckas who I'm supposed to have a hit on, and all this kinda shit. Nigga you trying to get me put away for life."

"That's probably why Stink and JT left town so quick," Fo Tre added.

"Exactly. Now I gotta be on the lookout for them niggas, Tank, *and* 40 Grand. So for all your transgressions, you get to go in the pit while you still breathing. Nuff, talk. Get yo' bitch ass up!"

Romell and Fo Tre each grabbed an arm as the man continued to struggle and plead through his duct taped mouth. He looked for a window he could dive out of if he managed to break free, but all he saw was armor guard. His legs stiffened as they continued to pull him in the opposite direction of where he wanted to go. Resistance was pointless, but for a man fighting for his life, all he had was resistance.

As they cleared the threshold, they stood at the landing to the basement, which was held together by two beams. The ravenous gators were fully aware of their presence. It had been a solid month since they had been fed, and they were ready to demolish whatever came their way.

"Thanksgiving is coming early, muthafuckas," Romell shouted.

"Nooo, noooo!"

They tossed him in the water.

His body hit the water with a splash. The screams were deafening. The two of them looked on, captivated by the gators as they relentlessly ripped flesh apart. It was the kind of thing that became more exciting each time they saw it. The screaming stopped, and they knew their associate was no more. His legs were inside one gator's mouth, while his head was in another's. It was a sight like no other.

Romell's cell phone rang, snapping him back to reality. He stepped away from the basement and into the blood room for privacy. He hated anybody listening in on his phone calls, even Fo Tre. When he looked at the phone, he recognized the Indiana area code.

"What up," he answered.

"What up, my nigga." It was Lucky, a friend and protégé for many years, who had came up under Romell. He had since become his own man and ventured off to Indiana.

"You got it, playboy. What's the deal?" Romell said.

"Well, you know I relocated from South Bend to Gary, since I had that situation.

"Right."

"But I still got a couple hoes in South Bend I go through and bang from time to time."

"Okay."

"So, I'm in South Bend yesterday, and I hear some familiar names."

"Oh yeah, like who?"

"Like Stink and JT."

"You bullshitting?"

"Dog, you know I don't even bullshit like that. I remember you used to talk about them dudes and how you couldn't wait til they came home. I know you and me shared shit that we ain't shared with a lot of niggas. Them niggas here, dog," Lucky revealed.

"Yeah, I know them dudes bounce around a lot, so I ain't been able to greet 'em like I wanted to. I really do need to get in touch with them."

"Well, we ain't even gotta say no more. I'll find out if it's official or not, and then I'ma come holler at you and see if what I know is worth its weight in gold."

"That sound like a plan to me."

"Bet that."

Romell hung up the phone and began stroking his goatee. Things were really starting to come together just the way he wanted. Just as he was beginning to lose too many soldiers to the war with Tank, he found out Tank had been hit with a conspiracy charge and was now behind bars. If he did manage to get out, he'd have much bigger problems, so Romell felt he could now turn his attention to 40 Grand and the rest of his enemies.

Romell knew Lucky wasn't real quick to get into gun play these days. He had been shot too many times, and lived to tell about it. But he had goons, and his crew was an extension of Romell's army. He could only hope that Lucky's lead turned out to be a solid one.

CHAPTER 17

JT roamed around the used car lot, looking at cargo vans. He wanted something that could hold a nice stash spot, and didn't scream out, drug dealer. If things went right, he would get at least one big trip back to Indiana were they would slaughter the city with twenty-dollar rock boulders big as a shoulder. His eyes fell on a white van with dark windows that had a price of seventy-five hundred written across the front windshield.

He was attracted to this van in particular, because of the tints. It was perfect for what he was trying to do, and he knew that this was about as low-key as it was going to get. He thought about how the snow would be coming soon, and he wouldn't have any problems getting around in a cargo van. Stink two-wayed in.

"Where you say you at?"

"I'm at the car lot on Michigan, by the Jukebox.

"I'm right here. I don't see no fucking... oh, I see it straight ahead."

JT walked around the van, inspecting it inside and out. It had brand new snow tires, clean inside and out, and the mileage was extremely low. It was a steal for that make and model, but JT didn't know or care about any of that. As long as he could stuff it with bricks, he was good. He figured that even if he had to get rid of it, he could easily sell it to a construction company or something for a small profit.

Stink walked up. "Fuck you looking at this for?" he asked.

"Cause it's some low key shit. Bet we can get bout thirty bricks in this bitch." Business was booming for JT, so he was thinking ahead on how to capitalize while the getting was good. Things were going ok for Stink, but he had his mind on the next gank move.

"I been doing my research, right. I found out this nigga Face could be worth a couple million." Stink said, waiting for a reaction.

"Oh yeah?" That caught JT's attention. There was no sense in grinding it out if they could get the same money all in one wop.

"Yeah nigga, you know I stay on my inspector gadget shit."

"You found a way in, yet?"

"Hell naw, I still think the daughter is the way in. What you think?"

"What you talking 'bout, kidnapping the bitch?"

"I don't know, maybe." They turned around as they heard the car salesman's hard bottoms crunching across the gravel."

"I thought you was bringing Toya so she could drive my Caddy back to the spot."

"I did bring her. She in the car talking to that good

pussy eating nigga she be talking about all the time." Stink said.

"The nigga she call Head Hunter?"

"I guess, man."

The salesman began his pitch about the van, but JT told him he could save it.

"I want this van. We can go get the paperwork started."

Later that evening, they took the whole crew to University Park Mall in the new van. Rob nicknamed it the snowmobile, because of the color, and because he knew what JT had planned for the van. All of the workers were given cash to go and shop, while JT, Stink and Toya stuck together. JT was busy explaining to Stink why he and Toya's operation on the Southside was coming together so easily. He and Toya had snuck in like a thief in the night, laying out all the groundwork before setting up shop, whereas Stink had chosen to force feed niggas on the eastside, off his connection to Big Pooh.

Stink realized he should have played his hand a little differently, but right now, it really didn't matter. All he really had on his mind was taking money. After they hit the lick in Columbus, his mind began to run in a different direction. He still loved the hustle, but there was nothing like the feeling of waking up a hundred thousand dollars richer than you were the night before.

They went inside the jewelry store, and Stink immediately began casing the joint. No security guard inside the store, two salesclerks and no cameras. Although they had never discussed robbing a jewelry store, Stink always thought he could pull it off. He had watched enough gangster flicks to believe he could pull off anything.

"Stink." Toya called out.

"Huh?" Stink said, snapping out of it.

"Come look at this watch." It was a women's black leather band Rolex.

Stink didn't think much of it. He didn't see the point of a leather band Rolex.

"It's aiight."

"You crazy," Toya said, appalled. "This is classy. See you got flashy and you got classy, you gotta be able to switch it up." Toya's cell phone rang.

"Well, I'm flashy 24-7." Stink said, shaking his iced out gold Rolex in her face.

"Hold up, Head Hunter on line one," Toya said.

JT glanced over at Toya as she wandered off to the back of the store. He felt a hint of jealousy that he didn't understand, but he brushed it off. He knew Toya didn't really like any of the guys she dated, but it seemed she was digging the Head Hunter a little.

As the salesclerk brought JT's customized chain and pendant out, Stink noticed a girl with her back turned. JT smiled when he saw his initials glistening in diamonds. When she turned her head, Stink got a side view of her face. From where he stood, the girl bore a striking resemblance to his target's daughter, Carmen.

He slid to the other side of the store to get a better view. Once he was closer, he could see if it was definitely her. He became overwhelmed with excitement, thinking it had to be fate that she was here, standing only a few feet away from him. He knew this was his chance, and it could be now or never.

He rushed over to JT and pulled him to the side. "Aye. That's her."

"Who?"

"The bitch, Carmen. Face's daughter."

By then, Toya had ended her phone conversation and began one with Carmen. Stink and JT just watched for a second, not knowing what to do next.

"Go put Toya up on game." JT finally said.

"Bet." Stink moved slyly to the back of the store, eavesdropping on the conversation.

"I knew this was a nice watch. My homeboy just a hater, that's all it is to it," Toya said.

"Toya, come look at this one." Stink called out.

"That's some bullshit." she responded before even seeing the watch.

"Just come look at it," he asked a second time.

She sashayed over. "Which one?"

"That's not what I wanted. Remember the nigga Face I been telling y'all about?" he whispered.

"Yeah."

"That's his daughter. Don't look back at her, play it

off! You still don't like it?" Stink said loud enough for Carmen to hear that they were still talking about the watch.

"Hell naw, it look like silver to me." Toya said, referring to the platinum Rollie.

"I need you to see if you can get her phone number or something. If not, give her yours, but just—"

"Aiight, aiight, I got it."

Toya walked away from Stink, knowing what the mission was. Toya was the best person for the job. Not only was she a female, but she was a people person in every sense of the word. She was sure she could charm anybody with her vivaciousness.

"So you think I should get it, girl?" she asked Carmen.

"Yeah girl. If you can afford to, why not treat yourself?"

"You right, too. I should treat myself. I love that bag you rocking. I need to treat myself to one of those too."

"Oh thank you, I picked this up at Neiman Marcus last week."

"I love Neiman Marcus! How much was it? About twelve hundred I bet?

"Fifteen, but girl I ain't gon' front. I don't wanna see nobody rocking this purse but me. Now there is a nice little store inside Scottsdale Mall that a lot of people don't know about. They keep a lot of nice bags and accessories or whatever."

"Scottsdale? I ain't familiar with that one. See, I'm from Detroit."

As Toya continued to schmooze, JT paid the balance owed on his chain and placed it around his neck. The pendant held thirty diamonds in all.

Stink lifted the chain off JT's chest. "You starting to look like a meal to me, nigga."

Toya exchanged phone numbers with Carmen, and they agreed to go shopping together the following week. Stink was so excited, he kissed Toya on the lips.

****

There was nothing suspicious about the friendship in the beginning, because Toya never really had to initiate anything. Carmen had seen her around town, and after a few phone conversations, she was convinced that her and Toya were cut from the same cloth. It felt good to have somebody around that could hold their own, and didn't need anything from her. They had breakfast every Sunday at IHOP, and they took turns treating each other. It wasn't long before Carmen began inviting Toya to her home.

"Shit, I don't need validation from no nigga. I don't care if I'm single until the day I die." Carmen announced about the upcoming holidays.

"That's what I'm saying, fuck a nigga. It's only one thing I need from a nigga. No, two things. Yo' south pole and ya mouth hole." They laughed and hi fived.

Carmen flipped through the channels on her Direct TV, while Toya reclined in the sofa that was becoming her favorite spot in the house. Carmen had plush white carpet all through the house and she made everyone who entered take their shoes off at the door.

"I need to find somebody else to do my nails and pedicures," Toya said, extending her legs to look at her toes.

"Why?"

"Cause I cussed the bitch out that used to do 'em."

"Girl, you always cussing somebody out."

"If muthafuckas would do like I asked them to do, then they wouldn't be getting cussed out. When I'm spending my money, I want shit done right."

"I hear that. So, what you doing for Christmas?"

"I don't know. I'll probably go to a party or something."

"I heard they throwing one at The Factory. I would go, but my dad be tripping. He don't like me going to shit like that. He really don't like me going out to clubs at all."

This was the first time Face had come up in a conversation. It was the perfect opportunity to pry.

"Why he don't want you going out?"

"Well, you know everybody knows my dad, and he worries that somebody might do something to me to get to him. He made me cut almost all my girlfriends off cause he said they was all just broke hoes, hanging around looking for a bone. A lot of 'em was though, but some of them, he just didn't even give 'em a chance. I gotta do what he say, cause he give me whatever I want, and more. I know he gonna like you, doe."

The doorbell rang and she steadied herself with the palm of her hands to push her chubby frame off the sofa. She peered through the peep hole.

"I just talked this nigga up," she said with a giggle.

The tall, brown-skinned man slid in through the barely cracked door. He had to be in his early forties, and his standout feature was his strong face. It was big, and defined with thick eyebrows and deep creases. His face looked like you could punch him as hard as you could, and it wouldn't faze him.

"Daddy, I was just talking about you, nothing bad either."

"Whose Jaguar is that in the driveway?"

"That's my friend, Toya's car. Daddy, this is Toya. Toya this my daddy, Face.".

"How you doing?" Face spoke with a hint of flirtation in his eyes.

"I'm fine, how are you?" Toya replied.

He looked forty, but he was dressed like he was twenty. His multicolored diamond Frank Muller watch was the only thing that separated him from a dude on the corner. When Toya's eyes landed on the watch, she tried her best not to stare or look impressed. She wanted to make a good impression, so that she didn't get the boot like the rest of Carmen's friends.

Face commented that he had never seen her around,

and then he roamed to the back of the house. Toya heard his footsteps travel down the basement stairs. She wondered what was down there.

This was only the second time Stink and JT had been to Big Pooh's bachelor pad. Stink was ready to leave already. No women were there and it was a Friday night. Lately, he'd been occupying his time with a lot of different women just to keep his mind off Naomi. He had talked to her again and hung up again. His gut told him she was pregnant with his baby, but he continued to deny the facts because he never planned to step foot in Columbus again.

He refused to believe it, because once he believed, he'd have to act. As the days went by, the whole thing began to eat away at his conscience, so he decided to talk to JT.

"Did I tell you Naomi said she pregnant by me?"

"You know damn well you ain't told me no shit like that!" JT lashed.

"Yeah, she said she know for sure it's mine."

JT was concentrating on rolling a blunt. "It probably is yours, nigga." he responded.

"Why you say that?"

"Cause that was yo' bitch! Nigga I know you was fucking her every night. You cut off all yo' other lil broads for her. Come on, now."

Big Pooh had come in with a bottle of 1738 and weighed in on the conversation. "Tell you something, my nigga. Them out of town hoes always trying to trap a nigga. They know them D boys bout that bread, so they just trying to get a meal ticket. Bitch tell me she pregnant I'ma put my backhand down." He raised his backhand and swung in a slapping motion. "Bitch, I stay strapped, quit playing wit me!"

"Aiight um, Goldy." JT interrupted. "I know this nigga, and if he feeling a broad, he gonna run up in her raw with the quickness. I can't count how many times I woke up and this nigga was gone to the clinic early as hell in the morning. I try to offer him a drink later on, 'cause I know what's up. Nigga go in his pocket and pull out some medication."

Everybody laughed, including Stink, knowing everything JT said to be true.

"Shut yo' punk as up." Stink finally said.

"I'm for real, though. If you know you was shooting up in the bitch, you can't sit here and act like it ain't yours."

Stink was silent for a moment. "I'm gon' call her, man." It wasn't something he looked forward to, but he knew JT was right. He had to at least talk to her and see what was going on. What was on her mind?

On his way back to the hotel, Stink called Naomi in the car. He didn't know what to say to her, so when she answered, he hung up.

Two minutes later, his phone rang and he saw Naomi's number on the caller ID.

"Hello."

"Did somebody just call my cell phone?" Naomi said.

"This Stink."

Naomi snorted. "What, Stink?"

"You still pregnant?"

"Yes I am. Five months."

"How you know it's mine?"

"Psssssh. Whatever. I don't got time for this."

"I'm asking you an honest question. You can't give me an honest answer?"

"Stink, the month I got pregnant, you were at my house almost every night. Who the fuck else is the father?"

Since he came home, Stink's weed habit was out of control. All the timelines were a blur. He tried to recall something different than what Naomi was suggesting, but he failed.

"What made you want to keep it?"

"Well, it was irresponsible of me to get pregnant, not knowing where things were going with us. But now I have to be responsible for my actions. Besides, they say it's never a perfect time to have a baby, so why not now? If you don't want to be there for your child, it doesn't matter to me anymore."

Stink took everything into consideration. Naomi seemed to be convinced she could take care of a child with or without him. She wasn't anything like the girls Big Pooh had described earlier. Even though Stink had spoiled Naomi in the beginning stages of their relationship, she had never asked for any of it. The Pretty Mike situation weighed heavy on his mind every time he even thought about Columbus, not to mention everything else.

"I wanna see you, but I can't come to Columbus."

"Why not?"

"I just got too much going on where I'm at."

"I don't know if it's a good idea for us to see each other anyway. I don't need the stress, you know, arguing and carrying on."

"You think I would wanna see you just to pick a fight? I can do that shit over the phone. I'm sending you a plane ticket."

"I'll think about it," Naomi replied.

He could hear in her voice that she was happy. It made him happy to know he still had the same effect on her.

CHAPTER 18

Toya paid for dinner and then proceeded to get Carmen too drunk to drive. As they filed out of the restaurant along with the other patrons, Toya realized she was concerned about Carmen's safety. *What the hell?* Why was she concerned about someone she was supposed to be playing like a video game? Was she getting soft?

"I think I gained about ten pounds since I met you." Carmen said, slurring each word.

"Yeah right, don't say that. But is you sure you can drive?"

"Yeah girl, I'm straight."

Carmen swayed with each step she took, making Toya question her sincerity. They were parked right next to each other. Toya's Jaguar and Carmen's BMW 540i. Carmen leaned against the car, fumbling through her purse for her keys. Her small silver pistol fell from her purse to the pavement, shimmering from the pole lights in the parking lot. The sound made Toya peek over in the area just enough to see what had fallen. She thought it sounded like a gun, and sure enough, it was.

"Girl hurry up and put that away.

"Shut up. Ain't nobody see it."

Until now, Toya never even knew Carmen carried a gun. "Call me when you make it home." Toya said.

In the car, she thought about all she had learned about Carmen over the past few weeks. They had become closer than she intended. Even though Toya had completely fabricated her life story to Carmen, in the back of her mind, she was wishing things were different. Toya had claimed she had money from a big lawsuit when a fire truck crashed into her while she was eight months pregnant. It supposedly changed her life forever. Toya had really began to enjoy having another female in her inner circle, because there was really nobody in all of Indiana besides dudes, that she had a relationship with.

It had to be that way because of the life they were living. She couldn't afford to befriend some chick who might slip up and see too much or hear something she wasn't supposed to hear.

Even Trouble seemed to have a life of her own now, and was growing distant. If Toya and Carmen had met on different terms, she was positive that they would have stayed friends for years to come, regardless if she went back to Detroit or not.

Her mind began to drift back to the murders in Ohio. She hadn't given it much thought after she knew it was a good chance they had gotten away with it all. She only hoped for Carmen's sake, that things didn't turn out that way again.

At the hotel, Toya keyed her door and fell in, dropping her purse on the floor. She crashed on the bed, staring blankly at the ceiling.

JT two-wayed in. "What up?" he said.

She knew what he wanted. The pressure had been coming down from Stink and Big Pooh to speed up the process. Toya was making good money on the block and wasn't in a hurry to betray the only girlfriend she had in town. But this was the plan all along, and her feelings were just something she was going to have to shake off and get over.

"What up?" she answered.

"Tell me something."

"Yeah, I think it's something in the house. I know it's something in the house for sure. We not even gonna have to do all that other shit, you feel me?"

"Cool, you seen dude again?"

"Yeah I seen him once more since the last time."

They had been contemplating whether they were going to have to kidnap Carmen and hold her for ransom or if there was something in the house worth doing a straight kick door. It didn't seem like a man of his status would leave his daughter as a sitting duck, but at that level of the game, there was not a lot of people you could trust.

"And you fo sho it's in the crib?" JT asked.

"It's something in there. Nigga go in the basement every time he stops by. But he don't come in carrying nothing and he don't leave out carrying nothing. He probably just be tucking the shit, you feel me?"

"Aiight, we should talk tomorrow."

"Aiight."

Stink picked Naomi up at the airport the day before Christmas Eve. Her pregnancy was evident in the roundness of her belly, but she hadn't gained much weight elsewhere. Her face had an extraordinary glow that made Stink smile the moment he laid eyes on her. He put away her things at the hotel, and they went to The Grill for lunch.

Stink tried the grilled swordfish, just to be different, while Naomi went for the lemon herb chicken. Her long dark hair rested on her shoulders with a bang in front that Stink thought was cute. As she swept her hair behind her ear, Stink got to see her one carat diamond earrings for the first time.

"So where you get the knock offs?" he teased.

"Boy please. Just cause you know you didn't buy 'em they gotta be knock offs, huh? My mama bought me these for Christmas. She was a lil sad when I told her I was leaving for the holidays, so she had to give them to me before I left."

Stink was glad she clarified where the earrings came from, because it would have drove him crazy thinking about it.

Naomi's mind seemed to drift off to some private place. "This is gonna be our first Christmas without my brother, and I should have stayed with my family, but... I just don't wanna sit around thinking about him and be all depressed. I know that's what would happen if I stayed home. I hope they understand, I'm just trying to keep a healthy mind. My brother told me if something was to ever happen to him, don't ever stop my life. Don't mourn his death, just celebrate his life. It's been hard, but that's what I've tried to do."

"I know it's been hard. I've never really lost anybody I cared about that much." Stink said.

He was very uncomfortable with the subject of Pretty Mike, but he couldn't be insensitive to Naomi's pain.

"Don't you worry sometimes about something happening to you, Stink? I mean my brother took every precaution in the streets and he still ended up getting killed."

"Well, I hate to say it like this, but if it's gonna happen, it's gonna happen"

The wrinkles in Naomi's forehead let Stink know she was clearly upset about his nonchalant attitude toward death. He couldn't help the way he felt.

"But you have a child on the way. What's the point of getting involved if you not gonna be around to help raise this child?"

"Listen, I didn't mean it like that. I don't plan to die anytime soon, but it just ain't the type of thing I like to talk about over a meal."

"I know. You right." Naomi backed off, but she knew they would have to talk soon about his plans for the future.

After lunch, Stink took Naomi to the mall where

she informed Stink that she had already purchased just about everything the baby needed, except the clothes, since she didn't know the baby's gender yet. Instead of baby shopping, Naomi went shoe shopping and Stink paid the tab. Even though her feet were swelling, she figured she might as well let Stink spoil her now, in case he flipped the script again later.

Stink never complained the whole time they were at the mall. He let Naomi have her way, as usual.

"How you gonna fit all these shoe boxes in your luggage?" he asked, lugging her load.

"I'm not. I'm leaving the boxes and taking the shoes. They probably gonna collect dust until after I have this baby, anyway."

"So what you wanna do now?"

"I'm tired. I wanna lay down."

Back at the hotel, Stink turned up the heat and stripped down to his boxers. It was no way he wasn't about to get some before she called herself turning in early.

Once the heat kicked in, Naomi was forced to come out of her jeans and sweater. She changed into a nightgown and slid under the covers. Stink slid right behind her. He cupped her breast and nibbled on her neck. Her breasts were bigger. Firmer.

She wiggled her ass across his stiffness, pretending to be getting in a more comfortable position to go to sleep.

He continued to nibble at her neck, knowing she was probably just as horny as he was. He slid a hand inside her panties.

"What is you doing?"

"Come on, girl. Quit playing," he mumbled.

"You didn't say anything about this part when we discussed my coming to visit you for the holidays. I'm on my period," she teased.

"As much as I miss your sense of humor, this is not the time for jokes." He continued to kiss behind her ear, knowing it was her spot.

She couldn't pretend any longer. It had been months since she had sex, and her hormones were at the boiling point. She moaned slightly, giving Stink all the encouragement he needed to take her.

It was Christmas day, and JT had spent most of it trying to iron out the details of the lick with Big Pooh. It was time to hit Carmen's crib, but it seemed she had left the house for the holidays to be with family. They couldn't break in, because Toya had assured them the security system was way too tight. Even if they could, it would probably be best if Carmen was there to make sure they got what they were looking for; money or dope. They had no choice but to wait until Carmen came home, to make their move.

JT had already started to plan his departure from Indiana. It was rumored that more and more cats were beginning to ask about all the Detroit niggas surfacing in the city. He knew that would mean heat in one form or another.

They didn't want to actually sit and wait for Carmen. She was known for circling the block before she went home, so the clique decided to hit downtown for one last night out.

JT hadn't seen Stink in three days, but he knew Stink was laid up with Naomi. JT expected him to be more involved in the final plans with Carmen, but he didn't complain. After all, it was his idea for him to call Naomi in the first place. Still, he wanted to hang out with his man tonight, so he gave him a call.

"Hello," Stink answered.

"Merry Christmas, you bitch ass nigga!

"Watch yo' mouth, soft ass nigga. Merry Christmas."

"Do you think you can break curfew for one night and come fuck with the homies?"

"Nigga fuck you! I just been chillin' and catching up, you know what I'm saying?"

"Yeah, I hear you and I know Naomi loving that. Since we can't put nothing in motion on that other thing right now, we taking the day off. The whole crew coming. What's happening?"

"Where y'all meeting up at?"

"Big Pooh's crib."

"Aiight, I'll be through after I put it on this nigga lying next to me, and knock her ass out for the night."

"Boy you ain't all that!" JT heard Naomi say in the background.

"Aiight, in a minute."

"In a minute? Oh, you got jokes too!" Stink said.

"Man, bye!" JT hung up.

It wasn't such a good idea, but this is how it happened. The crew hit The Factory twenty deep, rocking Detroit fitted caps. It felt disrespectful from the start, the way they roamed and around flaunted their money like they owned the joint.

Stink was the only one without a fitted cap. He rocked a green Detroit skull cap with a green fox trimmed Marc Buchanan Pelle Pelle and green fox trimmed gator boots. The diamonds in his chain glistened proudly on his chest as he clutched a bottle of Cristal.

Lil Rob and his crew were there, and JT had decided to let Rob wear his chain and get his shine on. Rob had been essential to his success in South Bend, and JT wanted to show him and his crew some appreciation.

"Everything on me tonight." JT announced before pointing to Big Pooh and company. "Except for y'all niggas. I ain't paying for y'all. Shit, y'all niggas got more money than me, fuck that!"

Big Pooh got excited at the chance to talk trash. "Nigga you right. Nigga I'll buy the bar in this muthafucka right now." He pulled out a wad of cash, stunting for his homies. "M.O.B Nigga!"

All eyes in the club were on them, male and female, as they began to spread out and break off into different areas of the club.

Stink watched his brother Rob for afar, getting his mack on. Since their business relationship went south, the two hadn't spoken much. He thought about how stubborn he'd been toward his brother, and was realizing tonight that life was going too good for both of them to be carrying on a senseless feud. He was making money with other guys in Rob's crew, so he was still glad his brother had come. He promised himself he would patch things up before the night was over.

JT came over to the bar where Stink was hanging out.

Stink noticed that he was sweating profusely.

"The fuck? You been dancing, nigga?"

"Hell naw. It's hot as muthafucka in here. Whassup man, you ain't fucking with these broads tonight, hun?"

"I'm good, my nigga. I'm waiting for a bitch to choose me. You know what I'm saying?"

"Damn, you finally learning some game."

"Yeah you know I done ran through half the town, anyway." Stink exaggerated.

"Stop lying, nigga. We ain't even been here that long."

"Aye... I move quick."

JT knew Stink's mind was really probably somewhere else, like back at the hotel with Naomi.

"So why Toya ain't come out?" Stink asked.

"She said she chillin' with Head Hunter. She claim she tired of hanging out with a bunch a niggas all the time. I'm like, fuck you then."

"She ain't never had a problem with it before."

"Same thing I said. Whatever, you know?"

After the club, the crew split up and went their separate ways. Stink and Rob had made up, and Stink even let Rob take his Benz. He wanted Rob to impress the young dimepiece he had bagged. Stink could see she was hot and ready. He played the backseat and told Rob to drop him off at the hotel.

Stink's new theme song, Big Tymer's "Number One Stunna" blasted through the system. Stink rapped the song verbatim, all the while, believing in his heart he'd get a chance to stunt like Baby, one day soon.

Rob stopped at the Always Open to grab some blunts and some condoms. The gas station was packed as always, on weekends after the clubs let out. Dudes parking lot pimping, girls tricking, and niggas rolling up weed, watching out for the police.

Stink began flirting with Rob's date as soon as he went into the gas station. It wasn't that he wanted her. But for the purpose of his ego, he had to know that if the opportunity had been there, she would have chosen him over his little brother.

Rob walked out of the gas station, swag on one hundred, pants sagging, chain swinging and diamonds gleaming off the streetlights. Stink wanted to finish their talk, but he knew he wouldn't get a chance that night. He'd get up with Rob in the morning after he brought the car back.

Stink spotted two dudes quick stepping in Rob's direction and they didn't look right. They looked hungry, and at first glance, he thought they could be carjackers. They wore puffy coats and big hoods. From there it all seemed to happen in slow motion.

Rob was only ten steps away from the Benz when they pulled their guns and opened fire. The barrage of bullets spun Rob completely around and sent him crashing to the ground, face first.

By the time the shooting stopped, Stink was out of the back seat with his gun out. He aimed at the fleeing assassins, bursting off round after round until both men dropped near the back of the building.

He kneeled down over his brother's limp body. It didn't take but a glance to know that Rob was dead. It was total chaos at the Always Open, as the female passenger ran screaming from the Benz. All cars skidded out in fear for their lives before more gunplay could erupt. Stink ran up on the men who lay bleeding to death behind the building. He grabbed the closest one and stuck the gun to his neck.

"Who sent you?"

The man tried to speak, but began coughing up blood before his eyes started to roll to the back of his head.

Stink shot him in the neck and went to the other

gunman who was still breathing. He laid face down, but Stink flipped him over.

"Who sent you?" he asked with the gun firmly planted right between his eyes.

"You gon' kill me anyway nigga," the gunman said.

Stink took the gun from his forehead and shoved it between his legs with the barrel aimed at his dick.

"Who the fuck sent you?"

"Romell." his victim barely managed.

Stink went blank. Puzzled.

Blah! Stink pulled the trigger, blowing his balls off before firing another shot to his head.

He ran back towards the Benz, stopping at his brother's twisted torso, leaking blood all over the cement. His chest began to tighten as he realized he couldn't stay with him. He had to go. He reached down, grabbed the chain off Rob's neck, and jumped in the Benz.

He bailed out as fast as the German engine would allow him.

CHAPTER 19

The first person Stink called was Toya. He needed her to call the ambulance and police to report Rob's shooting. He also needed her to find someone who would be willing to go to the morgue and identify his body. He couldn't help but think about the conversation he had with Naomi when he said he'd never lost anyone that close to him. Now he was feeling the same pain as she, and it was the worst feeling he'd ever had to deal with.

As he floored the Benz on the freeway, he told himself that this was the life they'd chosen, but it didn't ease the pain. He called JT and told him to gather up the crew and meet him at Big Pooh's house. He didn't call Big Pooh until he was in his driveway.

Big Pooh opened the door in his bathrobe, clueless to what was going on.

"Let me in, nigga. What the fuck?" Stink said pushing his way inside.

"You tell me, nigga. It's 2:30 in the morning."

"It's beef on the floor." Stink said.

That was all Big Pooh had to hear. He scurried to the bedroom and Stink could hear the two female voices in commotion.

"Come on, y'all gotta go." Big Pooh said.

The two girls came stumbling out of his bedroom with heels in hand, complaining and gathering their things. He escorted them to the door and shut it behind them. Before he could take three steps, the doorbell was ringing.

"That's probably JT." Stink said as he paced the floor.

JT came in with his pistol in hand. He was angry and paranoid. No one knew what was going on.

"Bitch ass niggas killed my little brother, man." Stink finally said.

"What? Who?" Big Pooh said.

"Some hired guns. Who the fuck is Romell?"

"Romell?" Big Pooh and JT repeated at the same time.

"Ain't no nigga round here by that name. Especially a nigga with that that kind of clout." Big Pooh explained.

"Tell us what happened, dog." JT coaxed.

"Man, Rob was driving my Benz. We pulled up at the Always Open. His lil hoe was in the front, I was in the back. Rob went in to get some blunts. He come out, two niggas just ran up on him from the side and started bussin'. I got out and clapped both of they asses before they could run off, but they had already hit Rob up like ten times."

"Shit! You killed 'em?" Big Pooh asked.

"Yeah, but first I ran up on 'em with the mag. The first nigga was bout dead, so he couldn't talk. I put the gat on the other nigga balls and I said, 'who sent you?' He said 'Romell'. Then I clapped his hoe ass."

The three of them sat in the living room puzzled, because by now, they knew all of the major players in South Bend. Anyone that would be a threat to them was already under the radar. This Romell dude was unheard of.

"I don't know if the niggas thought he was JT or me, cause he was driving my car and he had on your chain, so it was meant for one of us."

JT's face went blank. He knew Rob could have easily been mistaken for him, even without the chain. Both of them were tall, slim and dark skinned from the D. Guilt penetrated his heart and expanded across his chest, settling in his stomach.

Big pooh got on the phone and began to call around to see if he could find out anything about this Romell cat.

"I know what you thinking, JT, but this shit ain't our fault." Stink said.

"Man, this shit is crazy." JT said as he walked to the bar to pour himself a drink to calm his nerves.

"Make me one too, dog," Stink said.

Minutes later, Toya walked in. Her eyes were glossy and you could tell she'd been crying. Even though she hadn't known Rob for that long, she was extremely affected by the death of one of their own. This was a first for all of them. They had never seen the other side of the game, when you lose the gunfight and have to bury your own people. Everyone knew it would come one day, but now that the day was here, it was a reality check in the worst way.

"I need a drink." Toya said as Big Pooh ended his conversation.

"You hear anything?" Stink asked.

"Well, my manz and them is talking about Romell from yo' hood. They say he got people down here that been floating back and forth for a minute. I don't know who they talking about though, cause the names he threw out didn't ring a bell. But y'all ain't got no beef with that nigga, right?"

The room fell silent. Stink and JT's eyes locked on each other. Could it be that some shit they had done at the tender age of thirteen had come back to haunt them? Was it possible that Romell had rocked them to sleep? Caught them with their drawers down?

"That can't be it." JT refused.

Everyone had heard about the beef between Romell and Tank, and it didn't seem likely that Romell would make the time to track them down to avenge Dusty's death. The only thing they were sure about, was that Romell hadn't forgotten about Dusty.

"Call Scurvy and see if he heard something." JT suggested.

Stink roamed through his phone book until he

found Scurvy's number, while everyone else conversed about the possibilities. Everyone agreed that it was time for Stink, JT, and Toya to get the hell out of Indiana.

"Scurvy's phone is cut off." Stink informed.

"Damn, I can't believe this shit!" Toya spat as she downed a stiff shot of Hennessy.

Everyone followed by killing the cup they were holding, trying to numb the pain. Stink's cell rang and he saw it was Naomi calling from the hotel phone. He excused himself and took the call in the kitchen.

Big Pooh spoke in a low tone, so Stink couldn't hear. "I don't mean to sound foul or insensitive, but if y'all leaving soon, then we need to make a move on that lick, ASAP."

"I can't think about that shit right now, dog." JT said.

Toya, on the other hand, agreed with Big Pooh. She had no love for Carmen at this moment. Her ruthless side had surfaced again and she was ready to let the dog off the chain on any and everybody.

"I talked to the bitch earlier today. She said she would be home in the morning.

"Ok, you talk to Stink about it. I don't think I should be the one to bring it up." Big Pooh said to Toya.

When Stink reentered the room, everyone was quiet. Toya was the one the break the silence.

"Stink, I know this ain't the time for this shit right

now..." Toya started.

"Time for what?"

"It's just that we really need to get the fuck back to Detroit."

"I know that, but I got handle this shit with Rob first. Shit, we ain't even identified the body yet, and y'all talking 'bout dipping already?"

"Naw, it's not that," JT jumped in. "Ain't nobody trying to leave you high and dry my nigga... we was just talking about the Carmen thing. If we still gon' do it, we gotta move fast."

Stink couldn't think about money right now, but he knew they were all looking for an answer from him, since it was all his plan from the start.

"I don't even wanna talk about that shit right now, but ... it is what it is. Fuck it. Let's do it!"

They all got drunk and passed out at Big Pooh's house.

In the morning, Stink went back to the hotel to send Naomi back to Columbus. After that, he and JT had the workers drive their cars back to Detroit.

____

Toya paid a dope fiend to go down to the morgue and identify Rob's body. Her mood was somber, but she tried to turn it up as she pulled into Carmen's driveway that afternoon. Carmen greeted her with a smile as Toya entered the house bearing gifts, wearing red and white with the Santa hat to match.

"You didn't have to buy me nothing! Now I feel bad cause I didn't get you anything. I wish you would have told me you was buying me something."

"Girl, don't worry about it. It was spur of the moment anyway."

As she handed Carmen the two gift wrapped packages, Toya pretended to lock the door behind her.

Carmen ripped open the first package, which was obviously a card. As Carmen read the card aloud, Toya took a seat, thinking about the irony of it all. The words on the card actually described the way she wished things were with her and Carmen.

"Awwww," Carmen squealed and went to give Toya a hug.

Toya reluctantly received her, but it was cut short by the ring of her cell phone. It was JT calling, and she knew she had to answer.

"What up?" Toya said.

"You over there already?"

"Yeah..."

"You leave the door unlocked?"

"Yeah..."

"Aiight. We gone be pulling up in a few minutes.

"Aiight."

Toya got antsy as Carmen opened her second gift, which was a Coach belt. She was hoping Carmen wasn't gonna try to hug her again.

"You is so sweet. Ain't none of them other bitches I been knowing for years buy me shit. And they never do, that's why I'm so in shock right now."

Toya eased over to the blinds to peek out front just in time to see the Snow Bird pull up. Stink and JT hopped out, pulling hoods over their heads. They calmly walked to the house, as if they were visitors.

Toya turned to Carmen. "Well… it's been real."

"What, you leaving already?"

"Um, not just yet."

"So what do you mean by that?"

"It's been real, but it's bout to get real ugly!"

Toya pulled her pistol from her waist as Stink and JT entered Carmen's house.

Carmen wasn't slow, so she knew exactly what was happening. She made a run for her purse. Her chubby frame moved quicker than expected, but JT hawked her down by the threshold of her bedroom door.

He smacked her up. *Wop, wop wop!* "Bitch we don't got time to play no fucking games with you." he barked as he dragged her back into the living room.

"No, this way. It's in the basement." Toya ordered.

"I don't got shit in this house. I don't know what y'all looking for, let me go!" Carmen struggled as she was forced into the basement.

Stink had his gun out, ready to cut short all the nonsense from Carmen. "Where it at?" he asked calmly as JT searched around.

Toya patted Carmen down as she pleaded her case. Toya then went to an old-fashioned stereo that was covered with cardboard. She removed the cardboard, revealing a twenty-pound safe.

Stink had the gun in Carmen's mouth. "Bitch, I'ma blow yo' fucking head off and find it myself!"

"I found the safe." Toya called out.

They drug Carmen over to the safe. She tried to act as if she was unaware of the safe's existence. JT put Carmen in a submission hold, twisting her arm behind her back and up to her shoulder blade.

"What's the fucking combination?"

"Aaahhh I don't know, I don't know!" she cried.

"Move." Stink said as he aimed his pistol at Carmen's leg.

As soon as JT was out of the way, he fired a single shot into her calf muscle.

Toya winced as Carmen fell to the floor, screaming in pain. Toya decided to take charge before things went from bad to worse.

"Let me talk to her."

She stood over Carman as she cried out in a miserable squeal that echoed through the basement.

Toya called out to her in a voice of reason. "Carmen, if you don't give us the combination, they're gonna have to kill you."

"Y'all gon' kill me anyway." she cried.

"No we not. We leaving town anyway, so there's no need for you to die. Now come on before it's too late because this is your last chance."

"I'm tired of this tough ass bitch." Stink said, aiming his gun at Carmen's head.

Toya held him with one arm, signaling for him to wait just a few more seconds.

Stink started a countdown. "Five, four."

"All we want is the money or the work, Carmen." Toya pleaded.

"Two, one."

"Okay, okay. Promise me they won't kill me, Toya!"

"My word ain't shit to you, look what I'm doing here! Just give us the combination and we will be on our way."

Carmen looked her fake friend in the eyes, knowing she'd never trust anyone again. She gave up the combination, and as soon as she did, Stink duct taped her hands behind her back. Carmen's blood had seeped through her jeans and on to the basement floor.

The safe came open on the first try, revealing two kilos. No one was satisfied. They duct taped Carmen's legs and mouth, and then left her on the floor bleeding, while they ransacked every room in the house.

Stink's cell phone rang. He knew that that it was Big Pooh alerting them that they had been in the house too long.

He picked up. “We’ll be out in five minutes.”

“I heard a shot.”

“That was me... tough ass bitch ain’t wanna act right.”

“Five minutes is too long, dog. If I heard it, somebody else heard it.”

“You right. Two minutes.”

“Bet.”

The search uncovered an AR-15 in the closet, a 40-caliber pistol under the mattress, and a bag full of cash in the drop ceiling. Stink didn’t think it was much cash, because it was so easy to find, but he was glad he found it. When his phone rang again, he knew it was definitely time to go.

“Come y’all, we gotta dip.”

If anybody saw them go in the house or heard the shot in the basement, the police were probably on the way. They piled out of the house as quickly as possible, giving a fuck less about the neighbors watching.

Toya hopped in her Jag as Stink and JT climbed in the Snow Bird and stabbed out. As long as they could make it off the block and to the expressway, they were home free with what they would find out later was two bricks of not coke, but heroin.

KING BENJAMIN'S PERSPECTIVE

My, my, my. If only these cats had enough sense to apply some of their guts to taking a chance at getting out of these streets, they just might a be a force to be reckoned with for real. Stink has a baby on the way, so it seems he should be more focused on slowing down. Sometimes it ain't all about the money.

CHAPTER 20

Back in the D, they held a private funeral for Rob, and buried him right outside the city. Rob's friends, along with a few relatives were allowed to attend. Stink and JT attended the services rocking bulletproof vests under their mink coats, armed with 17 shot pistols. They were wanted dead in three states now.

They rode towards dangerous grounds in the Snow Bird to take Diamond, who was feigning for a rock, back home. Stink noticed Diamond had picked some of her weight back up and was looking better than he expected.

"Y'all ain't gotta drop me off, just let me out up here at the corner." Diamond insisted.

"You been acting strange about going to your crib since I been back home. What's up, Mama?" Stink asked.

"I ain't had a hit all day. That's what the fuck is up!"

"You just buried your son, and all you can think about is a hit?"

"Don't start with me muthafucka, cause it's yo' fault I had to bury my goddamn son!" Diamond screamed.

"Come on y'all, chill out." JT intervened.

"Man, take her straight home." Stink told JT. "She don't need to be on the block today."

"Don't tell me what I need, Stink. Last time I checked, I was yo' mama."

"We taking you home, Diamond. Where you go from there is up to you." JT said.

Diamond sighed, realizing she had no choice. "Ain't this a bitch."

When they arrived at the house they grew up in, Stink spotted a young man on the front porch talking on a cell phone.

"Who is that?" he asked.

"Nobody." Diamond said, moving quickly for the door.

"What you mean nobody? Who the fuck is he?"

"My friend."

She jumped out the van, signaling the young man to follow her into the house.

JT pulled the van from the middle of the street to the curb, and Stink got out. JT soon followed. They both knew that something was obviously going on that Diamond didn't want them to know about.

Stink twisted the doorknob, only to find it locked. He banged on the door. "Ma, open the fucking door!"

The house was quiet for a moment, and then the door sprung open. The dude standing in the doorway wasn't the same dude that was just on the porch.

As Stink and JT entered the house, they counted four young cats about their age or younger, just chilling like they were at home. Diamond sat in the corner with her crack pipe in hand, looking disgraced. Caught.

"I already told them they can't stay, now that y'all back. So don't even trip," she said.

"You got niggas selling dope out the house?"

"I said they was leaving Stink, what the fuck?" Diamond said jumping defensive.

The crew of unfamiliar faces sat silently.

"Y'all niggas gotta go. Now," JT ordered calmly.

The crew stared at each other to see if anyone wanted to protest.

Stink and JT waited for a response.

The crew of amateurs recognized they were in the presence of some real Gs. They got up and left.

After the funeral, they had a meeting with a gun dealer they had been referred to by Big Pooh. The meeting took place in the suburb, Sterling Heights. They purchased a complete arsenal. 40 Cals, Sig Sauers, P-22s some AR-15s and a couple of MP-5 HK's. It was about to be on.

Toya pulled her dripping wet Jaguar out of the automatic car wash and parked in front. She lit a cigarette while the workers applied Amor All to her tires and dried her car with towels. She thought about the funeral, and how it seemed that her and JT were more affected by Rob's death than Stink. Some people just didn't take death hard, she conceded. She wondered if her life was in danger in Detroit. Technically, she hadn't wronged anyone except out-of-towners, but she knew in the streets, it was sometimes guilt by association. She brushed off the thought and held firm to her belief that scared money never won.

From the car wash, Toya drove to Trouble's house. She hadn't seen her since she'd been back in town. She was hoping that Trouble would help her get in touch with some of the old hustlers she had lost contact with when she left town. She had half a kilo of raw she needed to get off, ASAP.

She pulled up to the house and noticed Trouble's car with dents all over it. *It's time to junk that piece of shit,* she thought.

When she entered the house, the smell of marijuana smacked her in the face. She strolled into the dining room where Black Joe, Trouble's boyfriend, sat smoking a blunt. It was the first time Toya had seen him since he'd gotten out of jail.

"What's up, Joe?" Toya said.

"What up doe?" he returned. Black Joe had put on a couple pounds since he'd been gone.

"Good to be home, ain't it?" Toya asked.

"Hell yeah. That bitch ass county ain't no joke. I heard you riding Jag now."

"Yeah, it's outside." Black Joe got up and went over

to the window to peek outside.

"So what's up, bitch?" Toya said to Trouble.

"Shit, I been just chillin'."

"I know. You don't even call a bitch no more."

"Girl, most of the time, Joe have my cell phone. I told him he need to hurry up and get his own."

"Shut the fuck up." Black said, reentering the dining room.

"You shut the fuck up."

"Y'all still crazy, I see." Toya said.

"That Jag is hard," Black complemented.

Toya downplayed it. "It's straight. I need a house, fuck that car."

Toya glanced around at the less than humble crib Trouble had come to call home. The carpet was screaming for a vacuum. The blinds had gone from white to a dirty tan. It was obvious Black Joe hadn't made any major moves since his release. Trouble should have been dying to get at her and make some moves of her own. She just didn't get it.

"Let's go get something to eat." Toya suggested to Trouble.

"Like where? Girl you see my hair all over the place."

"Bitch, Wendy's. I don't give a fuck. I'm hungry."

Trouble threw on a baseball cap and a jacket that matched her Timberlands. "I'll be right back, bae."

Black Joe didn't seem too happy about Trouble leaving, but he didn't say anything.

They rode down Gratiot, listening to Missy Elliot's new cut, "Hot Boys," and singing along. Toya turned the volume down but Trouble kept singing.

"Listen, do you still got a number for Flip and his people?" Toya asked.

"Hell naw."

"What about Kean?"

"Nope, I think Kean in jail."

Toya thought for a second, trying to remember who else dealt with heroin that she could reach out to. She knew two heads was always better than one, so she was hoping Trouble could help.

"I need to get rid of this blow," she said. It was the term used widely in the Midwest for heroin.

"You got a lot?" Trouble asked.

"I got enough to handle Flip and n'em. I just need to find 'em."

"Well, you know I had to take all them niggas numbers out my phone when Joe came home." Trouble turned the music back up and went back to singing. It was like she was complacent.

Toya was trying to help her out of inertia, but she didn't seem the least bit interested. Things had definitely changed since Black Joe came home.

"What Black been up to?" Toya asked.

"Just trying to get on his feet any way he can. All his so called homeboys acting like they ain't got shit, but always see them niggas in the club popping bottles all night. Niggas ain't shit."

"Ask him do he want some of this blow," Toya suggested.

"Aiight. Hot boooys baby you got what I want," she sang as if Toya's words went in one ear and out of the other.

Back at the Trouble's house, she and Black chewed down on the food that Toya bought for them. Toya was so mad, that she had lost her appetite. She was waiting for Trouble to tell Black Joe about the heroin. Out of respect for her girl, she waited patiently for Trouble to introduce the idea. She tapped her nails on the stain-covered glass of the dining room table. Finally.

"Oh, Toya got some blow." was all she said.

I hate this hoodrat ass bitch, Toya thought.

"Oh yeah, how much?" Black asked.

"Shiiiid, how much you want?"

"You gonna front me whatever I cop from you?" Black asked.

"You got a spot?"

"Hell yeah, I just buss that bitch open. If I can get some samples out today. You know tomorrow the first, so if it's good, I'm gonna bang."

"Tell me what you want and I'll go get it right now." Trouble had left the room, ducked off into her bedroom. She came out with a sandwich bag with about ten ecstasy pills in it.

"When the last time you had one of these?" she asked Toya, shaking the bag in her face.

"It's been a minute."

"You want one?"

Toya cut her eye at Trouble with a look of disgust. "I'm straight." She answered in a condescending tone.

Trouble noticed the tone and rolled her eyes.

Toya didn't care. "So what's up, Black?"

It was 12:30 on New Year's Day. Guns banged out all over the city. JT rode around, getting more pumped up by the minute. He drove through the Black Bottom as if the Snow Bird was bulletproof. Every time he heard a barrage of bullets, he would try to guess what kind of gun it was, and how many rounds were left in the clip. They had done enough research to find out that it was in fact Romell, who had sent the hit men at them in Indiana. It was revenge time, and his adrenaline was on high.

With all the money Romell had, his moms had always refused to leave the hood. Romell ran the hood with an iron fist, so no one had ever even attempted to throw a rock at her window, until now.

Romell could never be caught slipping at his mom's house, but on holidays, his uncles, cousins and some of his closest friends would hang out and enjoy his mom's food all day, until the wee hours of the morning.

JT and Toya had rode by an hour earlier, just to make sure the crowd was still around. It was about forty degrees that night, perfect weather for gangsters to hang outside, keeping warm with shots of liquor while shooting guns at the stars in the sky.

As JT cruised down Superior past his targets, he didn't look any of the thugs in the face. He just wanted them to notice him. He picked up the phone and called Stink.

"Where you at?"

"We just getting to the alley now." Stink replied.

"Okay, it's about six or seven of'em outside."

"We ready." Stink said, referring to himself and three of Rob's closest friends.

"Aiight, walk slow. I'm about to make my second round."

JT circled the block, but this time, when he got near their target, he stomped the gas and sped past. Shots rang out, but JT just kept speeding by. It didn't matter if they were shooting at him or shooting at the sky, he just wanted them to shoot until they ran out of ammo. The third time he circled the block he had their full attention. He pulled over well before he got in shooting distance of the crew standing in the middle of the streets, guns in hand, staring at the white van that seemed to be up to something sneaky. Stink and the three ski masked gunmen crept up from the blind side with assault rifles in hand.

"Whassup hoes?" Stink yelled as they unloaded.

Blocka blocka blocka, blaw blaw. The street quickly filled with people falling and dying, or running on bleeding, wounded legs.

JT pulled down slowly as he watched Stink get busy. His AR-15 was surgical as the 223s punched holes in nigga's backs. He chased one down in the neighbor's backyard. Once he entered, he realized the wooden fence was too tall to jump. Stink had his victim trapped in a corner, holding on to a gun with no bullets.

As Stink ran up on him, the man tried to block bullets by throwing his hands in front of his face.

"Stink, bitch!" he yelled before letting off four rounds in his head and chest.

JT and the rest of the crew sat in the van, nervous as shit, waiting for Stink. There were five bodies lying right out front.

JT had one foot on the brake, about ready to pull off on Stink until he saw him running from the neighbor's backyard.

"Come on, muthafucka!" JT yelled.

Stink ran up and hopped in the van along with his AR-15, and JT peeled out like a madman.

KING BENJAMIN'S PERSPECTIVE.

I just gotta say. These young niggas don't play; I gotta give it to 'em. They will lay it all on the line in a heartbeat if it's what they believe in, and I respect it. And Toya... for a female, she got a lot of balls. It seems like she is not shook by anything that comes with this life, so I guess she really cut from that cloth. I just hope they ain't bite off more than they can chew with this Romell dude.

CHAPTER 21

Romell was at the Marriott Hotel with the famous Sherida. She was giving him head in the Jacuzzi. Drunk off Don P, he held tight to her long ponytail braid. Her head game was vicious, and although he was used to it by now, she was still the best head hunter on his team.

As he felt the explosion about to erupt from his manhood, he yelled out, “Happy New Year, beyotch!” He came in her mouth.

She began to choke, and tried to back up off his penis, but he held her head as she spit out cum. He pumped her mouth until he was finished releasing.

His cell phone rang for the third time in the last two minutes. He climbed out of the Jacuzzi with cum still dripping down his leg. “Yo’,”

“Maaan, we just got ambushed, dog.” The lone survivor, Romell’s uncle yelled.

“What you talking about?”

“They got everybody, nephew. Everybody!”

Sherida had gone into the bathroom, and came out bitching about what had just transpired in the Jacuzzi. “I told you about doing that shit, with yo’ stupid ass. You know I can’t swallow that shit.”

"Bitch, if you wanna keep them teeth in your mouth, I suggest you shut the fuck up."

"Romell!" his uncle called out.

"What!" he yelled.

"I don't think that dude JT is dead, man."

"Don't even say nothing else over the phone. Just meet me at the spot."

Romell left Sherida at the hotel and drove straight to the House of Horrors. He called Fo Tre and told him to be there as well. For the first time, he felt a small trace of fear running through his body, alerting him that he was human. From the looks of things, he might have finally met his match with these dudes.

He was glad to see Fo Tre and his uncle were already there when he pulled up. Just when he had gotten rid of Tank and his bitch ass crew, here comes a whole other set of problems that were already costing him valuable people.

Romell hopped out with his sixteen shot Glock in hand. Fo Tre was holding the front door open for him.

"What up, cuz?"

"That's what the fuck I'm trying to figure out," Romell replied.

His OG uncle came from the back room, explaining things as much as he could.

"Man, you gotta believe what I'm about to tell you. The nigga, JT, that your people said they bussed out in Indiana ain't dead." he said.

"Really?"

"You remember I had just came home and paroled to your house when all them little niggas started coming around, back when y'all was kids. I remember all them lil niggas and I thought I had seen the nigga JT riding around in a white cargo van earlier. It was the same white van that kept circling the block before them niggas came from the backyard and started shooting."

"So they got my man, Screw too?"

"Man, they got everybody except me. I'm just a the luckiest muthafucka in the world right now to make it out that shit, cause I was the first muthafucka in the wind when I peeped the play. Them bitch ass niggas gotta die."

"I'm ready right now cuz, what's up?" Fo Tre growled.

Romell leaned against the wall, engulfed in the pain of losing half of his crew, all in one night. He took a deep breath. "The nigga Stink's mama live on Kirby. Go kill that bitch." he calmly ordered.

"Which block?" Fo Tre asked.

"Matter of fact, I'm going with you." As the two headed for the door, Romell's uncle called out to him.

"Nephew."

"What up, Unc?"

"You know yo' mama can't never go back to that house right?"

"Yeah I know... it is what it is."

The killing spree was the big story on all the local news stations. That night, Diamond's drug habit saved her life because she was out searching for drugs when her door was kicked off the hinges. The hood was on fire with police in the days after. The whole crew was laying low, letting things cool down.

Toya, with the help of her Aunt Kiesha, had purchased a home near Gross Pointe, but still had a Detroit address. It was a four-bedroom brick colonial style home with a finished basement, a fireplace, and stucco paint throughout the first floor. Today, she was about to meet the furniture company at her house so she could get settled in and spend her first night in her new home.

She pulled into her driveway, talking to an old friend, Flip, whom she had finally caught up with. Toya was pissed. First, he pretended that he was getting too much money to buy his dope from her, which she knew wasn't true. Then, he tried gearing the conversation towards sex, which she had no interest in at all. He obviously had her confused with the old Toya.

"Yo' dick ain't all that, Flip. I'm just being honest."

"Oh yeah? So why the fuck you used to be paging me in the middle of the night?"

"For your head game, pussy nigga."

"Watch how you talk to me. I'll have to see you and slap the shit out cha."

"Yeah right. You are what you eat, pussy nigga." She hung up on Flip.

JT hadn't been out the house for days, for fear of homicide lurking any and everywhere, looking for answers. The only runs he made, were from his apartment to Stink's and back. He was headed to Stink's house again, thinking about Diamond and how she had just escaped death. She was probably pulling her hair out now, because she had been stuck at Stink's apartment for days without drugs. He chuckled at the thought as he parked his Cadillac near the entrance and his cell phone began to vibrate.

"What up, doe?" he answered.

"This Chase, man."

"What up?" Chase was a good friend of Rob's and was one of the soldiers that helped put in work on Romell's crew.

"Shiiid, we kinda hurting out here, we need work."

"I'm gonna get with you on that today, my nigga. We ain't bout to leave y'all out here like that."

"Aiight, I'll be waiting by the phone."

"Bet."

Inside the apartment, Stink and Diamond sat on the couch watching reruns of Good Times and smoking weed. Since Diamond couldn't get any crack, she had to settle for whatever she could get.

"What up, JT?" she said after she finished coughing from a strong pull of the blunt.

"You know damn well you don't smoke weed." he responded.

"Well shit, y'all got a bitch in rehab up in here. I keep telling Stink, the 12 steps ain't working for me."

"Fuck that, this is our intervention," Stink teased.

"Whatever, fuck y'all."

"Last night, I caught her trying to sneak out at four in the morning."

"She ain't have the plasma TV with her, did she?" JT joked.

"Fuck y'all. That shit ain't funny. Give me a cigarette," she told JT.

JT pulled out a pack of Newports and handed her five. "I just got off the phone with Chase. Them niggas is hungry."

"I know, man. We need to do something for 'em," Stink said.

"Let me open the house on Kirby back up." Diamond suggested.

Stink nodded in agreement. "Put that blow in there, huh?" he said to Diamond.

"Hell yeah, them other young niggas had blow and rocks. They clientele is already there. All you gotta do is open up shop."

"You think the hood still hot?"

"That can't stop the hustle, regardless." JT finally commented.

"Yeah, you right, dog. I haven't even touched that work I got.

"Me neither. We need to find Scurvy too. He might know where Romell is hiding.

Scurvy came through and asked about y'all about a month ago. I didn't have a phone number for either one of y'all, so I just told him to check back with me," Diamond said.

Stink rubbed his goatee, thinking of a master plan. "Ain't nobody in the streets fucking with Scurvy but us. If anything, he might can help us move some of this blow."

"He did tell me to tell y'all he still live with his girlfriend."

Just then, JT's phone rang and it was Toya. "What up?"

"What y'all doing?" she asked.

"Shit, chillin'."

"Good. You think y'all can come over here and help me put this bed and this pool table together?"

"Hold on." JT put the phone down while he relayed the message to Stink.

"What's in it for us, 'cause I ain't fucking you." Stink said loud enough for Toya to hear.

"You heard him?"

"I got some bomb ass weed, some Henny, and a couple bottles of Moet."

"Okay. Wait until it gets dark and we'll be over there."

"Okay," Toya agreed before they ended the call.

"She said she got some bomb ass weed, some Henny, and couple bottles of Moet."

"I wanna see the crib, anyway," Stink said.

"Yeah, me too. I can't believe she done bought a crib and we renting apartments. We gotta step our game up." JT said laughing.

"I'm hip," Stink agreed.

Stink, Diamond and JT walked around the inside of Toya's house. It was only the second time her and Diamond had ever met. Toya was just hoping she didn't try to steal anything. She'd hate to have to whoop on Stink's mama.

"Girl, this living room is sharp." Diamond said excitedly.

"Thank you." The color scheme was a violet blue

and grey through the house, giving it a very unique feel. Kiesha had ordered her an antique violet rug as a housewarming gift. It sat under a gold trimmed circular glass table in the living room. The ceramic fireplace was lit and the 47-inch plasma played videos on BET.

"You can have a seat." Toya said to Diamond, as she flopped down on the sofa herself.

Upstairs, Stink began to separate the bed frame parts and screws while JT twisted up a blunt. He had to smoke before getting off into something that felt like real work, something he wasn't used to at all.

"This is a nice crib, man." Stink said, ripping the plastic off the pack of screws.

"Yeah, it is. It ain't like I can't afford it. I just know I can't put no shit like this in my name, and I ain't got nobody else to do it. That's what I was gonna use the bitch Tasha for."

"Yeah, speaking of Columbus chicks, I gotta call my baby mama and see how she doing." Toya came upstairs with two glasses of Hennessy on the rocks.

"This gonna make us lazy. You should've gave us this shit when we was finished." JT said.

"Well, drink the shit when you finished, nigga." She turned to leave.

"My old bird downstairs getting on your nerves?" Stink asked.

"Naw, she good. We bout to drank and be merry."

By the time they were finished with the pool table

in the basement, the four of them had drunk two bottles of champagne plus the fifth of Hennessy. Stink and JT had smoked three blunts and they all sat around in the living room giggling about everything.

"This place is a fucking dump," JT teased referring to Toya's new house.

"Fuck you, hater."

"On some real shit doe, how your pack been moving?"

"I gave a little something to Black Joe, Trouble's nigga. He been doing ok with it. But Diamond just told me y'all about to open Kirby up, so I want in."

"Fuck that three-way split! You stay working on Joe Black or whatever the fuck his name is," Stink spat.

"If you remember, Chase was working for me. Not you and not JT. Besides that, y'all need somebody around that can show their face all the time. Y'all is too hot to be in the hood like that right now."

Once again, Toya had presented her argument convincingly. Stink and JT needed someone to keep tabs on the soldiers while the murder thing died down.

"You a greedy muthafucka," Stink said.

"You is too." Toya shot back.

JT rose to his feet. "We bout to be out."

"We is?" Diamond asked, not ready to leave.

"Hell yeah, before I pass out on this couch."

"You can crash." Toya assured JT.

"Naw, you probably got a head hunter coming over."

She didn't, but she wished.

After everyone left, Toya found herself alone in the big empty house. Empty because she now felt the loneliness creeping in, knowing she would have to spend the first night in her house all by herself. She wished JT would have stayed.

She popped in a DVD of the movie, *Love Jones* and settled in with a blanket on the couch. It felt good to be in her new house, but it still put a damper on her night, knowing there was no one to share her bed with. As the movie progressed, she analyzed the idea of love, something she hadn't done in a very long time.

Now that she was back in the D, where her reputation was still no good, the idea of her meeting somebody new who was worth taking seriously, seemed ludicrous. Toya hadn't had sex since she left Indiana. She had to laugh at how ironic her life was. When she was younger, she had all these dudes and no money. Now here she was all grown up with all this paper and no dude.

The heroin was slow money compared to what they were used to, especially having to split it three ways. As the weeks passed, the clientele increased and half of the blow they'd gotten from Indiana was almost gone. Toya did most of the drop offs and collected the money while Stink and JT laid low.

Stink hadn't been to a barbershop in so long, his bald head had turned into a mini afro. He found a unisex salon in Southfield that looked quiet, so he strolled in to get his head shaven. While he waited, he called his apartment to make sure Diamond was still there. She had snuck out so many times, he just decided to get her a key made and buy her a cell phone. She didn't answer the house phone so he called her cell phone.

She didn't answer the cell phone either. He hated having to worry about her whereabouts all the time. Stink planned to let Diamond stay as long as he needed to, but hoped he could convince her sister to let Diamond move in. His phone rang, but it was Naomi.

"What's up?" he asked.

"What you mean, 'what's up'? You called me earlier. I'm just returning your call."

"Calm down baby, why you so hostile. I called you 'cause I miss you."

"So, I guess you miss me like once a month or something."

"Come on now, stop acting like that. You my baby mama and we might get married one day, who knows?"

"It ain't in the cards." Naomi quickly assured him.

"Whatever. So you gained a lot of weight since I last seen you?"

"Not really. Probably about five pou—"

"Oh, it's my turn in the chair. Let me call you back."

Naomi hung up before he could.

Twelve o'clock that night, Stink hopped in the Benz and headed to the Bottom. Something was wrong. He still hadn't heard for Diamond, and he had called her phone all day. It was still a possibility that she was somewhere getting high and ducking his calls, but now Toya was calling and saying nobody was answering their cell phones at the spot. She was on her way to investigate when he called her back and told her to just stay put. He had to go to The Bottom to look for Diamond anyway.

First, he stopped by his aunt's house, who he never really visited. He blew the horn. She opened the door and knew it was him, because of the Benz.

"You seen my mama?" he shouted from the car.

"No, I haven't, baby."

"Aiight."

He sped off and dialed her number again. No answer. When he reached The Bottom, he hit crackhead Yvette's house first. He blew the horn.

Yvette finally came to the door after a few minutes of peeking out of the curtains.

"You seen my mama?"

“Who is yo’ mama?” she said squinting to see who was inside the vehicle

“This Stink.”

“Oh, not since earlier today.”

“Ok, if she come back, tell her to call me.”

As he drove away, he felt some relief that she had been seen around the hood. He figured he’d find her sooner or later, as long as he checked the right spots. His next move was to check on the house on Kirby. As he bent the corner with the gun on his lap, he eased on the brakes as the flashing blue and red lights froze him like a deer. Two of the seven police cars were parked nose to nose blocking off the street.

He glanced at the police officers standing on the porch of his spot as he threw the car in reverse. The last thing he spotted was what looked like a coroner van, but he couldn’t be sure. Something in Stink’s gut told him that he had lost his mom.

CHAPTER 22

Things were bad, real bad. To the police and the media, it was something out of a horror movie. Diamond had been found with her head severed in the basement. Everyone who was in the house was dead, except for Chase, who was clinging to life by nothing short of a miracle. Doctors said he only had a forty percent chance of making it. The saddest part was, no one would even visit him in the hospital, because no one wanted the heat. Five people were dead, and it wasn't a damn thing they could do about it.

Romell was a heavyweight in the game and he could afford to lay low just as long as they could, and a lot longer. Romell never had to show his face on the streets if that's what he chose to do.

"All of this, over some shit that happened when we was kids, dog." Stink vented, holding a cup of Hennessy as his nostrils flared in anger.

JT took a long pull from his cigarette. "It ain't just that, dog. You do dirt, you get dirt. Remember Big Pooh always used to say that shit. Shit hurt like hell but it's true, dog. We ain't been home two years and look how much shit we done did. Everybody we know is animals, so it ain't like we wasn't gone never bump heads with nobody. You know that was like my moms too, so we gone ride til the wheels fall off on this one, however it ends."

"I'm through hiding from niggas, doe." Stink said. "I'm a frontline nigga anyway. I ain't no lay low ass nigga. I been a thoroughbred since before I could spell it. This nigga done killed my moms dog! My moms? I ain't holding nobody up from here on out."

That night, they drove to Toya's house in separate cars so they could discuss things as a team. They knew at this moment, they only had each other. They rang the doorbell and Toya came to the door in a night-gown."

"Where y'all coming from?" she asked as she let them in, not wanting to look Stink in the eyes. She felt bad for him, knowing what he was going through. But she didn't really know Diamond that well, and wasn't deeply affected by her death.

The only person she was close to that was in the house, happened to be the only person still alive, and that was Chase.

"We just coming from JT's crib," Stink said.

"Oh, I finally slid up in the hospital to see Chase," Toya said.

"What's up with him?"

"They said he gonna make it, but he gonna be blind."

“Man, that’s fucked up.” JT vented.

“Better than dead.” Toya said flatly.

Stink went to Toya’s mini bar and poured a stiff shot of Hennessy. He reached in his pocket and pulled out his cell phone and it began to ring. He saw Naomi’s number and stepped into the kitchen for some privacy.

In the living room, JT and Toya sat looking depressed and burdened by the past day’s events. They were both thinking the same thing about how everything seemed to be catching up with them so fast, but Toya was the one to speak on it.

“I just keep thinking, when is all this shit gonna end, man? When is we just gonna be able to make money and just live our lives?”

“I been wondering the same thing, but right now, it looks like never. I’m like this, if you cross me, I’m gonna hunt you down. But I know I’m not the only nigga that thinks like that. That’s just how the game goes, and that’s how it’s always gonna be. But you know what I was thinking?” He didn’t wait for and answer. “We made way more enemies than friends, and that was our biggest mistake.”

“Hell yeah,” Toya agreed.

“We made enemies everywhere we went.”

“The whole city of Columbus and Indiana! Can’t never go back to neither one of them! Not to mention, 40 Grand and niggas in our own city looking for y’all.” Toya said.

“But you know what? I think we could work the shit

out with 40 Grand."

"How you figure that?"

"Because Romell is just as much a problem of his as he is of ours. But if we take care of that problem and make him think we did it for him, that would kinda make us even, I would think."

"How'd you come up with all this?"

"Because he had already asked us about it. Well, he didn't, but Hammer had brought it up to Stink about us hitting Romell."

"How Stink feel about all this now?"

"I haven't talked to him about my ideas on 40 Grand. Right now, he just on some kill everybody shit. And I feel him on that, trust me I do. But we did do them niggas wrong on some grimy shit, cost them a lot of business, and started some beef. If it's anybody we could make peace with, it should be them cause them was our peoples."

Stink had heard the tail end of the conversation as he walked into the room, wiping tears from his face. "Man, fuck peace. If y'all scared, go to church! I ain't about to make amends with no muthafucking body." Stink barked.

Toya was caught off guard. "You ain't heard the whole story yet, and you just come up in here popping off at the mouth."

"I heard peace, that's all I needed to hear. My mama dead, my lil brother dead, ain't nobody getting a pass. I don't give a fuck about nothing no more, so y'all with me or against, plain and simple."

JT knew Stink's emotional state at that moment, so he just let him rant and let it go in one ear and out the other. "Whatever, nigga."

"Yeah, whatever, nigga. I ain't got no second thoughts about the life I chose. It was either this or be a bum ass nigga. I know I'm gonna die in these streets one day, and I can live with that. Can y'all?"

JT hated for anybody to raise their voice at him. He never had a real mother or father, so he couldn't see anybody talking to him like he wasn't grown. Stink was way too loud for him to continue to sit there and listen. He stood up and headed towards the door.

"You out?" Toya asked.

"Yeah," he answered, twisting the locks on the door.

When JT left, Toya was hoping Stink would too, but he stayed. She didn't like being around him when he was all in his beast mode. She made them both some drinks, even though she could tell that Stink had probably had enough for the night. Toya wanted to try to explain thing from JT's perspective, but the way Stink was acting, she doubted if she could talk some sense into him.

As he sipped his Hennessy and flipped through the channels, Toya tried to change the subject to a lighter topic.

"Who was you on the phone with, yo' baby mama?"

"Yeah," he said dryly.

"Why you always leave out the room when you on the phone with her?"

"Cause I don't want y'all in my business, that's why."

"Damn nigga, I'm just making conversation. You ain't gotta be snapping at me and shit." Toya was on the verge of telling Stink to take his ass home.

"My bad, I know I've been tripping since I got here. I'm trying to get Naomi to move to the D with me, but she keeps telling me I need to get my life in order first."

"Well, on one hand, I agree with her because of all that's going on. On the other hand, I think with all the deadbeat dads round this muthafucka, she should be glad you trying to be a part of your kid's life."

"Yeah, I know right now she probably safer in Columbus, but soon, I want her to come live with me for good. I can't see my kid in Columbus, and the longer I stay away from there, she gonna wonder what I did to make me never come back."

Toya understood how Stink felt, but still didn't think it was a good idea. She hoped Naomi stayed in Columbus, along with all their dark, ugly secrets. But Stink was feeling like he needed something in his life that was family, now more than ever. If something happened to his seed, it would take him right over the edge and he knew it. It was selfish of him to even think of bringing her to Detroit at this time, but still it was all he could wish for.

"I know what you thinking right now, Toya, but I'll never let none of my people get touched ever again. Ever again!" Stink's speech was slurring and his eyes were as low as they could get without being closed.

The spaghetti strap on Toya's nightgown fell off her shoulder, exposing the top half of her left breast, almost to the nipple. She slipped it back on, but not before Stink caught a glimpse.

"All these channels, and ain't shit on," Stink slurred.

"Hell naw," Toya said as she balled up in the corner of the couch. Her strap fell again, but this time she didn't notice it for a while.

Stink sat next to her, getting a hard on from staring at her firm brown chest. She finally noticed it and fixed her strap again. Stink slid close to her and pulled it back off her shoulder.

She fixed it for the third time, wondering what the hell Stink was thinking. "You done had too much to drink, nigga."

He leaned into her.

"Toya let me get some pussy," Stink blurted out.

"What?" Toya shouted, not believing her ears.

"I'm serious, just this one time." Stink eased closer and slid his hand up her thigh, while moving in to kiss her neck, but she stiff armed him."

"You tripping, nigga!" Stink was a good-looking guy, and if they had met in the streets, she wouldn't have thought twice about fucking with a guy like him. But this was Stink. A guy she considered to be the brother she never had.

"Come on man," he persisted.

Toya sprung from the couch just before he could make another advance. Stink watched her ass jiggle away as the silk gown pressed tightly against her body. If he wasn't so drunk, he would have gotten up to follow her upstairs to see if the third time would be the charm.

Toya came back downstairs with a blanket and a pillow.

"You too drunk to drive, and your head ain't right. You just need some time to yourself to think." She threw the pillow and blanket at him. "I'm going to bed."

"I need some pussy! That's what I need," Stink slurred as Toya headed up the stairs.

JT cruised in his Cadillac, with his mind drifting from Toya, to Stink, to Romell. He was concerned for Toya's safety. Romell was obviously a maniac that had to be dealt with, in order for them to stay alive in Detroit. Meanwhile, he couldn't lose anybody else he cared about, especially Toya. He flipped out his cell phone and called 40 Grand just to see if he still had the same number.

"Hello." 40 Grand answered.

"Is this Keith?"

"Who?"

"Keith."

"Wrong number, dog."

JT hung up, recognizing 40 Grand's voice. He turned down the heat in the Caddy as he began to break a sweat under his bulletproof vest. He made a right on the street he remembered Scurvy lived on last time they spoke. He remembered the block, but not the exact house. His eyes roamed up and down the block, hop-ping to spot Scurvy's Caddy in the driveway. Scurvy was the only other friend he had in Detroit that he felt like he could trust. He had to shake his head at the thought. How far the trust would go with a guy whose name was Scurvy, only God knew.

A light snowfall rested on preceded flakes, now half slush. No noise, but the light squeak of the wipers brushing softly against the window. *Pow!* A single shot rang out and JT ducked off instinct and cocked the hammer back on his pistol.

Once the single shot wasn't followed by another one, his head came up slowly, observing his surround-ings. He spotted a man on the next block with no shirt on holding a rifle. He noticed the house he was in front of also had a Cadillac in the driveway. The closer he got, the more the guy looked like Scurvy and the car looked like his girlfriend's Cadillac.

He pulled over in front of the house, facing the op-posite direction of all the cars parked on that side of the street. Rolling down his window, he could tell Scurvy was drunk and paying him no attention.

"Call the police, bitch! I got something for 'em." Scurvy cocked the lever action 22 rifle, but didn't point it at his girlfriend.

JT blew the horn, grabbing Scurvy's attention for

the first time.

He spun around, scowling. "Who the fuck is you?"

"It's JT, nigga. What the fuck is you doing?"

Scurvy leaned sideways, peering inside the car. JT could see his hair was thick and nappy. He looked like he was starving as he girlfriend come to the door.

"If you're a friend of his, you need to take him with you, 'cause the police is on the way," she shouted from the doorway.

Scurvy finally realized it was his friend and comrade, JT, and he couldn't have shown up at a better time.

"Aww bitch, this my nigga! That's aiight. It's on now!"

"Take him with you!" she continued to shout.

"Shut up, bitch! It's on now. Pop the trunk."

JT opened the trunk.

Scurvy tossed the rifle inside, then hopped in the car with no shirt or shoes on. "Pull off, dog. That bitch just called the police on me."

JT pulled off, shaking his head and wondering what the hell had he drove up on. More drama.

"We can stop and toss that punk ass deuce-deuce rifle in the dumpster somewhere, 'cause we sure won't be needing that." JT said.

"Man, that bitch was talking about having her cousins and brothers come over there and jump me, like I'm some type of punk. I was gonna shoot the first nigga that ran up on me."

"Y'all been fighting?"

"Man, I'm not even into putting my hands on women, but ever since I been starving, she just been tryna dog a nigga out. It's like she don't got no respect for me no more."

"So you should have just got the fuck on."

"I mean, I slapped her up a little, just 'cause I was tired of her dogging me."

JT never felt it was justifiable to put your hands on a woman, unless of course, in a robbery. Then, anything goes. He could use and abuse them, but he would never lay a hand on them.

"You can come to my crib, dog." he heard himself say. He thought about it after he said it. Maybe it wasn't the smartest idea he ever had, but Scurvy was his friend.

After bending a few corners, they stopped in an alley and got rid of the rifle. JT only fucked with big guns and high-powered shit.

"Fuck you doing with a deuce-deuce rifle anyway, nigga?"

"Man, I don't know. I'm fucked up out here."

"Shit been real crazy out here, man. You know Stink done lost both his moms and his lil brother."

"What? His moms and lil brother? What you talking about?" Scurvy yelled. He was pissy drunk, which made him super hype and angry when he heard the news.

"You heard me."

"What? Man who the fuck did that shit? Tell me you know who responsible, so we can go kill them muthafuckas."

JT knew Scurvy was drunk, but he also knew he meant every word he was saying. He thought about how Stink was acting back at Toya's house. The two of them would be perfect together right now, two drunken maniacs.

"Who did this shit, JT?"

JT wasn't ready to disclose all the information at this time. Scurvy was in no position to help anyway, right then. He reached in his pocket and pulled out a fat sack of weed.

"Roll up."

JT moved Scurvy in for a couple of weeks to get himself together. He had an extra room and felt that after a while, Scurvy might be a lot more useful than he thought. It turned out, Scurvy had big plans, and they were the kind the crew loved to hear about. Stink and JT hit him off with a couple thousand each, until they could put the plans in motion. They got scurvy a vest and gave him a Sig Sauer and eventually told him all about the beef with Romell.

Scurvy didn't care. He was always loyal to Stink and JT, and after they brought him back to life this time, there was no limit to what he would do for them. His name was so bad in the city; he was totally disconnected from the streets, but still wanted dead or alive. The same as them.

Stink came out to play, just as he said he would. He went wherever he wanted, when he wanted, and he drove his Benz that everybody knew about. JT soon followed, realizing that things had to come to a head one way or another. It was on-sight beef, and that's just how they had to live their lives—ready for whatever.

Three weeks passed while Scurvy scoped out their target, just going over the basics. What time did they arrive? How many people? Did they seem to have weapons? Scurvy would report back to them, and once they were sure they could pull it off, they went for it.

On March first, they hit up the Romanian liquor store owner for one hundred thousand dollars cash. It was income tax time, and most of the money was there for the purpose of cashing checks. It was that perfect time, and they ended up with more money than they had expected. It went off without a hitch, and although they had never robbed anyone but drug dealers, they believed it was more potential in these types of licks now that they were back in Michigan. Besides, they couldn't really rob drug dealers anymore; they had actually run out of safe places to hide.

Since everyone was in on the lick, they split the money four ways, 25 racks each. They rode in the Snow Bird after the lick, recalling the events that had just taken place.

"We is Gank Masterz, dude. We have mastered the

art of taking people's shit." Toya said from the back as she counted and recounted her take.

"That should be the name of our clique. The Gank Masterz, baby." Stink said.

"Yeah. You earn it, we take it." JT joined in.

"Did y'all see the look on that muthafucka's face when I flashed the Sig on 'em?" Scurvy asked.

Everyone nodded, giggling at the thought.

"He had the nerve to try and clutch that brief case like he wasn't gonna come up off it."

"Hell yeah. Scurvy let that Sig go one time and he dropped the bitch like it was hot," JT said.

"I needed that shit. It's time for me to pay my bills," Toya explained as they pulled the Snow Bird into her garage next to her Jaguar.

JT took off the stolen license plate, while the rest of them headed inside. It wasn't quite ten o'clock in the morning.

"Y'all want some breakfast?" Toya asked as she headed upstairs to her safe.

"You know it." she heard Scurvy call out.

Upstairs, she spun the combination and pulled the safe open. She put twenty in the safe and left five thousand out for bills and shopping. Life was starting to feel good again. She flopped down on her bed and went over a few bills and her things to do list. There was a knock at the door.

"Who is it?" she yelled, like she was answering the

door at a crack house.

“JT.”

“Come on.”

JT stepped in, observing the bedroom for the first time. He took a seat on the opposite side of the bed from Toya.

“So you cooking everybody breakfast this morning?”

“I shouldn’t have said that shit, cause I really don’t feel like doing it. Them niggas can cook they own food if they hungry.”

“Mmpt,” JT said nonchalantly. It didn’t make him a difference one way for the other. His appetite wouldn’t kick in until he had smoked at least one blunt.

“You know Chase came home from the hospital today,’ he said.

“Yeah, we gotta go see him.”

“I told Stink and he didn’t say nothing else about it, so it might just be us two going to see him.”

“That’s fucked up. Stink be on some other shit sometimes.” She was thinking about the night Stink had come on to her. She never brought it up after that night, and they were able to get past it easily, but it made her wonder about his mental state.

“He still pretty fucked up about everything, you know.” JT said, defending him.

“Yeah, I guess.” Toya agreed in a gloomy tone that darkened her mood. She hated to think about all that had happened.

JT sat still with his head down, making her wonder what was on his mind. She didn't have to wonder long. "You ever think about getting a job?" he questioned.

Toya stood, glanced over both of her shoulders and even looked in the closet, making sure no one else was in the room.

"Who you talking to?"

JT laughed.

"I'm talking to you."

"Hell naw, why?"

"Why not?" he countered, sounding a bit irritated.

"This is me, JT. This is who I am. Didn't I tell you about my mama? This shit in my genes, you know? I'm my mama's daughter." she said, throwing her hand up as if that was all that needed to be said. Toya had told JT about her mom but didn't go into detail.

"Whatever," JT said.

"I mean, I'm not just talking about the Ganking and shit, because honestly, I'd rather get mine grinding. But if a lick is on the floor, I'm not gonna turn it down, either."

"So your moms never had a real job?"

"Fuck no! My mama is five times worse than me. But hey, if you wanna chill out and look at other options, can't nobody be mad at that."

JT laughed at the thought. "I wasn't talking about

me. I know how my story ends."

"So what you worried about me for?" She was heated now and ready for an argument. She didn't understand what his beef was. Her eyes shifted back and forth from the money lying on her bed to JT.

"My own life isn't really my concern. I just don't wanna lose nobody else I care about."

"I mean, I ain't gon' never grow tired of getting no money. So, as long it's some money to be made on these streets, I'm gon' get it. I ain't built for none of that nine to five shit, but I am built for this, so this what it is.

"JT, I will never, ever, ever be a broke bitch again. I don't care what the price to pay is. If my mama would have kept her head on straight, she would be a millionaire by now. That's why I stopped popping all them pills and shit, cause I knew what I could do if I kept my head on straight. If I stay focused, I'll be a millionaire by twenty-one, guaranteed."

For the first time since meeting her, JT realized just how much he and Toya were alike. Their thought patterns ran parallel, and they were bonded by a fear that lay deep within. The fear of being a broke ass nobody.

JT rose from the bed and extended his arm for a hug. "Come here."

She rushed to his arms faster than she intended. They embraced long and hard. They embraced because life was short and there could come a time when all they had were memories of each other. They both knew at that moment that they had found the deepest connection a man and woman could find in each other.

JT wanted to tell her he loved her, but the words wouldn't form to come out of his mouth. He hoped she knew. The length of their embrace said it all for both of them. JT made his exit without saying another word.

When he left the room, Toya's emotions were bungee jumping. She hated that feeling and tried her best to shake it off as quickly as possible.

The rest of the day was uneventful, except the airing of the liquor store robbery on the news. Stink was happy because Naomi had finally agreed to move to Detroit, but only if he found her a good pediatrician, which was what he was supposed to be doing that day. Everyone except Stink thought it was the dumbest idea Stink ever had.

JT knew there was no way Naomi knew what she was walking into with becoming a full-time member of Stink's world. Not only was he putting her in jeopardy, but also the life of his unborn child. He didn't even tell them the craziest part about him having to travel to Columbus to get her because was no way she was traveling anywhere by herself, eight months pregnant.

Later that evening, JT and Toya went to see Chase at home. His mother let them in and escorted them to the basement, which she had set up to accommodate his disability. She had no idea that the people she had let in were partially responsible for her son's tragic fate.

Once she made sure nobody wanted drinks or food, she left them alone and went back up the stairs. Chase's face was still swollen, and one of his eyes appeared to have no movement. His left eye moved around as if he was watching everything and everybody, but Chase had already informed them he was permanently and completely blind.

"How you feeling, dog?" JT said

"Just glad to be alive, man." Chase said truthfully.

"We gon' get they ass, Chase. I swear to God, man." Toya vowed with passion in her tone.

"I know y'all don't play." Chase said with a smile.

It was good for Toya and JT to see him in high spirits. Toya stared at the skully Chase was wearing, wondering what the bandages under it would reveal. She didn't really want to know.

They told Chase about the lick they hit and they both hit him off with some stacks from their own stash. Toya wished she could do more to help, but it was what it was. She knew money was the last thing Chase would be thinking about for a while, but it was all they had to offer.

"When you feeling up to it, we gonna get you some girls over here to keep you company." Toya said.

"Yeah, that would be nice."

"I'm talking bout some bad bitches, too. Ass like blaw, titties like blaw!" Toya continued, trying her hardest to keep a smile on Chase's face. It seemed to be working for now.

"You been eating and shit, my nigga?" JT asked him.

"Yeah, my appetite is coming back slowly. But let me ask y'all, what the fuck happened? Like where that shit come from?"

Toya and JT glanced at each other, unprepared to answer. JT knew that Chase had a right to know why he was blind for life.

"To be honest, that shit goes back to when me and Stink was 13 years old. It didn't have nothing to do with y'all or that house. But I promise you this, muthafuckas ain't gonna live too long to brag about it."

Chase held out his hand to slap fives. He still believed in his crew.

They left Chase's house feeling better than before the visit. He was taking it like a soldier, but they knew deep down he had to be completely traumatized for life. On the way home, Toya thought about the conversation she'd had with JT that morning about visiting her mom. She always wondered about JT's parents.

"You don't never think about trying to find your mom?" Toya asked.

"Hell naw, that bitch ain't never came looking for me. Find her for what?"

She could tell she had upset him by even bringing his mother up.

"I don't know, to see if she still alive?"

"Shit, it don't even matter, Toya." This was the one thing JT never liked to talk about.

"I understand, I guess." She decided to leave it alone and JT quickly changed subjects.

"Chase looks fucked up, though."

"Yeah, I hate that shit. He was gonna be a beast. Lil nigga wasn't scared of shit."

"Yeah, he was gonna be a beast," JT agreed.

When JT pulled into Toya's driveway, he noticed she was staring at him with a strange look in her eyes. She wanted to invite him in, but couldn't think of a subtle way of doing it without him getting inside her head. They had been together all day, and JT hadn't even been home to stash his take of the money from the lick.

Her reckless eyeballing made JT feel a little guilty about shutting her down when his moms came up. Now he was thinking that maybe he had hurt her feelings. Toya had always opened up to JT about all the intimate details of her life from the beginning. He wanted her to know that her trust in him was appreciated and returned. He decided to share some of himself with her that he never had.

"I left my crib when I was about twelve years old. My mother was so cross-addicted, I don't even think she noticed I was gone. If I wouldn't have left, the people from social services would have showed up eventually and took me, anyway. A year later, I went to juvenile, and since I been home, I haven't looked for her and she hasn't looked for me."

Toya could relate to being abandoned. She never knew who her real father was. "It's fucked up that people just made us and left us to raise our fucking selves. That's why I will never have kids. I know I can't handle that much responsibility."

"Right, me neither." JT said. "I wouldn't dare bring a muthafucka in this fucked up world to have to struggle the way I did."

"I mean, you probably would be a good father if you wasn't in the streets."

"Why you say that?"

"I don't know, I just can't see you being one of them foul ass niggas that have a baby and then walk around acting like they don't exist."

"Naw, I don't see myself like that either."

"So, where you headed now?" Toya asked.

"Home, get me something to eat and some sleep."

"You and Stink hanging out today? I know y'all wanna blow some of this paper."

"Naw, I been up the past few days. I'm tired."

Toya wanted to tell him to come back later. She felt like she should kiss him goodbye or something, but she ignored all the thoughts floating around in her head.

"Aiight, I'll see you later." she said, reaching for the door handle.

"Later." JT said.

He watched her go into the house, then backed out

of the driveway.

The next day, Stink and Naomi arrived in Detroit around 5:30 pm. Stink wanted to get Naomi home before dark, so he hit the Southfield freeway straight home. She had slept most of the ride, but now that she was awake, her brain was racing again. She was adamant about having a good doctor in Detroit and she was praying that Stink's life had really slowed down, the way he said it had. She always knew his abrupt departure from Columbus had probably been a matter of his freedom or his life. Naomi was sharp, and she had dealt with enough street life with a brother like Pretty, to know what time it was.

When they arrived at the apartment, Stink retrieved her duffle bags from the trunk and led her to the elevator. Upstairs, he keyed the door and moved out of her way so she could get in and sit down.

She scanned the apartment, taking it all in and thinking it looked just about as she expected. Expensive television, stereo, nice furniture, but no real thought put into the decorative scheme. It was a bachelor's pad, in serious need of a woman's makeover.

What did come as a huge shock was that the baby's room was already set up. The crib was already put together, and there were boxes of pampers aligned against the wall, along with baby bottles, bibs, etc.

She walked over and peeked in the closet to find a rack full of boy's clothing. She was confused, because she never asked the doctor the sex of her baby.

"Why did you buy all this boy stuff? What if it's a girl?"

"It's a boy." Stink assured her.

"But what if it's a girl?"

"Then we'll go get some girl stuff and work on making a boy." Stink said with a sly grin.

She glared back with her no nonsense look. She decided not to start a situation on her first night in town, but she had no plans on having back to back kids, no matter what. Right now, she was just glad to see him man up, and all ready to be a father. He agreed to reimburse her for all the money she had spent on the baby items that she had to leave in Columbus. Naomi believed him when he said he would take care of everything. What she didn't know, was that Stink needed this baby. He needed the baby to be with him all the time for his own sanity and peace of mind.

The reality of the losses he'd suffered were eating at him on a daily basis. He shoved the feelings back down each day as they tried to rise, getting stronger but weaker now, as Naomi came back into his life. Before today, he was hating life, but still in love with money. It was the only thing he could count on to bring him some form of pleasure.

Stink's fears of poverty were five times stronger than anyone in his crew. He had come a long way in a short period of time, and could never go back. He had lost his only real family because of the life he had chosen, but that was something he denied every day.

He told himself that they too had chosen their own lives, because that's what he had to do to rationalize things.

"So what did your friend, JT, say when you told him I was coming to live with you?" Naomi asked as she hobbled to the bedroom and eased down on the bed.

"Fuck JT. His opinion don't count for nothing," he said jokingly. "He likes you though. He always said I should be with you."

"He don't even really know me."

"He knows what I tell 'em and everything I tell 'em is the truth." Stink felt better already just having someone in his home he could trust... someone he could talk to about things. He didn't have to sleep in a hotel and wake up next to a stripper or some girl he just met. He could come home to his girl.

Naomi noticed the twenty-pound safe in the corner. "Stink what's in that safe?" she asked.

"Why?"

"Because if it's guns or dope you gonna have to get it out of here. I'm not gonna have my baby around that shit."

"Ain't no dope in here." he said honestly. And the guns are not somewhere a baby would be able to get to."

"That's not the point. If something was to happen with you and the police wound up in this apartment, they could take my child for that kinda stuff."

"No they won't, just tell 'em you didn't know about

it. This ain't your apartment."

"Why you just can't take them somewhere else?"

"Aiight, whatever." he agreed, just to shut her up.

Stink left to get the Chinese food he had promised Naomi. She was shocked to see him come right back home with the food, instead of running around for a couple hours the way he used to do in Columbus.

After they ate, Stink rubbed her feet and they talked at length about their relationship and their future. They both laid down all the ground rules and deal breakers. Stink's biggest concern was that Naomi not try and change him, but accept him for who he was. Naomi's thing was quality time. She refused to be the girl calling his cell phone all kinds of night trying to find him.

That night, they made passionate love and even though her belly was huge, Naomi's loving was even better than Stink remembered it.

CHAPTER 23

JT was on his way to pick up Scurvy, who had moved back in with his girl. He wondered if Scurvy was to fall off again, would he be back on the street. *Probably,* he thought. They were supposed to be at the paint shop by now, picking up the Snow Bird, which was now painted black. He was running way late, because Chase had called and asked for a ride to the Social Security office. He and his mother were in the process of applying for disability compensation.

He honked the horn in front of Scurvy's house and Scurvy shot out the door quickly. They now had half an hour to make it to the shop before it closed. Lately, JT had been wearing black skullys and black shades everywhere he went. The reality that he would come face to face with his enemies one day began to make him uneasy again.

He stopped hanging out once Stink brought Naomi to town. In reality, he was happy he didn't have to hang out and watch Stink's back, because he had grown tired of the club scene. He knew the women he took to the hotel most nights didn't care if he lived or died the next day. They'd turn on him in a heartbeat for a few dollars.

As he pushed the Cadillac up Seven Mile, he thought

about how bad he wanted this beef shit over, once and for all. They arrived at the paint shop fifteen minutes before closing. They paid for the van and Scurvy followed JT in the Cadillac until they reached Toya's house. She was supposed to be home, but the garage door would have been up so he could park the Caddy if she was. He two-wayed her to find out where she was.

"Where you at?"

"I had to take care of some business. You was supposed to be at my house two hours ago." Toya reminded him.

"What kind of business?" he inquired.

"The kind of business that ain't none of your business, nigga."

He wondered to himself if she was with a dude. He couldn't remember the last time she had mentioned one.

"Well, we out front waiting on you." JT said.

"I'm on my way. I'll be there in about ten minutes."

As soon as he finished with Toya, JT two-wayed Stink. "Where you at, my nigga?"

"On the e-way. I'll be there in about twenty minutes."

"Ok, me and Scurvy already here."

"Aiight, bet."

Thirty minutes later, they were all in the van headed to Oakland County. They were going to case out a jewelry store that Stink and Scurvy had been checking out for two weeks.

JT and Toya wanted to see the place for themselves, just to make sure they hadn't missed anything. A mini police station, hidden cameras, alternative escape routes. Stink had gotten the idea from an Italian jeweler he had met in the strip club months earlier. He found out that the Italian jewelers and the Chaldean jewelers didn't care for each other that much.

Stink found it particularly interesting that this Italian jeweler found it funny when his Chaldean competitor got robbed last year. Stink got his card, and started to build a relationship with him. He bought some nice earrings for Naomi, and a few days later, he brought JT in to buy a watch. They had to get comfortable enough with the Italian jeweler to open up to him. Feel him out, see if he was the type to bend the laws and look the other way for a few bucks.

He seemed to take a liking to JT, so JT took it upon himself to coach the game plan from there. Just yesterday, they brought Toya in to purchase a pair of Cartier diamond earrings. Afterwards, JT gave her all her money back and told her consider it a gift. He didn't mind doing something nice for Toya. He had come to the realization that he had real feelings for her, even though he wasn't sure what to do about it. That day he had a long talk with the Italian. The conversation was vague, to make sure it wasn't incriminating to either party, but they reached an understanding. It was on.

When they reached the Chaldean jewelry store, they parked down the street near the pet store. Stink stayed in the car while JT and Toya made their way to the store. Toya walked about forty-five seconds ahead of JT, so she was first enter the store, as planned. She looked around for a few seconds while the Chaldean owner serviced another Caucasian woman.

"Can I help you with something?" the owner asked after finishing up.

"Do you sell wedding rings?"

"Sure do, right this way," he said motioning her to the far end.

JT walked in, and Toya faked surprise with a buck-eyed look.

"Shhh," she told the owner, attempting to hold him to secrecy.

It only took JT ten seconds to see what he wanted to see. He strolled over to Toya.

"What you doing?" he asked.

"Nothing." she said shyly.

"Come on then, we running late."

"I was just window shopping, dang. Sorry to bother you, sir." Toya said as she followed JT to the door.

"It's no bother." the store assured her with a giggle. He thought they were cute.

They each took one more glance around as they went for the door.

"I think it'll work." Toya said outside.

"Me too," JT agreed.

"I think we should wait a few more days, though. He got a pretty good look at me."

"They ain't gonna wait, you know Stink."

Toya knew he was right. Stink was always a little too impatient in her eyes.

They climbed in the van.

"Toya wanna wait a few days," JT said.

"Why? Y'all see something?" Stink said.

"Naw, just cause… you know, she was in there for a while and dude got a pretty good look at her."

"Man, fuck that. We already knew he was gonna get a good look at her. Fuck waiting. Matter of fact, Toya, you can drive the van and stay behind the wheel while we run up in the spot."

Toya looked at Stink, appalled. "Do I look stupid to you, nigga? Y'all ain't about to run up in that bitch and shortchange me. You got me bent."

"When did we ever shortchange you, Toya?" Stink asked.

"I don't know, but it won't be tomorrow."

JT interrupted. "First of all, she can't stay in the van, cause we gonna need all four of us in the store. We can do it tomorrow or we can wait, but we gonna do it all together."

There was silence in the van as JT drove towards the freeway.

"I ain't trying to wait, fuck that." Stink insisted.

"I don't give a fuck. We can do it tomorrow, shit." Toya finally said.

Stink came home at a reasonable hour as always, nowadays. Naomi had cooked some steak and potatoes and was feeding her face. He thought she looked so comfortable and beautiful, wearing one of his old T-shirts with nothing underneath. Stink got turned on, looking at her thighs as the T-shirt rose high when she came in and sat down on the bed. They had sex just about every night and he didn't plan on tonight being any different.

"How was your day today?" Naomi asked.

"Productive," he said.

"You make mama some money?" she teased.

"Shut up." He pushed her shoulder lightly.

Naomi got up to use the bathroom. There was a splash, and to Stink it was like a water balloon fell from her vagina to the floor.

"Oh shit," Naomi said, staring at Stink wide eyed.

"What the hell was that?"

"I think my water just broke."

Stink hopped up, not really sure what to do. "You bout to have the baby?" he asked just be sure.

"Yeah." Naomi said calmly. "Bring me a dry towel."

Stink scurried to the bathroom and came back with

a big white towel. She dried herself and told him to get her sweat suit she had set out for the occasion.

“You gonna have to help me get dressed,” she said.

He laid her clothes on the bed. “You sure is calm for a mafucka that’s about to have a baby.”

“That’s because I’m not having contract… ooh shit, time to go.” Her first contraction was a big one.

“You want me to call an ambulance?” Stink asked.

“No fuck that, you drive.”

———————

They arrived at the hospital fifteen minutes later and Naomi’s contractions were still slow in coming. Once she was set up and changed into a hospital gown, they began to speed up. She squeezed Stink’s hand tightly and he stayed right by her side. Around two o’clock that morning, Naomi gave birth to a baby boy who was a mirror image of Stink.

They named him Donald Morehouse Jr. They were both elated beyond words and Stink spent the night at the hospital asleep in a chair. He woke up in the middle of the night and never went back to sleep. He just sat there thinking and watching Naomi sleep. He was a father now, and he felt like a weight had been lifted off his shoulders. He felt whole again.

———————

The next morning, JT couldn’t figure out what the

hell was going on. Stink's cell phone kept going straight to voicemail. He called the crew to see if anybody else had heard from him, but they hadn't. He called Naomi's phone to see if she had some answers but she didn't answer. That's when it struck him that Naomi had probably had the baby.

Twenty minutes later, Stink called and confirmed that he was at the hospital with Naomi.

"My bad, my nigga. I know we had some business on the floor this morning."

"Fuck that, nigga. You just had a son, nigga. A lil bald head ass junior. Nigga, don't nothing come before that."

"I know man. That shit is a crazy thing to see with your own eyes. But we can just do it in a few days like Toya said, man."

"Yeah, yeah, fuck all that. I wanna see the baby," JT said. He was almost as excited as Stink was. He was the godfather, and was looking forward to playing a role in the little boy's life.

"Ok, just meet me at my house and we'll go back to the hospital together."

"Aiight, bet. I'll scoop Toya. I know she wanna see the lil nigga too."

"Cool. That will give me some time to get cleaned up."

"Aiight, in a minute." JT said.

"In a minute." Stink returned.

Stink spent the next hour showering and changing

clothes. He thought about how things would be completely different for his son than it was for him growing up. His son wouldn't be going to school with ran down shoes and no deodorant on. Not while he was alive and breathing. Matter of fact, even if he wasn't alive and breathing. He was gonna make sure his Jr. was straight, no matter what.

The three arrived at the hospital around noon. Naomi and her son were awakened by Stink's loud mouth. She had met JT a few times before, but she was sure she had never met Toya. She did always know of Toya, but this was the first time she was able to put a face with the name.

For some strange reason, her face looked familiar. Toya introduced herself and asked to see the baby. Naomi passed the baby to Toya, studying her face. It was at the tip of her brain, but she just couldn't finger her.

"He looks just like yo' egg head ass, Stink." Toya teased.

"Shut up hater, this the most handsome lil nigga ever."

"So, since I'm the goddaddy..." JT said.

"Godfather." Naomi corrected.

"Yeah, godfather. What y'all need me to do?"

"Well, since Stink got everything but a stroller, that's what you can get your godson."

"Not a problem."

They all stayed in the room talking and enjoying the moment for about an hour. Before Toya and JT left, they called Stink out into the hallway for business.

"I was thinking we should kick back until Friday." JT said.

"Yeah, that will give me some time to get Naomi settled in at home." Stink agreed.

"There it is, then." Toya said, happy she had gotten her way.

Three days later, they pulled in front the jewelry store twenty minutes before it opened. They had to go in and strike early, before a lot of customers hit the store in numbers, causing confusion. JT was behind the wheel while Stink rode shotgun. The adrenaline rush consumed them both, knowing they were about to risk it all once again for the almighty dollar. Something they had never tried before, a jewelry store.

"Make sure y'all shit off safety." Toya shouted from the rear.

Scurvy thumbed the safety off his 40 cal. JT would be the first one inside. Everyone trusted his judgment under pressure, so they felt comfortable following his lead. Everyone was dressed to fit the early April weather, but also to conceal bulletproof vests and firearms. They all rocked hoodies, puffy vests, and no masks.

Within two minutes of the store opening, they

quick-stepped single file to the door and barged in, drawing pistols simultaneously. JT snatched up the owner and pointed the gun at his temple. Stink grabbed the unarmed security while Scurvy and Toya secured the owner's assistant and a lone customer that had managed to beat them inside

"Aiight, everybody in the back." JT ordered.

They forced everyone into the back room where the jewelry was cut.

"Lay down!" JT ordered loudly.

The male customer was hesitant.

"Lay the fuck down." He ordered again, this time, aiming his weapon at the customer who grew nervous and immediately complied.

"I don't think none of y'all ready to die about this shit. Go get started," He order Scurvy. As Scurvy went back up to the front room, the rest of the team removed their plastic handcuffs and began cuffing the hostages' hands behind their backs. They could hear Scurvy breaking open glass casing with his pistol.

As soon as everyone was tied up, they all joined him. They smashed all ten cases loaded with rings, watches, chains and earrings. They loaded all the jewelry in pillowcases as fast as they could.

JT checked his watch. "Thirty seconds," he yelled out.

Everyone continued to pick through the broken glass with gloves, trying not to get stuck by sharp points. Time was running out.

"Come on, let's go!" JT called out to everyone.

They stomped and shattered more glass, bailing for the front door, but stopped on a dime and backed back up into the store. They followed Stink's lead, looking at the expression on his face.

"Fuck, the police out there!" Stink said.

"Where?" JT said, peeking around Stink's shoulder cautiously.

Stink pointed to the squad car directly across the street, involved in a traffic stop.

JT peeked out again and saw that both cops' backs were turned to them.

"Man, fuck them. Go, go, go!" He shoved everyone in front of him out the door and slid out behind them.

They scurried to the van and piled in. JT cranked up the van and pulled out slowly, trying his best to look natural and calm. Inside, he was on a hundred and about to explode. The cops still had their backs turned as the crew pulled out to the main road and turned left in the opposite direction of the squad car. It took a few minutes before everyone was able to take a sigh of relief.

They had done it again. Gank Masterz, they were.

CHAPTER 24

The news reported the jewelry heist and stated that an estimated 1.5 million dollars in jewels had been stolen. They all thought it was an exaggeration until they took some of the jewels to the Italian jeweler who estimated that some of the watches they'd stolen were worth thirty and forty thousand dollars. The jeweler took as much of the jewelry off their hands as he could, without drawing suspicion to himself. About one fourth, at half of its value.

There was no rush to unload the rest of it after that they had stung the biggest lick of their criminal career, all right under the nose of the Pontiac police. Money problems were officially a thing of the past. Stink kept a lot of his jewelry for himself, giving Naomi a ten thousand dollar bracelet and a pair of 2 carat diamond earrings. JT bought a Cadillac Escalade and threw some twenty-fours on it.

Scurvy copped a Q-45 Infinity and paid off all his street debts. This opened up communication with all the hustlers who could afford to take some of the jewelry off their hands at a reasonable price. Some paid in drugs, some paid in cash, but within a month's time, they had gotten rid of almost all the jewelry without getting hot. They had been partying all week for the fuck of it, so when Stink and JT's birthdays rolled around, they just kept the party going. Ménages, strip clubs, trips out of town. By the time Stink's birthday was over, he couldn't even get out of bed. He slept the afternoon away.

Every once in a while, he would roll over to catch Naomi's evil eye peering at him. She wasn't happy one bit. Things were going good at first, but now he seemed to be trying to shower her with things to replace time spent. There had already been nights Stink didn't come home at all, and lately, he seemed to have no consideration for her feelings and the deal breakers she had laid out.

He finally woke up around eight o'clock that evening. He asked Naomi if she cooked anything.

Her answer was, "Pshh."

She avoided him most of the day, staying in the bedroom with the baby, hoping he would get the hint that she was pissed and stay home. She had given up her whole life in Columbus for this bullshit. She didn't care about how much money he had. She knew he was about money from the moment she laid eyes on him, but she never led him to believe she was impressed by it. She wanted loyalty more than anything, and was beginning to think she was looking in the wrong spot for it.

After an hour or so of the silent treatment, Stink knew something was up, but didn't have a clue as to what it could be.

"Fuck wrong with you?" he asked.

"Are you staying home tonight?" she asked.

"Come on man, you know it's JT birthday. Look, I promise after tonight, I will spend the next week with you, and I'll start back coming home early every night. Tonight is just gonna be like one last night on the town. You don't understand what we been through to get here. Everybody understands that tomorrow ain't promised, so we just want a chance to enjoy this shit as a team, you understand?"

"No, I don't understand. I thought that's what you been doing for the last month. And what's your idea of enjoying yourself? Cheating on me? Coming home too drunk to even be behind the wheel of a car?"

"You may be right about the drunk driving, but I never cheat when I'm out in the streets. That's not what this is about." he lied.

Truthfully, it was exactly what it was about. The six weeks it took for Naomi to heal from giving birth had given Stink time to find some of the baddest bitches with fire pussy and dream head the D had to offer. No way he could just up and stop now, it was a lifestyle. Popping bottles fucking models.

"So you want me to believe in this last month that we haven't been able to have sex, you've been hanging out with JT all night?"

"Pretty much." he said sticking to his story.

After being locked up for all those years, he couldn't believe she was expecting him to deny himself the opportunity to bust a nut. The whole idea of it was ludicrous, but he loved her, so he would try to convince her otherwise.

"I thought we had an understanding, Stink." Naomi said, shaking her baby to sleep on her knee.

"Listen, just this one more night, let me go do me. Tomorrow is a new day and we gonna start fresh, I promise."

"Whatever you say," she said rolling her eyes.

"I'm serious. Next month, we gonna start looking for a house we can call home. If you decide you wanna go back to work, that's cool. If not, that's even better. I just want us to be happy, you feel me?"

"Us or you?" she asked seriously.

"Us, baby." She just stared at him as he leaned in for a kiss that had a little resistance to it. She hoped he meant it all and wasn't just sweet talking her.

Stink laid out his bulletproof vest and a pair a Timberlands as he began to get dressed. He put on two platinum chains and two watches that were exactly the same. He also put on a bracelet and a pinky ring on each finger. If he ever went to jail with that jewelry on, he was gonna have some serious questions to answer. But in true Stink form, he just didn't give a fuck.

Naomi just rolled her eyes as his Nextel alert went off. It was Toya.

"What up, doe?" he said.

"What's up? You ready?" she asked.

Toya had decided to hang out with them tonight. Normally, she'd stay home and watch the Sopranos, but since it was JT's birthday, she knew she had to be there.

"Where you at?" Stink asked.

"I'm coming off the freeway. Meet me at the Amoco."

"Why?" Stink said. He thought it was strange that she didn't just come to the house.

"Just do it, nigga. I got a surprise for you."

"Aiight."

He sprayed on some Issey Miyake as he caught a glimpse of Naomi rolling her eyes. He knew it was about the two-way conversation she had just overheard, but he was done explaining himself for the day. He gave her another kiss on the cheek as he finished getting dressed.

He kissed Stink Jr. on his way out the door.

When Stink got to the Amoco, he Spotted Toya's Jaguar parked off to the side. There was a black stretch Hummer parked next to her. He pulled up next to the Hummer, but the tints kept him from seeing inside. As he got out, he saw Scurvy stick his head out the back window.

"Get your ass in here, nigga!"

"Where Toya at?" Stink asked.

"She in here with us." Scurvy said.

Stink opened the door and peeked in.

"What up, nigga?" Toya shouted. She sounded like

she was already turned up. There was a row of well-known strippers sitting across from Scurvy and Toya.

Stink grinned. "You rented this?" he asked Toya.

"Yeah, get in." Toya said, excited about what she had put together for the night.

As Stink climbed in, he scanned the faces of all the women. He stopped at one whose face just jumped out at him. He couldn't believe it was her, but he couldn't have been happier to see her on a night like tonight.

"Sherida?" he said, staring at her.

"Hey Stink," Sherida said flirtatiously.

They hadn't seen each other in almost seven years, since the age of thirteen. Sherida was cold as ever. He could see why she would have chosen to capitalize on the beauty God had bestowed upon her. He snuggled in right between her and another gorgeous young lady he was familiar with, but his attention was completely on Sherida.

"I been looking for you, girl." he said with a grin.

"You ain't been looking too hard. I been working at Chocolate City for over a year.

"Well, I ain't really been in the city like that, you know what I'm saying? I'm an interstate, mobile type nigga. You feel me? I like to take my show on the road." he boasted.

"I like to take my show on the road too, when I can," she shot back.

A few seconds later, JT pulled up and Stink stuck his

head out the window, overly excited.

"A nigga! Come here, you ain't gonna believe this shit!"

JT swaggered over to the limo, smiling. He was clearly in a great mood. When he opened the door, he was taken aback by all the girls inside. He looked directly at Toya.

"Happy Birthday, my nigga." she said, holding up a bottle of Cristal.

JT was happy and a little confused at the same time. Just when he was beginning to think he knew Toya.

Meanwhile, Toya was feeling good about how she had put all of it together with no help from the boys. The stretch Hummer, the strippers, the drinks and the weed. JT just continued to stare at her in amazement.

"You a muthafucka," he said smiling.

"Boss bitch, that's all." Toya returned.

After her and JT were done with their moment, Stink finally showed him what he was so excited about."

"So you just gonna act like you don't even know me, right?" Sherida said.

She sat so far into the back, JT hadn't gotten a good look at her, but when he focused in, his eye widened.

"Oh shit, Sherida?" He burst into laughter. "Where the hell you come from?"

"My mama pussy. What's good, nigga?"

"Everything good, baby, everything good. So that's why this nigga, Stink, showing all his teeth and shit, huh?"

"That's right, nigga. My boo on deck, now let's roll." Stink said.

"I see who going home with no money tonight." JT joked as they pulled out the parking lot.

Toya tried to pour drinks without spilling it everywhere.

"Shut the fuck up, nigga. Driver, turn this bitch around so you can drop this nigga back off at the gas station." Stink said.

"Y'all ain't changed a bit." Sherida giggled.

JT had to admit, Sherida was looking better than ever. She wore a short skirt and low cut top. Cleavage leaving nothing to the imagination.

"So, where your cousin, Kizzy, at?" JT asked, taking a cup from Toya.

"She lives in Atlanta now, but she still pops up in the summertime."

Toya had passed around a cup to everyone and was ready to toast.

"Aayeee, aayeee, aayeeee, drinks up everybody! Drinks up. To the birthday boy, I love you and to all my niggas from The Bottom, straight to the top. I love all y'all niggas til death and beyond."

Everyone toasted, even the strippers, and tossed their drinks back.

“That was a special kinda toast. You know what I’m saying? I think I see a tear in JT’s eye.” Stink taunted. “Is you crying, nigga?”

“Roll the weed up, punk ass nigga.” JT answered.

In truth, he was a little in awe of Toya at the moment. It was a feeling he never felt in the presence of a woman before.

“I got a few rooms downtown, already paid for and everything.” he heard her say.

Surrounded by bad bitches, JT’s mind wasn’t on any of them. Toya picked up on the vibe and wondered why he wasn’t showing the girls any attention. She thought she had done a wonderful job at hand picking all the girls that her crew usually went for. Still, he looked happy, and that was all that mattered to her.

Downtown was live, and the traffic was backed up almost as if it was a big concert night or something.

“Y’all wanna hit the club first?” Toya asked

“For what? We got everything we need already.” Scurvy said.

“You right about that,” Stink agreed as he spotted a car full of girls alongside the limo.

He glanced at them and just off instinct, he could tell they were the type of stuck up girls that wouldn’t give him the time of day if he wasn’t getting money. He rolled down the window, digging in his pocket at the same time.

He stuck his torso out the window. “Aye! Aye bitch!

Catch this!" He threw a bankroll out the window, which hit the car, then flew in the air and drizzled on to the streets.

Everyone in the limo laughed hysterically. The driver turned the music down and complained about Stink hanging out the window.

"Man, hit the weed and be cool." JT said.

That was all the driver needed to hear. The driver asked to hit the weed, and after that, it was a party for real. They rode around downtown for a while. Toya gave another gangsta toast to her mom, who was still doing time, and then the music went up. They turned the vehicle into their own little club.

At the hotel, Toya had the driver to wait for her while she went inside and had one more drink with her crew. She didn't want to hang out all night, and she really didn't want to be around JT while he was fucking with strippers, even though she paid them to be there.

Their suites were all on the top floor and each one had a huge living room space, a bar, a Jacuzzi, and a kitchenette. They all wound up in Stink's room, still drinking. The liquor began to make Stink sweaty under his bulletproof vest.

He took off his shirt and the vest, and tossed it on the bed. Sherida noticed and commented.

"Damn, it's like that?"

"Hell yeah, it's like that. Niggas ain't trying to see us

make it to twenty-one out here." He set his strap inside the drawer on the nightstand.

Toya stayed for one drink and ended up having three. Now she was drunk enough to go home and pass out without thinking about JT having a threesome or some other dumb shit. She was having a ball, but the longer she stayed, it began to irk her that she had nobody around to even just come through and put some nice dick in her life and be gone. JT would be glad to, but then she wondered what would happen after that. Things were different now. She had alienated herself from everyone, due to part paranoia and part bitch nigga detox.

As things began to warm up and get freaky, she stood to leave. "It's been real, but I'm bout be up outta here."

"You leaving already?" JT asked.

"Yeah, what you want me to get in the hot tub with y'all too? Ain't I done enough already?" she said, smiling.

"Yeah, let us see what that bathing suit looking like." JT blurted out.

"Whatever. Ain't nobody in here giving me no dick tonight, so what I'm undressing for?"

"Don't speak too soon," JT said with a chic on his lap."

Everyone one in the room got quiet for a few seconds. It caught everybody off guard, especially Toya.

"I ain't with that freaky shit, nigga." she shot back.

Everybody laughed and went back to what they were doing. JT made the girl on his lap get up, and he made his way over to Toya before she could reach the door.

He grabbed her gently by the arm. "I'm not ready for you to go yet."

She was smiling a little, but tried to conceal it. "Really… really JT? You want me to stick around for this?"

JT had been strategizing the whole night on how to say it, but he knew he had to. He didn't want to spend tonight with some random girl he just met hours ago. He wanted to spend this night with someone who had genuine love for him. He was positive that Toya had more love for him than any woman on the planet.

"Hold on," he told her. He went to the bar and grabbed a bottle of champagne from the ice-chilled bucket.

Everyone's eyes roamed the room, following JT as it appeared he was preparing to leave.

"What's up, dog?" Stink asked

"We'll be back… maybe," he added.

Toya just watched him curiously, as he opened the door and gestured for her to walk first through the door. They walked a few doors down and JT pulled out his room card.

"What type of shit you on?" Toya questioned.

"Just come on and stop looking at me all crazy."

Toya was reeling from the bottle and a half of champagne she had drank by herself. She came in and sat down in the living room space. She slipped off her stilettos and waited for JT to say whatever it was he was about to say.

He came over and sat down next to her. "I don't want you to go home. I want you to stay with me tonight."

She still didn't fully comprehend what was happening all of a sudden, and why. "Huh?" was all Toya could come up with.

"Listen, I appreciate the love. The girls, the limo, champagne all that. I really do. But I don't wanna fuck with them hoes tonight. I wanna be around some love, you feel me?"

"I feel you but, I mean... I'm just supposed to fuck with you whenever you feeling some type of way? I don't understand what you shooting at right now."

She wasn't making it easy for him. She was trying to get him say to shit he hadn't ever said to woman before and meant it. He looked at her beautiful brown skin glowing in the night light. From her neckline to her toes, were things he wanted to taste, touch and smell.

"This what I'm saying. Shit about to change."

Without permission, he moved in, pecking her neckline while pulling her close to him.

Toya wanted to resist, because it was all happening so fast. His lips on her skin felt so good. His hand around her waist had her cornered. She couldn't move if she wanted to, so she let go of all resistance and relaxed into pleasure. Her first moan gave JT a boner that was bulging out of his jeans.

He kissed between her breasts slowly, while cupping the softness of her ass. He longed for the taste of her big, dark nipples as she guided them to his mouth. He knew she wasn't going to try and stop him now, so he immediately went to unbutton his jeans. She stroked his dick through his jeans, increasing his eagerness to unclothe her.

Once he finished, JT laid Toya out on the couch, holding one of her legs in the air. She reached out to began stroking his manhood. She was ready. JT fingered her pussy and kissed her inner thighs, getting her juices flowing. He palmed her ass and massaged her clit with his tongue. It had been so long since she'd had this much fun, and it was just the beginning.

Sounds of her moans roared throughout the room. He could feel her body start to quiver as he focused on her pleasure. *There is no better way to spend the night,* JT thought as he came up for air and grabbed her by her waist.

He flipped her over into doggy style. He zoomed in on her round, plump, apple bottom, squeezing her cheeks and enjoying the Jell-O feel of her ass until he couldn't wait any longer.

He eased inside of her slowly, and immediately, he remembered the feel of her. He slow grinded her at first, but he was eager to let her feel all of him. He positioned himself with one leg up and began giving her back shots like he'd never given before.

Toya tried to bury her screams into the couch pillows, but it felt too good to hide it. She had to let it rip. As she felt the climax coming, she began to throw it back until he took control of her positioning. He jabbed and roughhoused until he exploded inside her.

They collapsed on the couch, leaving the limo driver outside, waiting and wondering.

CHAPTER 25

Stink didn't make it home until daylight, and he knew it was going to be a problem when he woke up. He was not surprise at all when the minute his eyes opened, she was right there with the most unfulfilled look he'd ever seen in her eyes.

"You know what? I should have stayed my ass in Columbus like I started to."

He wanted to say, 'take your ass back to Columbus and leave me alone,' but he didn't. "Don't start."

"Don't start my ass! You act like you don't know you got a newborn baby at home. I mean, what are you gonna sit up and say you been doing all night that's not gonna sound fucking ridiculous? What Stink?"

"I'm not about to justify shit. I told you what I was going out to do before I did it. I told you I wanna chill, why you can't leave shit alone?"

"You know what? Fuck it. That's what I'm going to do, leave you alone."

She stormed out and Stink didn't budge.

In the shower, he let the water massage his mind and body as he began to feel guilty. He knew he was dead wrong for the way he had been treating Naomi, and he knew it was time to do better. He promised himself he would try to be a better man for his family. He still wasn't going to stop fucking around, especially now that Sherida was back in his life, but he still knew he had to do better.

His mind drifted back to Sherida. Tight, wet pussy, bomb head and she liked girl on girl action. A girl like her would keep him out of the strip club forever. She was everything he wanted in a sidepiece.

After his shower, Stink decided he would talk to Naomi, hoping she'd calmed down. She was playing with their son when Stink came in the bedroom.

"Naomi," He called almost in a mumble. He hated feeling apologetic towards anyone.

"What?" she responded in the nastiest tone. She set Stink Jr. down to turn and face his father. She waited, staring at him buck eyed.

"My bad, aiight? I know I been fucking up, but I'm gonna do better. I promise."

"If you wasn't ready for a relationship, you should have left me where I was. I didn't ask for this, you did."

"It's not that. I am ready. I'm just learning how to be in one and this shit is all new to me. You're a little older than me and you haven't had years took out of your life. I know I'm still immature, but you can't question my love for you. I give you any and everything you ask for. You even have the combination to my safe. If that's not love or trust, then I don't know what is." He threw his hands up, feeling he'd made a valid point.

"For the millionth time, I don't give a fuck about your money. Yes, it's good to have nice things, but you care about that shit more than I do. I just don't know about this anymore, Stink."

Stink ended the conversation because he saw he was in a lose/lose situation.

As the day went on, he played with his son and tried to make up for last night in any way he could think of. Naomi warmed up to him enough to cook dinner for two, and by the end of the night, Stink had convinced her to have a drink with him. They had champagne after dinner, and shortly after, Naomi dozed off and woke up to Stink rubbing between her thighs.

"Stop. You crazy if you think we about have sex, so leave me alone."

Naomi was asleep two minutes later, and Stink was horny and frustrated. He was always horny, but he was frustrated because it had been almost a month and a half since he and Naomi had intercourse.

His pager went off in the living room. He went to see who it could be. He didn't recognize the number, but he had an idea of who it might be. He crept to the bathroom, turned on the water, and then called the number.

Sherida answered the phone fast, as if she waiting by the phone.

"Hello."

"What's up?"

"Nothing much, you told me to give you a call

today, and I said I would. Just being a woman of my word."

"Where you at?"

"I'm at home. Why, you coming over?"

"Hold on."

Stink went to the bedroom and peeked at Naomi to see if she was still asleep. He knew the alcohol would probably have her out for the night. He could sneak out and be back before she even knew it. He went back to the bathroom and picked up the phone.

"I'm on my way," Stink said.

Stink arrived at Sherida's house without an ounce of guilt. He threw caution to wind as soon as he heard Sherida's voice on the phone. She came to the door wearing a pink teddy and house slippers. She let Stink in and they walked through the dark house, straight to her bedroom. They shot the shit about the night before, and Stink felt comfortable with her as they reminisced about old times. He didn't feel Naomi comfortable with her, but familiar comfortable, because Sherida's personality hadn't changed much.

They began to talk about the case that had sent Stink and JT to juvenile.

"So how do Romell feel about y'all now?" Sherida asked.

Stink knew better than to go into any detail about

what was actually going on with his crew and Romell.

"I don't know what's up with Romell, but if he got a problem with us, we ain't that hard to find. You know what I'm saying?"

"Right. Well, to be honest, you know I used to fuck with that nigga for a minute. I'm just speaking the truth, because if y'all ain't on good terms, I'd rather you hear it from me than the streets."

"I feel you."

Stink played it cool, but inside, he felt like a deer caught in headlights. His heart fell in his stomach as he realized how much he had been thinking with his dick the entire night. Here he was, acting like niggas wasn't out to kill him, and could have easily walked right into a nightmare. He was strapped, but he wasn't on point at all, until now.

"So what made you stop fucking with him?" Stink asked with a skeptical brow raised.

Sherida began shaking her head, as if the memory gave her a headache.

"That bitch ass nigga is crazy. He don't got no respect for nobody. I played myself for even fucking with that nigga. I mean, I do what I do, regardless. But a bitch do got some kind of standards for herself."

After last night, Stink didn't see her as a girl with a lot of standards, but he went along with it. Learning that Sherida had dealt with Romell, he knew couldn't be comfortable at her house after that. He wanted to leave, but he didn't want it to be a wasted trip. They ended up getting a quickie in, with Stink's hand on his Sig under the pillow, the whole time.

As soon as he busted a nut, he fled the house like it was a crime scene.

———————

JT had begun to spend the night with Toya every night. They had a connection that neither of them wanted to deny any longer.

When Stink told him about Sherida and Romell, JT used simple logic. That fact that Sherida even told him about it was probably a good indicator that she no longer had dealings with him. No woman in their right mind would give a cat the heads up on a situation like that if she had malice in her heart. He encouraged Stink to keep seeing her and feeling her out, to see if she could be a valuable asset; the missing piece of the puzzle to help catch and kill Romell once and for all.

He had just left Scurvy's house, plotting on another jewelry store heist. He pulled into Toya's driveway, feeling like he was home. His cell phone rang, and he noticed it was a Columbus area code. The only person he still kept in contact with was Tasha, who was still in love with him. He thought she was good people, even though he had tried to pimp her out of every dime she had.

"Hey Tasha," he answered.

"Hey. Why you don't ever call me back when I leave you a message?"

"Been busy lately, but how you been?"

"I've been good. I'll be better when you come and visit."

"I don't know 'bout that. I can't make no promises, but I wouldn't mind seeing you and putting this Boa Constrictor in your life."

"Yeah, yeah, talk is cheap. I know you spinning me like a wheel, but it's cool. That's not why I called, anyway."

"Oh, what's up?"

"Well you remember the boy that got killed when you were down here, he went by Pretty Mike? You said you knew him."

"What about him?"

"Well, his family has posted a twenty-thousand-dollar reward for information leading to an arrest in the case. They've been showing a composite sketch on the news of a female going by the name, Toya. It looks a lot like the girl you introduced me to, so I just thought you should know. I haven't talked to anybody but you about this, so you don't have to worry about that."

JT was caught off guard. It was the last thing he had expected to hear. "I really appreciate you giving me a call, but it's not my people they looking for. I'm sure of that."

"Well, that's good. Like I said, I just thought you should know."

"Okay, I gotta go. I'll talk to you soon."

"Okay."

JT was very uneasy about the news he had just received. Even though nobody had plans to go back to Columbus, the fact was that, Naomi, Pretty Mike's sister, was right there in Detroit. Not only was she there, she was a part of the circle. He immediately called Stink to relay what he had just been told.

Stink didn't answer, so he left a vague message on his answering service. He entered Toya's house with her spare key, which was now his key. Toya was in the front room running cash through her portable bill counter. He knew he had to tell her, but didn't know what to expect after he did. Worst case scenario was that she would want to kill Naomi to be on the safe side.

JT made himself a drink and took a seat next to her. He waited for the beep from the money machine before he said anything.

"Got something to tell you," he started.

"What's up?" Toya said, removing the money from the machine.

"I talked to Tasha from Columbus today."

"And?"

"They got a sketch of you they showing on the news, along with a twenty thousand dollar reward for information leading to an arrest in Pretty Mike's murder."

Toya's face was filled with alarm, but it didn't last long, as she processed what she was being told.

"Which means they ain't got no information at all."

"Basically." JT agreed. "Still, thought everybody should know."

"Right. You told Stink?"

"I left him a message and told him to call me."

"Okay, so let me ask you something." Toya said.

"What up?"

"You and the fat hoe still talking, or what?"

"Naw, she just called me to tell me what she told me. Why? You jealous?"

"Jealous? Naw, I ain't, but you know with us it's gonna have to be one way. I been thinking 'bout this shit for a couple days, but I just ain't said nothing. So I'm a give you a chance to keep it real with me. We friends, we family, business partners and all that; but we ain't 'bout to keep being fuck partners. You can have all the hoes you want, or you can have me, it's your choice. What you wanna do?"

JT didn't have to think at all for his answer.

"Toya, you know I don't give a fuck about a bitch."

In the language they spoke, that was all that needed to be said, and JT meant it. He didn't feel the need to have any other women in his life. He knew he had the one that would go to hell with gasoline panties on, if he was going too.

CHAPTER 26

Stink woke up the next morning, realizing the huge opportunity that was in front of him. He didn't trust Sherida by far, but he knew for the money, he could probably get her to be his puppet on a string as long as he needed. He continued to see Sherida on a regular basis, fishing for info. This put even more of strain on his relationship with Naomi. It wasn't even about Sherida, but he couldn't explain that to Naomi. It was all about making sure Sherida had no loyalty to Romell, before he went to lay down a play. He tried his best to balance time between home, plotting licks, and trying to get Sherida to warm up to his ideas.

It only took a couple of weeks and a few racks for Stink to convince Sherida to start seeing Romell again. Once she started seeing him again, Stink could see that Romell was just as generous was he was crazy. He threw money at Sherida like he was a Mega Millions lottery winner, which made Stink apprehensive of where her loyalty would lie.

The worst part was that Romell was very suspicious of Sherida from the day she popped back up. She reported back to Stink that he would he remain secretive about where they were going when together, but he also wouldn't allow her to use her cell phone. No incoming calls, no outgoing calls, nothing.

Stink wondered was it just her or did he treat all the women in his life that way. He knew Sherida's fuck game was proper, so he understood why Romell would choose to see her, untrustworthy or not. Stink kept the crew informed about what was going on from day to day.

JT had his own ideas as usual, but everyone knew Romell wasn't going to make it easy on them. In order to continue to exist, in order to survive, they came up with a plan straight out of mobster flick. There was going to be risks involved, and if things didn't go well, they would be under the jail or underground, no in between.

JT was also convinced they could kill two birds with one stone by smoothing out things with 40 Grand. He believed 40 Grand to be a reasonable man, and he knew how Romell had cost 40 Grand more than anybody else in the city that was still alive to bitch about it.

He rode down Mack Ave. on a rainy day, searching his phone for 40 Grand's number, hoping it was still the same. When he found the number, he made the call.

"Yo'." 40 Grand answered.

"What's up, this JT." 40 Grand paused for a minute. JT couldn't help but wait for a response, even though he recognized the voice.

"Well, I hope you calling me to tell me you niggas gathered up some money for me. That was some hoe shit y'all niggas pulled after all the love I showed y'all."

“Yeah, you right, that was fucked up. But I got something better than money on the floor.”

“Better than money? Speak your piece, nigga.”

“I’m about to solve that problem you and Tank had in the city for the longest. Since y’all ain’t been able to solve it, I think that should give me and my crew a clean slate in your eyes.”

A few seconds went by. Just enough for 40 Grand to process the information he was being given. He still had money on Stink and JT’s head, as well as Romell’s, but only one of them was a threat to him at this very moment. He had to side with the lesser of the two evils, for his own survival.

“How soon we talking?”

“We talking asap.”

“I tell you what, nigga. Tank about to come home, so if you can get it done before then, we got a deal.”

“That’s a bet. So you can pull them contracts up nigga, cause this is official,” JT said.

“They come up when you handle your business. Soon as I get the call, it’s official. You got my word on that.”

“That’s your word?”

“That’s my word.”

It was on now.

After a while, Romell began to loosen up a little. Once he did, it took almost a week of subtle fishing before Romell made the mistake of telling Sherida exactly where he was at and how long he would be there. When Stink got the call, everyone was ready to roll on a dime.

Stink, JT and Scurvy hopped in the Escalade with a stolen license plate, strapped with three AR-15's, locked and loaded.

As JT drove to the destination, doing slightly over the speed limit, he constantly checked his mirrors for police. As usual, no one said anything during the ride. Everyone was in thug mode, thinking about what was about to happen. They knew Romell wasn't alone, and they knew if they didn't get the element of surprise, it was be a gun battle until death.

It took twenty minutes to reach Strikers Lounge. As they pulled in the parking lot, JT tried not to look anyone directly in the face. He knew once the guns started bussing, nobody would be looking at faces, but instead, dodging bullets.

Romell, Fo Tre and two more goons sat inside the sports bar, watching a championship game between the Lakers and Pacers. As the game came to a close, Fo Tre began to celebrate by taunting everybody that had bet against the Lakers.

"Told y'all niggas we ain't playing no muthafucking games. LA in this bitch!"

"Calm your ass down." Romell said.

"Naw, dig in them pockets, nigga. That's what you do."

"It ain't shit, cuz." Romell went in his pocket and peeled off ten crispy hundred dollar bills and handed them to Fo Tre.

"Yeah, all y'all niggas dig in them pockets. What you waiting on?"

"That's cool, cause now we bout to hit you with the check." Romell shot back as he signaled for their waiter to come over. Before he could even take his hand out of the air, he looked up and saw the commotion that had stopped Fo Tre in his tracks.

Three men in black hoods with assault rifles headed straight at them. Romell ducked and reached for his pistol as he heard the roar of the AR-15s letting go. Everyone scattered in seconds as the shots continued.

Romell began to fire wild shots without a target ducking beneath the table. He saw Fo Tre crawling on the floor as one his goons fell dead on top of him. Gunfire was still being exchanged back and forth, so Romell used his dead goon as a shield to block bullets as he lifted the limp body up and emptied his clip at the gunmen before they came any closer.

JT ducked down between the bar and a dinner table as he saw Romell's pistol aimed straight at him. Stink never took cover; instead, he went toe to toe with Romell, knocking him and the already dead goon to the floor.

Wounded, Romell crawled towards the bathroom. He heard the shooting stop as he made it to the door. His injured leg was caught in the door. Still on the floor, he reached for his extra clip and heard four more rounds let off inside the bar. Just then, the bathroom door was pushed off his leg. He knew it was not someone coming to save him. He knew he wouldn't live to see tomorrow, but he wanted to go out fighting.

As he tried unsuccessfully to load his gun, he stared in the face of his childhood friend, turned enemy.

"Stink, bitch!" he yelled before emptying the clip in Romell's face and body, overkill style.

Stink gave the signal and everyone made a dash for the Escalade. Stink was the last one in. JT bailed out of the parking lot, burning rubber and bullying traffic until they were away from the bloody murder scene.

After disposing of all the evidence, the crew met back up at Toya's house to celebrate. As they relayed the story to Toya, each gunman had their own version of all the detail. Stink and JT were both claiming the most bodies. They waited on the replay of the eleven o'clock news, knowing that the massacre would be the top story.

"JT, you still gonna have to put that truck up for a while. Them black Escalades about to be hot as hell on the streets." Stink said.

"Put it up? Nigga that bitch going on the market for sale, fuck that truck."

"I hear that."

They filled their glasses with champagne and Toya gave a toast to the death of Romell.

“Playa haters, bitch niggas and all outside this circle. Fuck ’em all, die slow,” she shouted.

“Fuck ’em all, die slow,” they all repeated.

Stink had been searching for his phone for a while, but in all the chaos, he hoped it wasn’t lost somewhere.

“Let me see your phone, JT.”

“Where your phone?” JT asked.

“I think I left it at home. Shit, I been looking for it since I left the crib.” JT handed Stink his cell phone and he called, just to see what would happen.

“Hello.” he heard Naomi say.

“Fuck you doing answering my phone?” he snapped.

“Well, what the fuck you call it for if you didn’t want me to answer it? I thought something was wrong, but you must got something to hide.”

“Man, be quiet. Ain’t nobody hiding shit.”

“Really, so why you not at home with your son?”

“I can’t tell you all that, but I was on my way home. And you better stop talking to me like I’m some kinda punk.” Stink warned getting heated, but so was Naomi.

“You know what, stay where you at nigga, fuck you.” She hung up in his face.

Stink was completely floored as he stared at JT’s phone in disbelief. Naomi had never talked to him in that way. She was on the verge of getting a beat down worse than a runaway slave. His first instinct was to drive straight home and give her a backhand shipped all the way from Florida. He thought about it and decided he needed to calm down. He knew going home right now would create more problems than it would solve.

Today had been a monumental moment in his career on the streets. He had just taken out one the biggest gangstas the eastside had to offer. Once he really thought about it, he knew this was the best day he'd had since he lost his mom and one that he would remember for the rest of his life. Stink decided he was going to enjoy his night, and as much as he loved Naomi, he wasn't going to let her ruin this for him.

He decided to spend the night at Sherida's instead.

Naomi couldn't sleep after the phone call from Stink. She was shaking mad when she hung up in his face. Mad because of the continued disrespect and uncaring behavior Stink had displayed after she moved from her family and everything she had ever known. She knew he would explode when he got home, but Naomi didn't care at this point. She was ready for whatever.

Around four that morning, she realized he wasn't coming home. She began searching his phone for female names and numbers. He had to be laid up with some trick. She came up empty, so she began trying to break into his voice mail by figuring out his access code. She tried his beeper code he used in Columbus. No good. She tried his birthday, to no avail. After trying her own birthday, she was just about to give up, but something made her give it one last Hail Mary. Bingo, her son's birthday.

Once she cracked the code, she saw he had five unheard messages. Two from Sherida telling him to call, it was important. Two from Scurvy saying basically the same thing. The oldest message was from JT. She wasn't really interested in that one, but she paced the floor and listened anyway, just because she had already listened to the others.

What she heard next would change her life forever.

"Yo'... I just heard some wild shit, man. They got photo sketches of Toya on the news. Say they got a reward for her arrest on that Pretty Mike situation. She ain't tripping about it, but I just wanted you to know. We might need to keep your girl from around her for a while, you know. Anyway, come through when you get this. Later."

Naomi immediately felt dizzy. She had to flopped down on the bed before she fell out. She tried to calm her nerves, but she could feel herself unraveling fast. *Could he actually be involved? He couldn't be, this just couldn't be.* A chill went through her body as she thought about facing the truth of the man she had been living and sleeping with all this time. *What kind of heartless bastard could look me in the face every day and knowingly be hiding such a massive secret?*

Tears began to spill from her eyes as she buried her face in the pillow, weeping uncontrollably. The pain of know the true man she fell in love with was unbearable and her whole body jerked as she let out as much as she could, one breath at a time. She picked up Stink's cell phone and hurled it at the wall, shattering it to pieces. She loved and missed her brother so much, and this bastard, this low life monster knew all along who was responsible.

Stink woke up in time to catch the eleven o'clock news. He sat proudly in front of the screen as they replayed the massacre, as if it was his most shining moment.

Sherida rolled up a blunt, smiling at Stink's boldness.

"So you said you was gonna really look out for me when all this was taken care of. I hope you a man of your word."

"Of course. You did your part and I'm gonna do mine." *The bodies ain't even cold yet, and this bitch got her hand out. It's all about the money with her,* he thought.

Stink thought about his girl and son at home, and got up and began to get dressed. He had a lot of making up to do, but now he was ready for it. He counted out ten thousand and sat it on the nightstand next to Sherida's bed.

"I'll see you later," he said, heading for the door.

"You don't wanna hit this?" Sherida said, referring to the weed.

"Naw, I'm good. Later."

Now that everything was taken care of, Stink knew he had to cut Sherida's gold digging ass off. As he drove to the house, he tried to think of what he could say to make Naomi understand, without telling her too much. It was bad enough Sherida knew everything, but she was a necessary piece of the puzzle. Naomi, on the other hand, stayed in the blind about what was going on in the streets. Stink knew it was best that way. The important thing was that Romell was out the way for good, 40 Grand was satisfied, and now things could get back to normal.

When Stink got home, he noticed Naomi's car wasn't in the parking lot. She still didn't really know her way around Detroit, so he figured she couldn't have gone too far. On the ride up the elevator, he felt a hint of guilt about the way he had been treating her. This was it though, he was going to make things right, starting now.

He turned the keys and entered the apartment. The first thing he noticed was his cell phone shattered into pieces on the floor. *The fuck? She's more pissed off than I thought.* There was a note on the kitchen table in big letters. He lifted the paper to his face and held it with two hands. I CHECKED YOUR MESSAGES AND I KNOW Y'ALL KILLED MY BROTHER. PAYBACK IS A BITCH.

The words hit Stink like a bullet to the chest. He ran to the closet to see if her clothes were there, but most of them were gone. He quick-stepped to his son's room to find his clothes were gone too. His next thought was to flee the apartment, fearing police would be on the way. His brain was clouded with all kinds of thoughts racing through it, with not enough time to process.

He was so mad; he fumbled his keys, trying open up his gun safe to grab his other Sig Sauer. If police showed up, he wasn't going alive. They would have to kill him. He ran back to the closet to check one more thing. *He would kill her if she...* He tried to block out the thought of the worst. He punched the code frantically, but when the safe came open, all doubt was removed.

Naomi had taken every dime in the safe, over a quarter million dollars. Stink's knees got weak and he sat down on the safe. *Over a quarter million dollars,* he thought as his entire body grew hot with anger

It was all gone. Everything. He was ready to explode, yet he couldn't move. Everything he had robbed, stolen and killed for was gone. He thought about going after her, but he knew she was headed straight back home. There was nothing in Columbus for him but a lengthy prison sentence.

He rammed his head into the wall until he was dizzy. He couldn't think clearly. He went in his pocket and pulled out all the money he had. It was nineteen hundred dollars. He had to go after her.

Stink jumped up and grabbed his pistol, then darted for the door.

In the Benz, he continued to talk to himself as the hit the freeway, Columbus bound.

"Ain't no way this bitch about to leave me with nothing. Nineteen hundred? Bitch is you crazy?"

The more he talked to himself, the faster he drove. But the more he drove, the more it didn't make sense. As soon as he arrived, she would probably have police waiting for him. After about twenty-five minutes of driving, he got off the freeway and then got back on, headed to Detroit.

He wanted to call JT, but didn't have a phone. He weighed all his options as he drove in a daze.

"This can't be happening."

All he knew for sure, was that he refused to start over.

CHAPTER 27

Toya was tearing down a chicken salad when her doorbell rang. She wasn't sure if she should take her gun to the door or not. Nobody ever came by her house without calling. She paused the *King of New York* DVD she was watching and went to take a peek through the peep hole. She saw it was Stink and let him in.

"What's up, bald head?"

"Another day another dollar, that's all." Stink replied.

Toya noticed he looked strange and tense. He definitely wasn't himself.

"You aiight?" she asked.

"Yeah, I'm cool." Stink tried his best to conceal his frustration, but he could tell it wasn't working.

"Why you ain't call me and tell me you was coming?"

"My phone broke, gotta go buy me one real fast."

"Oh. I'm mad as hell about that jewelry store lick," Toya said.

"What about it?" Stink asked.

"You ain't talk to Scurvy?"

Stink shook his head. "I told you, my phone broke."

"Oh, right. He said we ain't gon' be able to hit the lick, cause the layout ain't right. Even if we could get away with it, he said from what he saw, it ain't worth the risk."

Stink had tuned her out after hearing the worst news he could hear, given his current situation. That's when he made up his mind.

"Yeah, that's fucked up, but I need a favor."

"What kind of favor?"

"I need to borrow like ten stacks til tomorrow. I gotta get this bitch, Sherida taken care of and I ain't been home yet. Once I do, I probably won't be leaving back out for a while."

"Okay, ten stacks ain't shit, nigga. You can spare me all the details. I got you," she said, rising to her feet. "I thought JT was supposed to be giving you five."

"He is. I'll get his half from him when I see him. I just wanna get her out of the way."

"Shit, we should just murk that bitch, she know too much. Be right back." Toya said.

"Aiight."

"I'm watching your favorite movie too," she said headed up the stairs.

Stink couldn't care less what Toya was watching.

Upstairs, Toya counted out ten thousand quickly, thinking about Sherida. She really felt the girl should die, since they had no more use for her. She made a mental note to mention it to JT before the day was over to get his opinion on it. She was about to close the safe when she heard Stink's voice behind her.

"Leave it open."

She spun around to tell Stink she wasn't giving him more than the ten he had originally asked for. When she did, all Toya could see was the Sig aimed at her face. Disarray and confusion took over as she considered if she could in fact, be dreaming.

"Leave it open for what?" she asked calmly.

"Cause I said so." Stink answered as he stormed in the room.

Toya quickly closed the safe and stood face to face with him. "Stink, what the fuck is you doing my nigga?"

"I'm not playing. Open the safe, Toya."

"Man you done lost your fucking mind."

JT was on his way to the Nextel shop to pay his bill, but not before he disputed some charges he noticed that didn't make sense. It wasn't about the money at all. It was about someone trying to get over on him in any kind of way. He realized he had left the bill at Toya's house. Since he wasn't that far, he made a U-turn and headed back to her house.

When he arrived, he saw Stink's Benz in the driveway. He remembered Stink saying he was going to stay in for the day and spend time with Naomi, so he was surprised to see him out and about so early.

JT turned his key in the door and immediately heard the commotion coming from upstairs. Toya and Stink were shouting fiercely at each other. He climbed the stairs two at a time, never once thinking of drawing his weapon

"You remember what that bitch, Carmen, got for trying to play tough." he heard Stink say.

As JT entered the room, he saw Stink grab Toya by the hair and shove her to the floor near the safe. JT went to tackle Stink, but Stink felt his presence and spun around before JT could reach him.

Without thinking, Stink fired a single shot that sent JT crashing to the floor.

Toya and Stink froze in their tracks at the sight of JT bleeding on the floor. Stink didn't move until he saw JT lift his hand up and grab his wounded shoulder. It was too late to turn back now. Stink had to go all the way with it.

"You wasn't supposed to be here, dog. This ain't got nothing to do with you." Stink said.

JT looked into the eyes of the mad man that used to be his friend. "You just shot me, dog."

"I just told you, nigga. You wasn't supposed to be

here. Naomi took everything, dog, and I can't start all over. I just can't"

"So you gon' stick me, nigga?" Toya shouted.

Stink knew he was dead wrong, but after Naomi left with his son and his money, he felt he didn't have anything else to lose.

He pointed the gun at Toya again. "You get the next bullet, Toya. Now open the safe," he demanded.

He pointed the gun back and forth, making sure JT wasn't reaching for anything.

JT couldn't believe his eyes. His best friend for as long as he could remember had a gun pointed at his face, watching him bleeding on the floor.

"Give him the money, Toya." JT said grimacing in pain.

"Fuck that. You gotta kill me, nigga, and carry this safe out of here on your back." Toya argued. She wasn't scared to die and she wasn't scared of Stink.

"Give him the fucking money. I gotta get to the hospital, now."

Toya looked down at the blood soaked shirt JT was now wearing. She knew he had to get to a hospital fast, so she went to the safe and opened it back up. Stink tossed her a pillowcase from her bed and told her to empty the safe.

He didn't even have enough heart to leave her with something. But she didn't have time to fight anymore, so she loaded up the pillowcase with all her savings and slung it across the room at Stink.

"Get out my house, you bitch ass nigga."

He wanted to shoot her so bad, but at the moment he felt like a bitch nigga and a coward.

He looked down at JT. "I didn't mean to shoot you."

"Nigga fuck you, you got what you wanted." JT said, wincing in pain. He walked back over to Toya and aimed the gun at her again.

"Come over here and lay down next to him." Stink ordered.

"I'm not laying down shit," Toya said defiantly.

Stink could see JT's free hand sliding down his waist, reaching for his weapon. Stink rushed over and pulled JT's gun from his waist. He racked the bullet from the chamber and tossed the gun on the floor, away from everyone.

"You gonna shoot me over this bitch money? It ain't your money." Stink said.

"You just shot me over it, muthafucka. After all the shit we been through."

Stink continued to point the gun at both of them, backing out of the room slowly. Toya had two guns under the mattress and plenty more around the house. Stink knew if she got her hands on one, she wouldn't hesitate to squeeze until her clip was empty.

"If I hear anybody hit these steps, I'm shooting." Stink warned.

He closed the door behind him and dashed for the

stairs.

JT lifted his shirtsleeve, trying to view the damage. The bullet had passed through his shoulder, but it was torn up pretty bad.

"Help me up," he said.

"You want an ambulance?" Toya asked.

"Naw, I think I can drive myself to the hospital." Now that he knew Toya was safe and out of harm's way, the pain in his shoulder was overshadowed by rage.

Toya couldn't even think straight as she helped JT off the floor. If it had been anybody but him, she would have left him lying there and went after Stink.

He had everything.

CHAPTER 28

Stink drove to a Red Roof Inn outside of the city and checked in. Images of JT lying on the floor bleeding kept flashing through his mind. It was the only part he truly felt bad about. He tried to block out the images, but they were stuck like a bug to a spider's web. He rolled up some weed and began to count his money. He had all his next moves planned out.

Tomorrow, he got off probation and he could just leave town for a while. As he counted his take, he realized Toya had more money in her safe than he had in his. Then he thought about how much money he spent each day, and he understood why she had more than he did. JT had to be a damn fool if he thought Toya deserved all that cash.

After a couple of hours, with smoke breaks in between, Stink was done counting. He had $435,000 in cash, more than enough to head south and start over.

JT got patched up and was released from the hospital that same night. Only thing on his mind was revenge and Stink. The betrayal stung in a way he couldn't understand. It was a feeling he had practiced giving others, but had never felt for himself. As far as he was concerned, he had stuck to the G code when it came to crew, but Stink had no limits and no loyalty. Not only had he turned on a member of the team, but he had shot his main man; his brother from another mother.

Toya was now his lady. If not his better half, she was certainly his other half. For Stink to even consider her a target meant he had no love. JT and Toya spent the night trying to figure out the next move. They knew after pulling something so low down and dirty, Stink wouldn't think of going home.

They did a few drive-bys past Sherida's house, but didn't see Stink or Sherida's cars at the house. They staked out a few more of his favorite spots, but came up empty.

At three in the morning, JT remembered something that woke him up out of his sleep. Toya heard him fumbling around in the bedroom and she woke up too. He was looking for the handheld calendar that always sat somewhere around Toya's nightstand.

"I think I know where to find 'em." JT said as he found what he was looking for.

"Where?" Toya said. She jumped up, looking for clothes to put on.

"He get off probation today. We was supposed to celebrate later on."

"So what we gotta do? Catch him at the probation office?"

"We don't got no choice. After that, he gonna be gone."

They got dressed and then realized it was only three o'clock in the morning. They tried to stay up for the remainder of the night, but neither of them made it to five am.

JT woke at nine o'clock, realizing they had overslept. The probation office opened at nine, and JT new Stink would be one of the first ones there trying to get in and out.

"Wake up, it's nine o' clock." he said, giving Toya a shove.

"Fuck!" she yelled, upset with herself for falling asleep.

They scurried around, grabbing their guns and extra ammo. They rushed out the door, knowing they didn't have a second to waste.

As they drove to the probation office, JT couldn't help but shake his head at the thought of what he was about to do.

"It is what it is." he said aloud.

Toya glanced over at him, and she instinctively knew what was going through his head. She wanted to kill Stink herself, but not just because it was her money that was taken. She knew JT would suffer sooner or later, knowing he had to kill the only brother he had ever known. Maybe not immediately, but eventually, it would take its toll.

As they made the right on their destination street, JT slowed the Cadillac truck to a creep. The probation office sat at the end of the block, but they were being held up by an eighteen wheeler backing up to a factory.

"Move this shit out the way!" Toya snapped as she looked at the time on the dashboard.

Finally, they had enough space to swing around the slow moving truck and get a good view of the parking lot. The plan was to catch Stink leaving out of the building, and hit him before he even made it to his car.

They cruised through the parking lot, searching for the Benz or any sign of Stink. Both JT and Toya were filled to capacity with adrenaline.

Stink took his last warrant lien and urine drop and said adios to the probation officer after getting his discharge papers. He was one step closer to hitting the freeway and not looking back for a long time. He was thinking about Mobile, Alabama. He had heard some good things about Mobile. He stopped by the bathroom to pick up the pistol he had hidden neatly away on the inside of a toilet. He hated that things had turned out the way they did, but he couldn't turn back time, so fuck it. It was what it was.

JT spotted the Benz, but it was empty, which meant Stink was still inside. He pulled the Escalade all the way to the end of the lot and concealed the truck by parking next to a Denali.

As soon as he threw the gear shift in park, Stink

came strolling out of the probation office, looking like he didn't have a care in the world. JT slapped it in drive, and pulled out, headed straight for Stink.

Stink immediately spotted JT's truck and reached for his weapon. He fired shots at the front windshield as Toya sent bullets whistling by, inches away from his head. Stink ran for safety behind a vehicle in the lot as JT and Toya hopped out to go after him.

JT let off round after round in Stink's direction but he couldn't see him ducked down behind the vehicle.

Stink felt the glass shattering and falling all over him from the windshield, but stayed in position until he heard the shooting stop. He rose up and fired five shots as he tried to make a run for his Benz, but Toya emptied her clip to make sure he didn't even come close.

Stink stayed low and avoided being hit by taking cover behind another vehicle. A random bystander thug heard the shots and must have thought they were intended for him. He hopped out his vehicle and began to fire shots in the direction of Toya and JT.

Toya took cover behind the Escalade as she reloaded.

JT went toe to toe, exchanging gunfire with the thug from out of nowhere.

This gave Stink time to crawl to his Benz, which was only a few feet away, and open the trunk. He grabbed the MP-5. His first target was the bystander thug.

He crept up on him and shot him in the back. He was

just adding confusion to the chaos that was already taking place.

JT heard the sound of the MP-5 and knew Stink had made it to his trunk. He grabbed Toya by the arm and told her to stay down. He slowly made his way to the back seat of the truck, and with one arm, he slid the AR-15 into his hands and flipped off the safety. They had both came prepared for a fight.

"Show yoself, nigga," Stink barked from a distance.

JT took the challenge and rose up with AR-15 in hand, and Toya followed. But as soon as they got a visual, all they could see were two Detroit Police squad cars slamming on brakes right outside the fenced in parking lot.

As the police car doors flew open, JT, Toya, and Stink turned their guns on the police.

Police didn't even have a chance to draw their weapons as the bullets from high powered assault rifles riddled their squad cars while they rushed to the back of their vehicles for cover.

Stink stopped shooting just long enough to flip the switch on the MP-5 from semi to fully automatic, but by then, the officers outside the fence had gone on attack, busting 40 Cal pistols with precision.

Toya was now out of ammo, and all she could do was take cover. Crouched down next to JT, she began to fear for her life as the bullets pinged through and off the metal of the Escalade. She felt JT grab her arm.

"Listen, I'm about to raise up and shoot. When I do,

I want you to run into the building."

She hated to leave JT, but without a gun, she knew she was no help to him anyway. Toya wanted to live, even if it meant the rest of her life in prison.

"Okay." she agreed.

JT rose up and gave the police all he had as Toya ran for dear life until she reached the front of the building.

Stink felt powerful with one of the baddest assault rifles known to man. He came from behind his shield and sprayed the police cars wildly, disabling radio dispatchers, engines and all.

He saw one police officer stretched out behind his squad car and he felt a pinch of joy, knowing he had got at least one of them. He heard close sirens and he knew it was backup coming, but there was nowhere to run with the exits blocked by squad cars. He had no choice but to stand and fight with JT.

He took cover long enough to flip the double taped clip around and continue to fight. They let off round after round, not giving police a chance to take aim. The squad cars filed in, taking up the whole street. Ten extra cars came along with swat.

Out of ammo, Stink saw the bystander's weapon. He went to grab it, but bullets hit him in the back and sent him to the ground. He was hurt, but due to the vest, he wasn't hit.

JT went down hard with a bullet to the same shoulder that was already injured and three bullets lodged in his vest. He tried to reach for his weapon, but the pain wouldn't allow it. As he lay on his back, he saw Stink's Benz coming straight at him. At first, he thought Stink was coming to his rescue, but the Benz swerved around him and stomped the gas.

Stink aimed the pistol at the police as he went crashing through the fence and mashed into a patrol car. Bullets tore the Benz apart as Stink's body danced and bucked as a result of being hit from every direction.

Over a hundred rounds were let off as JT lay listening to Stink's massacre.

"Hands up muthafucka! Let me see your hands." Swat yelled as they approached.

JT lifted the only hand he could as they moved in and began to kick and beat him severely. Once he was a bloody mess, they finally handcuffed him and placed him under arrest.

They lifted him to his feet and JT saw the Benz filled with bullet holes through blood filled eyes. As he was led away, moaning and groaning, he turned in time to get a glimpse of Toya watching from the window, bunched between a crowd of probationers. He cracked a smile, knowing he had managed to keep her out of harm's way.

For the next few weeks, Toya sat at home, mourning the end of an era. How she made it out of the situation alive and without so much as a misdemeanor was a question only God had the answer to. She played the scene over and over in her head. The part where she raised up and emptied her clip at the officers. She still didn't see how she wasn't ever searched for or brought to light. She watched the news, expecting them to say that police were searching for a female suspect, but nothing was ever said.

After a few days, she began to believe that she had truly escaped scott free, thanks to JT. She had called all the hospitals and county jails in search of him, but came up empty. Toya believed he was probably being denied many of the regular rights a prisoner usually got, because of his charges. The news reported he was being charged with the murder of the bystander thug, one police officer and countless attempted murder charges on other police officers.

She cried the first couple of nights, thinking about the seriousness of the charges. She even found herself grieving over Stink. They had made a lot of money and memories together. Now she was moving on to the acceptance stage and trying to figure out what to do now. She never thought the day would come where she would have to pick up the pieces all alone.

Her phone rang, and when she picked up, it was an automated machine telling her she had a collect call from an inmate. She accepted the charges and immediately, her spirits began to lift at the thought of hearing JT's voice for the first time in weeks.

"Hello?" Toya said.

"Yeah, what up?" JT said calmly.

"You aiight?"

"Yeah. I'm good."

"Why you just now calling?"

"Shit, I been in the hospital handcuffed to a bed. They wouldn't let me use a phone. When I left the hospital, they still wouldn't let me use the phone. They thinking I'm gonna try some slick shit, and they might be right."

"Just let me know what you need me to do, and I'm on it."

"I'm gonna call you again in a couple days, okay?"

"Okay... I love you til death."

"And I, you."

Toya felt a small thread of hope emerging and it felt damn good. She couldn't begin to imagine what kind of trick JT had up his sleeve, but it didn't even matter. Whatever it was, she was going to ride with it.

ALSO AVAILABLE BY KING BENJAMIN

Gank Masters 2: All or Nothing

Gank Masterz 3: Toya's Story

Cry Baby

Cry Baby 2: Father Forgive Me

Don't wait for word of mouth for King Benjamin new releases. Text Kingology to 31996 to get new release updates as soon as they hatch

JOIN KING'S CASTLE READING GROUP ON FACEBOOK

Subscribe to Kingbenjaminpresents.com

Instagram: Authorkingbenjamin

www.ingramcontent.com/pod-product-compliance
Lightning Source LLC
LaVergne TN
LVHW020527100826
845148LV00010B/1367

* 9 7 8 0 6 1 5 8 1 4 8 9 6 *